Test Theory

TEST THEORY

David Magnusson
University of Stockholm

Translated from the Swedish by
Hunter Mabon

ADDISON-WESLEY PUBLISHING COMPANY
Reading, Massachusetts · Palo Alto · London · Don Mills, Ontario

© Almqvist & Wiksell/Gebers Förlag AB,
1966, Stockholm

This is the only authorized English translation of the second
Swedish edition of *Testteori*, published by Almqvist &
Wiksell/Gebers Förlag AB, Stockholm.

Preface

This English version is a translation of the second edition of a Swedish book entitled *Testteori*, which was first published in 1961. This was in turn based on notes which had been used in the basic psychology courses at Stockholm University. Since its publication, *Testteori* has been used for teaching purposes in many universities in Scandinavia. The second edition is a revision based on the experience gained during the preceding years.

The primary purpose of the book is to give a theoretically and statistically coherent introduction to (a) basic theory in measurement of individual differences, (b) methods and methodology applied to dependability problems, and (c) models and methods for using differential psychology data in practical situations such as test construction, diagnosis, counseling, selection, and classification. The book does not aim to give a complete account of models and methods in test theory and test methodology. The presentation in each area is concluded when the purpose of the account has been achieved, without assuming that the reader has advanced training in statistics. Suggestions for further reading are presented for the benefit of those who wish to continue with more advanced study. These suggestions do not claim to be exhaustive but are merely examples of literature which can serve as an introduction to more detailed study of selected areas.

In every book on measurement, problems arise concerning the level of competence in mathematics and statistics which should be assumed, the amount of such material which should be presented as an aid to understanding, and the amount of relevant matter which should be excluded because the presentation would require knowledge which can neither be assumed nor dealt with in the book. This problem is particularly accentuated in a book of this nature. My aim has been to make it possible even for those who lack extensive training in mathematics and statistics to be able to read the book without special study. Certain sections are therefore devoted to statistical methods which are necessary for the understanding of the purely test-theoretical content. For obvious reasons, special attention has been devoted here to the concept of correlation. An understanding of this concept can be regarded as an essential requirement for grasping what is involved in test-theoretical and test-methodological situations.

A relatively large number of problems with answers is included for the benefit of the reader's own, active work on the subject matter of the book.

v

Experience has shown that even relatively simple statistical notation and derivations present difficulties for many students of test theory. Nevertheless, the derivations of the equations presented and discussed here are relatively complete, since it is my personal belief that an understanding of these derivations is an essential requirement for a proper insight into the reasoning involved. The presentation has been simplified technically in some respects as an aid to reading and comprehension of the essential content. For instance, the same notation has been used for population and sample values. This obvious weakness from the statistical point of view has had to be weighed against what experience has shown to be the considerable increase in difficulty for students when the problem of samples and populations is introduced into the notation. My experience is that the advantages of the method of presentation used here clearly outweigh the disadvantages when teaching at the elementary level.

A large number of people, only a few of whom can be mentioned here, have contributed in many different ways to *Test Theory* in its present form. Professor Kjell Härnquist was the original instigator of the work. Professor Gösta Ekman, Professor Sten Henrysson, and Dr. Anders Dunér have read the manuscript in its entirety and made many suggestions for improvements. My colleagues Dr. Leif Evaeus and Dr. Lars Nystedt have given me the valuable benefit of their experience while using the book for teaching purposes. The book has been translated by Mr. Hunter Mabon. Miss Barbro Svensson has devoted much careful work to the typing of the manuscript and Mr. Tryggve Johansson has drawn the diagrams. I should like to thank them all, as well as those not mentioned here who have in different ways contributed to the book.

Stockholm, Sweden   D. M.
May 1966

Contents

CHAPTER 1

Measurement in
Differential Psychology

1-1 THE PROBLEM OF MEASUREMENT

In everyday usage the word measurement has a fairly clear and concise meaning. For measurements whose results we make use of in practical situations it is usual to have instruments which give us fixed and precise results in the form of scores. This is the case for all those instruments with which we measure length, weight, space, time, etc., where the result is obtained in, for instance, centimeters, grams, deciliters, or seconds. Measurements of this type, which can be carried out with objective, physical measuring instruments, seldom present any practical problems, either when we are actually carrying out the measurement or when we are interpreting the results.

The situation is different, however, when we wish to measure psychological variables. A variable is here defined as any single property or characteristic which it is possible for different individuals to possess in different quantities. In measuring such variables as independence, neuroticism, ability to think logically, or learning aptitude we meet scaling problems of a complex nature. The problem of measurement in the field of psychology can thus be considerably more complicated than in fields where ordinary physical measuring instruments are used. Before dealing with this problem we must examine more closely what is meant by measurement.

The usual general definition of measurement is: To measure is to assign numbers to the quantities of the properties of objects in accordance with given rules whose validity can be tested empirically. We could express this more simply by saying that we give the extent of a certain property of one or more objects with the help of the number system.

Numbers when used in this way can convey varying amounts of information. It is convenient to distinguish three levels of measurement which differ with respect to the amount of information conveyed by the numbers representing the extent of the qualities. The numbers can give the extent on an ordinal scale, on an interval scale, or on a ratio scale.

1

A. Ordinal scale

At the ordinal-scale level the numbers give only the order of the objects with respect to the trait being measured. The numbers 2, 4, 7, and 9 for objects *A*, *B*, *C*, and *D* with respect to a certain trait mean only that the objects have the order *D*, *C*, *B*, *A* with reference to the extent of the trait. When the positions of the objects are known on an ordinal scale we can give their relation to each other by means of > (greater than), = (equal to), or < (less than).

Since the order of the objects is the only information conveyed by the numbers, the numbers 2, 4, 7, and 9 can equally well be replaced by 1, 2, 3, and 4, or any other numbers whatsoever which retain the same order. No information has been lost by this kind of substitution. The numbers still represent the same order of the objects.

When measuring psychological variables we do not usually reach a more advanced level of measurement than the ordinal scale without making some assumptions. When measurement has taken place at the ordinal-scale level, the numbers give nothing more than the order of the objects on the scale. We can say that *A* has more of a certain ability than *B* and that *C* is more independent than *D*. In many situations we would consider this an inadequate form of measurement. Measurement at this level does, however, give sufficient information in many situations of practical importance in psychology. There is also a well-developed statistical methodology for treating ordinal data.

The situation when measuring at the ordinal-scale level is illustrated in Fig. 1–1(a). We assume that the individuals take up certain positions on a continuum which represents the trait we wish to measure. The position of every individual on the continuum is an expression for the extent of the trait he possesses. This continuum is represented in Fig. 1–1(a) by a straight line, the arrowhead giving the direction of the continuum. All that is now known about the scaling properties of the continuum is its direction. This knowledge enables us to describe an individual's position only as greater than, equal to, or less than another individual's position.

B. Interval scale

On an interval scale the numbers also convey information about the size of the differences between objects with respect to the extent of the trait measured. The differences between the numbers can be compared with each other. If the numbers 2, 4, 7, and 9 give the extent of a certain trait for objects *A*, *B*, *C*, and *D* on an interval scale, we can say that the difference between *A* and *B* is as great as the difference between *C* and *D*. We can also say that the difference between *B* and *C* is 1.5 times as great as the difference between *A* and *B* or the difference between *C* and *D*. To be able to measure at the interval-scale level we must have equal units on the scale.

The situation is shown in Fig. 1–1(b). Now we not only know the direction of the continuum; we also have equal units on the continuum within the area where the individuals have their positions and where we wish to make measurements. We can thus establish the differences between the objects' positions and compare them with each other.

As was previously mentioned, when we wish to measure psychological variables such as memory, aggressiveness, or arithmetic ability, it is usually impossible to go beyond the ordinal-scale level without making certain assumptions. However, in many situations we are interested in the magnitude of the differences between individuals on the continua for such variables. We may be interested in differences between individuals on the same continuum, which are called *interindividual differences*, or in differences between positions on different continua for a single individual, which are called *intraindividual differences*. In such situations it is necessary to measure the extent of the traits by means of interval scales. In a later section of this chapter we shall see how this can be done.

(The meaning of the expressions "equal units" and "equal intervals" is not entirely clear. It will not be discussed in greater detail here but it is worth-while to draw the reader's attention to the problem. An example may show its significance. If individuals A, B, C, and D are broad-jumpers and jump 4.25, 4.50, 8.00, and 8.25 meters respectively, we can immediately state that in the purely metric sense the difference between the results for A and B is the same as the difference between the results for C and D. We can scarcely, however, draw the conclusion that the differences in performance are the same in any other meaning than the metric one.)

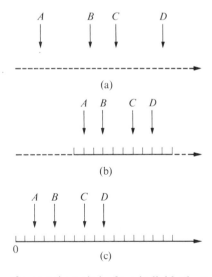

Fig. 1–1 Magnitude of a certain trait in four individuals on an ordinal scale (a), interval scale (b), and ratio scale (c).

C. Ratio scale

At the ratio-scale level the numbers give information not only about the rank order of the objects and the relative size of differences, but also about the relation between ratios. If the numbers 2, 4, 7, and 9 now represent the extent of a certain attribute for objects A, B, C, and D at the ratio-scale level, this tells us that B has twice as much of the attribute as A, C has 3.5 times as much as A, D has 2.25 times as much as B, etc.

Measurement at the ratio-scale level is based on the assumption that the zero point is known, and that we have equal units from this point along the whole length of the scale. Measurement at the ratio-scale level is illustrated in Fig. 1–1(c). We now know the direction of the continuum, we have equal intervals, and we can relate every individual position on the continuum directly to a zero point. Most physical measuring instruments give data at the ratio-scale level. When a certain property of an object is measured at this level we can establish the extent and give it as an absolute value. In view of what is to follow, it is perhaps worth pointing out here that this individual score can be established without knowledge of the scores of other objects on the same scale.

The problem of measuring psychological traits at the ratio-scale level has long been of interest to psychologists. Though early attempts were made (e.g., by Thurstone, 1928) it must be said that the problem has not been solved for the purposes of practical test construction. Before we advance from interval measurement to ratio measurement we must know the zero point in relation to the scores on the interval scale. We cannot draw the conclusion that a person is completely without the ability to solve mathematical problems of a certain type just because he has been unable to solve any of the items in a test containing this type of problem.

So far some general aspects of the problem of measurement have been presented, together with a number of problems relating to measurement of psychological variables, and we have pointed to the fact that in this field we encounter problems which we do not usually come across when carrying out everyday measurements. These problems concern both the construction of measuring instruments and the interpretation of the data which we obtain from these instruments. Later chapters will be devoted to these problems. This chapter is primarily concerned with the problem of measuring psychological variables at the interval-scale level. Before studying how this is done we must first know some of the properties of a normal distribution.

1–2 NORMAL DISTRIBUTION

If a coin is tossed we have an equal chance of obtaining heads or tails. This is true of every unbiased coin. If we then toss up ten coins at the same time, the most probable combination of heads and tails is five of each. It is probable that the combination six heads and four tails or vice versa will be obtained less frequently. We will obtain seven heads and three tails or vice versa even less frequently. The most infrequent combination is of course ten heads and no tails or no heads and ten tails.

It is now possible to compute with the aid of Newton's well-known binomial theorem the most probable expected number of, for instance, heads when we toss up ten coins a given number of times. In order to illustrate this, let us toss the coins 1024 times. Table 1–1 shows the expected distribution of the number of heads obtained when ten coins are tossed this number of times. With this total number of tosses it is likely that 252 tosses will yield five heads and five tails, while 120 tosses, for instance, will yield seven heads and three tails and the same number of tosses will yield three heads and seven tails. It is likely that only one toss will yield no heads at all, and the probability is equally small that all of the coins will show heads.

Table 1–1 Expected distribution, based on the binomial theorem, of the number of heads from 1024 tosses with ten coins

Number of heads	0	1	2	3	4	5	6	7	8	9	10	Total
Binomial distribution	1	10	45	120	210	252	210	120	45	10	1	1024

The distribution is obviously symmetric. It is equally likely that we will obtain three heads as seven heads, or nine heads as one head. This can also be seen in Fig. 1–2 where the binomial distribution is given. The distribution is also bell-shaped. The most frequent combination of heads and tails is five and five. The more the combinations deviate from this, i.e., the larger or smaller the number of heads in the combination, the less frequent they will be.

Let us now assume that we have a test consisting of ten items and that one point is given for every correctly solved item. Let us also assume that we toss a coin for each of 1024 individuals in order to decide whether he passes or fails on each item and then compute each individual score on the test. The most probable distribution of scores we would then obtain is that shown in Table 1–1 and illustrated in Fig. 1–2. The most frequent score would be five. The more a score deviated from this value, the less probable it would be. It is thus likely that the score zero would appear only once, as would the score ten.

It should be noted that the scores given in Table 1–1 give the most likely number of times we will obtain a given number of heads if we toss ten coins. If someone had in fact sufficient time to perform this number of tosses he would find that the actually obtained number of heads did not exactly agree

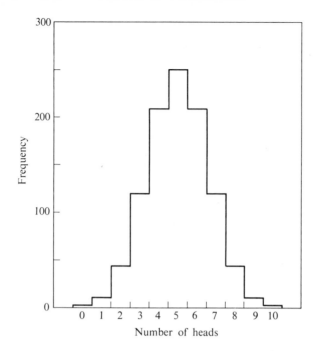

Fig. 1–2 The binomial distribution in the form of a histogram.

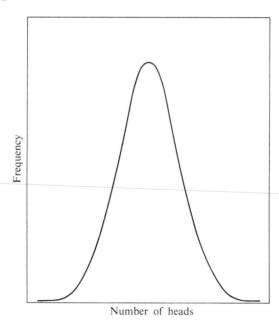

Fig. 1–3 The Gaussian or normal curve.

with the distribution shown in Table 1–1. The probable distribution which can be computed from the binomial theorem is merely a theoretical distribution of *expected* values.

The binomial distribution is presented in the form of a *histogram* in Fig. 1–2. The finer the grading for a given width of the distribution, i.e., the greater the number of coins included in every toss, as well as an increased number of tosses, the smoother the shape of the histogram will become. Its form will more and more approach that of the smooth curve shown in Fig. 1–3. This symmetric bell-shaped curve is the so-called Gaussian or normal curve, which is of considerable interest in test theory. The characteristics of the normal distribution are completely determined, and the frequencies for every given score can be determined individually from the equation for the normal curve:

$$Y = \frac{N}{s\sqrt{2\pi}}\, e^{-x^2/2s^2}, \tag{1–1}$$

where x is the deviation from the mean of the distribution, Y is the frequency of position x, N is the total frequency of the distribution, s is the standard deviation (see page 8), π is pi (3.1416), and e is the base of the system of natural logarithms (2.718). [Instead of a frequency, Y is often given as the ordinate of position x in a distribution with total area 1.0. This merely means that each frequency obtained from Eq. (1–1) has to be divided by N.]

Table 1–2 shows the probable frequencies of the number of heads that will be obtained by tossing ten coins 1024 times, when the values are computed from the equation for the normal curve. It can be seen that there are certain minor differences in frequencies between the expected values computed from the binomial theorem (Table 1–1) and those computed from the normal distribution (Table 1–2). The greater the number of classes of scores in the distribution, i.e., the finer the grading, the less significant these differences become.

Table 1–2 Expected distribution of the number of heads obtained when ten coins are tossed 1024 times, computed from the equation for the normal curve

Number of heads	0	1	2	3	4	5	6	7	8	9	10	Total
Normal distribution	2	11	45	117	210	254	210	117	45	11	2	1024

Certain characteristics of the normal curve are of particular interest in this connection.

(a) The normal curve is, like the binomial distribution, a theoretical distribution. Observed scores are scarcely ever distributed in exactly this way.   When we subsequently speak of a normal distribution of obtained scores we mean merely that the distribution does not deviate from the theoretical normal distribution more than can be explained by the number of scores in the distribution.   When we know the number of observations, we can compute the deviation which can be tolerated from the theoretical normal curve.

(b) The theoretical normal distribution is completely symmetric. Exactly 50% of all scores are located above the mean of the distribution, and exactly 50% below.   Any score which is a certain distance from the mean of the distribution has the same frequency as the score which is an equal distance from the mean on the other side.

(c) The theoretical normal curve is asymptotic.   The curve approaches the axis without ever actually meeting it.

Distributions of observed scores can have many different forms.   A number of measures are required in order to describe the characteristics of a distribution completely.   In order to describe a given normal distribution it is sufficient to give the arithmetic mean and a measure of the variation or dispersion of the data.   The arithmetic mean is obtained from the simple, well-known equation

$$M_x = \sum X/N, \tag{1–2}$$

where $\sum$ is the Greek letter sigma, and is used to denote "the sum of," X is any individual score included in the distribution, and N is the number of scores included in this sum.   The word "mean" will henceforth refer to the arithmetic mean.

A common measure of the variation of obtained scores is the *standard deviation*, which will be denoted by s.   It is defined as the square root of the mean of squared deviations from the mean of the distribution.   The standard deviation is thus dependent on the dispersion of scores in the distribution:

$$s_x = \sqrt{\frac{\sum (X - M_x)^2}{N}} . \tag{1–3}$$

If we wish to describe some position on the distribution as a deviation from the mean, we use the standard deviation as a unit.   We can express the relative position of an individual in a distribution by saying, for instance, that it is 1.0 standard deviation ($1s$) above the mean or 2.4 standard deviations below the mean ($-2.4s$).   What we are in fact doing is expressing every score as a *standard score*.   The standard score, which is usually denoted by z, is obtained for any score from the equation

$$z_x = \frac{X - M_x}{s_x} . \tag{1–4}$$

A standard score is thus a score expressed as a deviation from the mean with the standard deviation as unit.

It is clear that a distribution of z-scores will have a mean of zero and standard deviation 1.0. It should be pointed out here that scores on any distribution can be transformed to z-scores (see also Chapter 16). We are, however, particularly interested here in z-scores for a normal distribution.

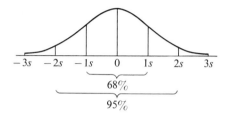

Fig. 1-4 A normal distribution with percentages.

One of the properties of the normal distribution is that fixed proportions of the total distribution are found between the positions given by standard scores of varying size. The approximate percentage distributions of the number of scores between standard scores -1.0 and 1.0 and between standard scores -2.0 and 2.0 are given as whole numbers in Fig. 1-4. Table 1-3 gives the proportion of the total area of a normal distribution which lies between the mean of the distribution and respective standard scores. It can be seen that approximately 68% of the scores in a normal distribution fall within the area between -1.0 and 1.0 in the standard-score distribution and approximately 95% between -2.0 and 2.0.*

For any standard score on a normal distribution, we can compute how large a part of the distribution lies above the standard score and how large a part lies below (see, e.g., Guilford, 1954, p. 83). Table 1-4 gives a cumulative frequency distribution, i.e., the proportions of the total normal distri-

Table 1-3 Proportions of the total distribution area which lie between the mean of the distribution and respective standard scores

Standard score	Proportion
±1.0	0.3413
±2.0	0.4772
±3.0	0.4987

* To be more exact, 95% of the scores in a normal distribution fall between $-1.96s$ and $1.96s$, i.e., between the standard scores -1.96 and 1.96.

Table 1–4 Cumulative distributions: proportions of the total distribution area which lie below respective standard scores

Standard score	Proportion	Standard score	Proportion
−3.0	0.0013	0.5	0.6915
−2.5	0.0062	1.0	0.8413
−2.0	0.0228	1.5	0.9332
−1.5	0.0668	2.0	0.9772
−1.0	0.1587	2.5	0.9938
−0.5	0.3085	3.0	0.9987
0.0	0.5000		

bution which lie below respective standard scores. If the proportions which lie above are plotted against their respective standard scores, we obtain a cumulative frequency distribution of the type shown in Fig. 1–5. For each standard score on the x-axis we can, from the curve, immediately read off on the y-axis the proportion (p) of the total distribution which lies above the standard score. Thus, if we take the standard score -1.0 on the x-axis in Fig. 1–5 and go to the point on the cumulative curve directly above -1.0, and then to the corresponding point on the y-axis, we find the proportion 0.84 for this standard score. This was previously established with the help of Fig. 1–4. Conversely, we can find the standard score for the position which splits a normal distribution in fixed, known proportions. This last possibility is useful in measuring psychological variables, as will be explained in a subsequent section.

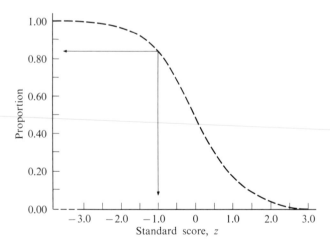

Fig. 1–5 Cumulative frequency distribution of standard scores.

1–3 AN ASSUMPTION

It was noticed long ago that, when human attributes are measured with objective measuring instruments which give the data on interval or ratio scales, the results are distributed approximately in accordance with the normal distribution. Such distributions are obtained for physical characteristics such as height, physiological variables such as temperature of human beings at rest, and performance variables such as hand strength measured by means of a hand dynamometer.

Table 1–5 shows the distribution of height for 62,372 Swedish men who registered for compulsory military service in 1962. Of these, 8,899 were in the class interval 166–171 cm (5 ft 5 in.–5 ft 7 in.), 20,773 were in the class interval 172–177 cm (5 ft 7 in.–5 ft 9 in.), etc. The class frequencies are shown in a histogram in Fig. 1–6. If the distribution had instead been given with the frequencies for each centimeter on the height scale, we would have obtained a histogram closely resembling the symmetrical bell-shaped curve, which is also shown in Fig. 1–6 and which has been drawn through the frequency score for each class average. We can now see that this rounded-off curve very closely resembles the normal curve shown in Fig. 1–3.

Table 1–5 Frequencies with respect to height for 62,372 men aged 18

Height in centimeters	Number	Percentage
154	29	0.05
154–159	155	0.25
160–165	1,631	2.61
166–171	8,899	14.27
172–177	20,773	33.31
178–183	20,492	32.85
184–189	8,560	13.72
190–195	1,684	2.70
196–201	138	0.22
201	11	0.02
Total	62,372	100.00

In view of such facts a fundamental assumption has been proposed for practical test construction, namely, that if we could measure the differences between individuals on an interval scale, we would obtain a normal distribution of individual scores.

We let Fig. 1–7(a) represent a performance continuum for a psychological variable which cannot be measured by means of physical measuring instruments, e.g., the ability to solve mathematical problems. Assuming that

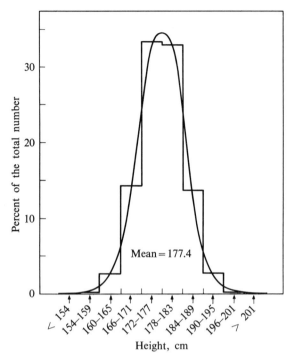

Fig. 1–6 Distribution of height of 62,372 men, 18 years of age.

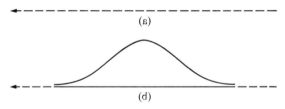

Fig. 1–7 Latent continuum (a) with known direction, (b) with known direction and a hypothetical normal distribution.

ability is a monotonic function (continually increasing or decreasing) of position on the continuum, we know its direction. An individual who has solved a greater number of items is assumed to have a higher position on the continuum than an individual who has solved a smaller number. It is thus possible to measure at the ordinal level. One important additional property of the scale, namely, equal units, is necessary in order to determine the magnitude of differences between different positions. In Fig. 1–7(b) the hypothetical normal distribution has been introduced on the same continuum. Observe that we now have a hypothetical distribution placed on a continuum about whose scale properties we know only the direction. The form of the distribution is based merely on an assumption, that of normality. The practical problem now consists of constructing a measuring instrument with such properties as can be derived from this assumption.

We have already pointed out that we need to know where the zero point lies on the continuum and to have equal units from the zero point along the whole length of the continuum in order to be able to carry out a measurement comparable to, for example, the measurement of height or of a broad-jumper's performance expressed by the length of the jump as an absolute number. We now see that our assumption of a normal distribution on the psychological continuum is of no help in solving the problem of the zero point. We have, however, approached a solution to the problem of equal units. If the assumption introduced is correct, equal distances on the continuum on which the normal distribution is placed are also equal units. If we construct an instrument which gives a normal distribution of obtained scores, we can thus express the positions of the individuals on this psychological continuum on an interval scale.

1–4   CONSTRUCTION OF AN INTERVAL SCALE

The level of accuracy required to measure variables in differential psychology varies from situation to situation. Sometimes it is sufficient to rank the individuals. In other cases we wish to compare differences, either interindividually or intraindividually. In such cases we need to measure on an interval scale. Since the latter situations are common and the step from measurement on an ordinal scale to measurement on an interval scale cannot be made directly, the principles involved in the construction of an interval scale will be given a comparatively detailed treatment.

Let us examine how we should proceed when constructing a test for measuring, on an interval scale, the ability to solve mathematical problems of a certain type. In order to simplify the presentation of the principle for scale construction we assume that all the test items measure exactly the same trait, namely, the ability to solve mathematical problems of a certain kind, and that the measurement of the extent to which each individual has this ability can be made without any error. It must, however, be stated that we will never have such a test in practice. We are thus only presenting a theoretical model for the construction of an interval scale.

We select a cross section of individuals sufficiently large to represent the population for which we have assumed that a normal distribution of obtained scores on an interval scale holds. Every individual in this sample is presented with a problem. Some individuals will manage to solve the problem, while others will be unable to do so. An expression for the degree of difficulty of the problem is obtained from the proportion of the total number of individuals in the sample who manage to solve it. This proportion is denoted by p. The proportion which remains of the total number of individuals $(1 - p)$ is made up of those who have failed and is denoted by q. It thus follows that $p + q = 1$. Let us assume that the item presented was solved by 84% of the individuals in the sample, which gives us $p = 0.84$ and $q = 0.16$ for the item. The frequency distribution of obtained scores for the item, which will contain only the categories 0 (wrong) and 1 (correct), will thus look like item i in Fig. 1–8.

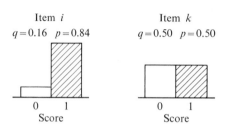

Fig. 1–8 Proportional distribution of obtained scores for two items, i and k.

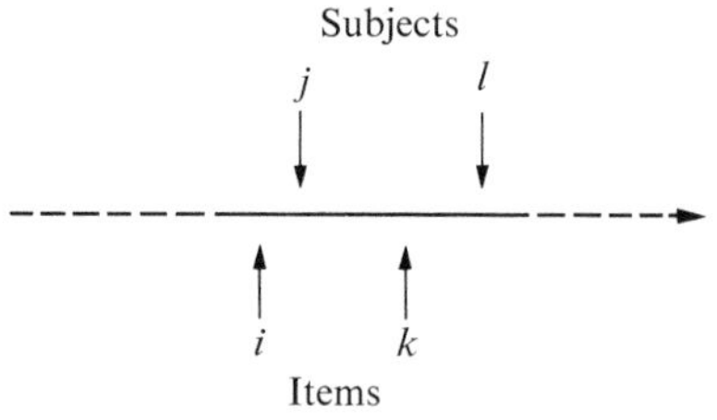

Fig. 1–9 The relationship between individuals (j and l) and items (i and k) on the same continuum.

The frequency distribution in Fig. 1–8 has obviously been obtained by splitting the individuals in the hypothetical distribution in Fig. 1–7 into two groups. Those individuals who gave correct responses to the item are found in positions farther up on the difficulty continuum than those individuals who gave incorrect responses. We must now find the position on the hypothetical distribution where the division has taken place. Since we know the proportion of the total number in the distribution who lie above this position—this is, of course, the proportion who gave correct responses to the item—we can now, with the aid of the cumulative distribution curve in Fig. 1–5, find the level of difficulty of the item in the form of a standard score on the hypothetical distribution. We start from the p-value 0.84 on the ordinate and find that it corresponds to the standard score -1.0 on a normal distribution. We can now say that those individuals who have managed to solve item i are above this standard score on the hypothetical distribution of scores for performance on this type of item, while those individuals who failed are below it.

The position of every individual has now been fixed in relation to the position of item i. But the position of the item has in turn been determined from the individuals' scores. It is an important fact that the positions of items and individuals can only be determined in relation to each other. The continuum on which we have determined the position of item i has been described as a difficulty continuum: the position of the item in relation to the hypothetical distribution of individual scores for performance ability gives the level of difficulty of the item. But it is therefore also an ability continuum when we fix the positions of the individuals: an individual's position on the continuum represents his ability. It is the relation between an individual's ability and the item's degree of difficulty which determines whether or not he can solve the item (cf. Coombs, 1952, 1956, 1964, who gives a model for different types of data). If the position of the individual on the continuum is higher than the position of the item, he will be able to solve it. If the relationship is the reverse, he will not. For items i and k in Fig. 1–9, individual j will thus solve item i but fail to solve item k, while individual l will solve both items.

We can now choose another item with some other level of difficulty but of the same type, e.g., item k whose frequency distribution is given in Fig. 1–8. Since 50% solved the item correctly, it follows that $p = q = 0.50$. This item divides the hypothetical distribution at another point which can be given as a standard score in the same way as for item i. This position will obviously be the standard score zero for item k, since the item has divided the distribution into two equal parts and must therefore lie on the mean of the distribution.

Let us now choose six items in the way described with p-values such that the distances on the continuum between the standard scores for the different items are always the same. In this case, we would obtain the test distribution t in Fig. 1–10 from the hypothetical distribution h, if we computed the number of correctly solved items for each individual and included his

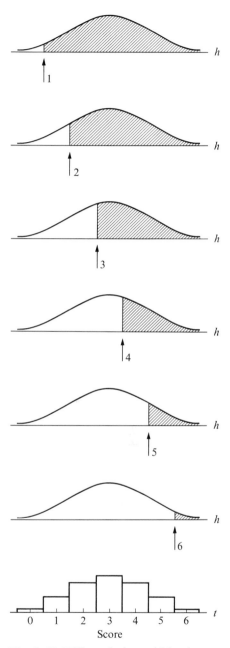

Fig. 1–10 Differentiation within the same hypothetical distribution (h) with six items of varying degrees of difficulty, and the distribution of obtained scores on the total test (t).

obtained score in the total distribution. The scale on which we have expressed the individual results can now be regarded as an interval scale with the step between 1 and 2 the same as that between 2 and 3, and so on.

With the given assumptions, we have theoretically solved the problem of the construction of an instrument which gives the result of the measurement of psychological variables on an interval scale. A number of practical problems which have been ignored in order to examine scaling problems will be dealt with in later sections.

In the above example the two important steps in the measurement on an interval scale of psychological variables are (a) the assumption of a normal distribution of individuals in the population and (b) the use of the variation among individuals as a unit of measurement.

1–5   TEST CONSTRUCTION WITHOUT ASSUMING A NORMAL DISTRIBUTION

For many practical purposes it is unnecessary, and sometimes it is poor strategy, to construct a test for measuring on an interval scale. For example, let us assume that it has been shown that a person must achieve more than a standard score position of 1.0 on a certain continuum to be able to handle duties of a certain type, but that it is of no importance for success in these duties how far above this position he may be. Clearly in this situation we ought to choose only items which divide the hypothetical distribution in the proportions 0.84 and 0.16. With a relatively small number of items of this type we can make a comparatively accurate differentiation within the area in question. In this situation we are not interested in differentiating at other points on the hypothetical distribution. Instead we attempt to obtain a distribution of scores in two categories, where one category contains 84% of a sample and the other the remaining 16%. In other situations, we may be interested in differentiating at more than one point without wishing to measure on an interval scale. In this case, the construction of the test is planned from the special requirements of the differentiation. It is obvious that we need not assume a normal distribution in situations where we do not intend to measure on an interval scale.

1–6   LATENT-CONTINUUM DATA

An important distinction which was made previously and which should be kept in mind is that between actually obtained empirical data and the latent, hypothetical continuum on which we assume that the individuals distribute themselves in a certain way. In Fig. 1–8 we have a distribution of obtained scores, i.e., a distribution of the data which shows how many subjects have solved a certain item and how many have failed. The latent continuum, which we have taken as representing the trait which we assume that item *i* measures, is illustrated in Fig. 1–7. We have also assumed that the individuals tested are distributed on a normal distribution with respect to this trait. Furthermore, we have assumed a monotonic relation between scores in the test and positions on the latent continuum.

In most measurements we are interested in the underlying trait which determines performance on a certain type of item. We assume a latent continuum, and we can make different assumptions both about how the individuals are distributed on the latent continuum and about the relation between the position on the latent continuum and on the distribution of observed data. The assumption made previously about the shape of the distribution is reasonable when the measurement refers to performance variables, as is the assumption that there is a monotonic relationship between scores on the test and position on the latent continuum. These two assumptions are not particularly satisfactory in other situations, e.g., when we measure attitudes. In this case, we must expect distributions with varying shape on the latent continuum in which we are interested, depending on the attitude measured. Nor can we always assume a monotonic relationship between scores and position on the latent continuum. Assume, for instance, that an affirmative answer to a question on a questionnaire requires an indifferent attitude toward religion. Then, individuals who are indifferent will lie in the indifference zone on the latent continuum and answer "yes." Those who have either a strong negative or a strong positive attitude will lie on different sides of the indifference zone, but nevertheless they will give the same *negative response* and be included in the same category of obtained data.

1–7   DIMENSIONALITY

In describing the construction of an instrument for measuring psychological variables on an interval scale, we have assumed that every item differentiates between individuals on one difficulty continuum, i.e., that (a) the items measure exactly the same trait but have different degrees of difficulty, and that (b) the model previously presented, which showed that the solution of an item is completely determined by the relation between the individual's position and the position of the item on the latent continuum, is correct. We pointed out previously that none of these assumptions can be entirely satisfied when we are measuring psychological variables. The first of the two assumptions given above concerns the dimensionality of the test. It is a question of central importance whether the data we obtain with a given instrument express individuals' positions on one or several continua. This problem will be dealt with in greater detail at a later stage in the book.

As was mentioned previously, the second assumption, that every item can differentiate without error in the distribution on the latent continuum, is never exactly satisfied when we are performing measurements in practice. The measurement will be contaminated with a number of errors, and in most cases it is of decisive importance for the application of the data that we should be able to estimate the size of this error. This problem will be dealt with in later chapters.

It is suitable to introduce here a concept to which we shall return, that of homogeneity. Different definitions of the concept have been proposed (cf. Guttman, 1950; Loevinger, 1947, 1948). Here we shall take homogeneity to mean a variable which gives the extent to which the two conditions discussed, about unidimensionality and freedom from measurement errors, are satisfied. We can then construct a homogeneity scale on which complete homogeneity denotes the extreme case, complete satisfaction of the given conditions. It is obvious that complete homogeneity is a purely theoretical case, since neither of the conditions can be satisfied when we are measuring psychological variables. In practical situations, therefore, we have varying degrees of homogeneity in the measuring instruments which we normally construct and apply.

1–8 SUMMARY

We can now sum up some characteristic features of the measurement of psychological variables.

1. The position of an individual on a continuum is not given as an absolute score but as a relative score. If only one individual is available, his position on a psychological continuum cannot be measured. We can only compare individuals with each other.

2. Instruments for measuring psychological variables on an interval scale are constructed by initially assuming a normal distribution of scores. For this interval scale we use the variation between individuals as the unit of measurement. The meaningfulness and correctness of the obtained scale depends of course on the correctness of the assumption.

It must be remembered that the assumption of a normal distribution of scores on psychological continua is used for the construction of tests in order to obtain scores on an interval scale. One cannot—as has happened— use the normal distribution of test scores as proof that even psychological variables give normally distributed scores, i.e., that the assumption is correct.

The assumption of normal distribution has been made the subject of empirical tests by, among others, Thurstone (1925, 1943). Thurstone showed that, if the assumption is correct, the standard score for single items in the score distribution for children of a given age will, under certain conditions, be linearly related to the standard scores for the same items in the score distribution for children in older age groups. The computations which Thurstone carried out on the basis of empirical data obtained from a number of tests gave results which support the assumption. The problem has recently been discussed and illuminated on the basis of empirical findings by Berglund (1965).

The discussion in this chapter has dealt mainly with technical scaling problems that we encounter when measuring psychological variables. An equally important problem, namely, the reliability and meaningfulness of the measurements, has scarcely been touched upon. These are problems of a kind we do not often encounter in everyday life, because most of the continua we come in contact with can be measured by means of instruments whose accuracy and reliability are entirely sufficient and need scarcely be questioned. In later sections, however, we shall show the importance of reliability in the construction of psychological methods of measurement and in the application of their results.

REFERENCES

BERGLUND, G. (1965). *Mental growth: a study of changes in test ability between the ages of nine and sixteen years.* Uppsala: Almqvist & Wiksell.

COOMBS, C. H. (1952). A theory of psychological scaling. *Eng. Res. Bull.,* No. **34.** Ann Arbor: University of Michigan Press.

——— (1956). The scale grid: some intercorrelations of data models. *Psychometrika,* **21,** 313–329.

——— (1964). *A theory of data.* New York: Wiley.

GUILFORD, J. P. (1954). *Psychometric methods* (2nd ed.). New York: McGraw-Hill.

GUTTMAN, L. (1950), in S. A. STOUFFER (Ed.). *Measurement and prediction.* Princeton, N.J.: Princeton University Press.

LOEVINGER, J. (1947). A systematic approach to the construction and evaluation of tests of ability. *Psychol. Monogr.,* **61,** No. 4.

——— (1948). The technic of homogeneous tests composed with some aspects of "scale analysis" and factor analysis. *Psychol. Bull.,* **45,** 507–530.

THURSTONE, L. L. (1925). A method of scaling psychological and educational tests. *J. Educ. Psychol.,* **16,** 433–451.

——— (1928). The absolute zero in intelligence measurement. *Psychol. Rev.,* **35,** 175–197.

——— (1943). *Primary mental abilities.* Chicago: University of Chicago Press.

Suggested reading

BJÖRKMAN, M. (1962). Measurement based on variability. *Studium Generale,* 15 Jahrg., Heft 2.

GULLIKSEN, I. H., and S. MESSICK (Eds.) (1960). *Psychological scaling.* New York: Wiley.

HEMPEL, C. G. (1952). Fundamentals of concept formation in empirical science. In NEURATH *et al.* (Eds.) *Inter. Encycl. of Unified Science,* **2,** 7.

LAZARSFELD, P. F. (1959). Latent structure analysis. In I. S. KOCH (Ed.) *Psychology: A study of science*, Vol. III. New York: McGraw-Hill.

LOEVINGER, L. (1965). Person and population as psychometric concepts. *Psychol. Rev.*, **72,** 143–155.

LORD, F. M. (1952). A theory of test scores. *Psychometr. Monogr.*, No. 7.

STEVENS, S. S. (1946). On the theory of scales of measurement. *Science*, **103,** 670–680.

——— (1951). Mathematics, measurement and psychophysics. In S. S. STEVENS (Ed.) *Handbook of experimental psychology.* New York: Wiley.

——— (1959). Measurement, psychophysics and utility. In C. W. CHURCHMAN and P. RATOOSH (Eds.) *Measurement: Definitions and Theories.* New York: Wiley.

SUPPES, P., and J. L. ZINNES (1963). Basic measurement theory. In R. D. LUCE, R. R. BUSH, and E. GALANTER (Eds.) *Handbook of Mathematical Psychology*, Vol. I. New York: Wiley.

TORGERSSON, W S. (1958). *Theory and methods of scaling.* New York: Wiley.

CHAPTER 2

The Single Item and its Variance

The data used in differential psychology can be collected by various types of basic methods such as tests, questionnaires, or ratings. An expression for the position of an individual on a given continuum can take one of several forms: a correct or incorrect response to a test item, an attitude to some statement, factual information in reply to a question, or a rating. Whatever form the data might have, they are used to determine the position of the individual on the continuum in relation to other individuals.

The presentation given in this chapter is based upon the assumption that the individual score can be expressed as 1 or 0, where 1 signifies a correct solution, a positive response to a question, or a rating of the person above some specific level. A score of zero will, of course, signify an incorrect solution, a negative response to a question, or a rating below the given level. Furthermore, it is assumed that the relation given in Chapter 1, p. 14, between the positions of individuals and items on the continuum holds when scores are expressed as ones and zeros.

2-1   THE SCORE MATRIX

For statistical treatment of the data the raw scores are placed in a score matrix. There will be only ones and zeros in the cells of the score matrix, since each response is placed in one of two categories. Table 2–1 shows the general notation which is used to avoid the risk of misinterpreting a single cell score or summation. We usually assign a row to each individual and a column to each item. A subscript system whereby the first figure gives row position and the second column position is used to identify raw scores. The general notation is therefore X_{ji} for the raw score which individual j obtains for his response to item i. The notation X_{73} would stand for the raw score of individual 7 on item 3.

In the following text, for the sake of simplicity, the score obtained by individual j on test t will be denoted by t_j, whenever this is sufficient to prevent misunderstanding. The value of t_j is obtained by summing the raw

Table 2–1 Score matrix showing general notation

Item

Indi-vidual	1	2	$\cdots$	i	$\cdots$	n	t_j
1	X_{11}	X_{12}	$\cdots$	X_{1i}	$\cdots$	X_{1n}	$\sum_{i=1}^{n} X_{1i}$
2	X_{21}	X_{22}	$\cdots$	X_{2i}	$\cdots$	X_{2n}	$\sum_{i=1}^{n} X_{2i}$
$\vdots$							
j	X_{j1}	X_{j2}	$\cdots$	X_{ji}	$\cdots$	X_{jn}	$\sum_{i=1}^{n} X_{ji}$
$\vdots$							
N	X_{N1}	X_{N2}	$\cdots$	X_{Ni}	$\cdots$	X_{Nn}	$\sum_{i=1}^{n} X_{Ni}$
f_i	$\sum_{j=1}^{N} X_{j1}$	$\sum_{j=1}^{N} X_{j2}$		$\sum_{j=1}^{N} X_{ji}$		$\sum_{j=1}^{N} X_{jn}$	$\sum_{j=1}^{N} \sum_{i=1}^{n} X_{ji}$

scores in one row of the score matrix. For the sake of clarity, such a summation for an individual over a number of items can be written in complete form in the following way:

$$t_j = \sum_{i=1}^{n} X_{ji}. \tag{2–1}$$

Since each response is rated as 1 or 0, the total score for individual j is obtained by counting the number of correctly solved items.

The frequency of correct response to item i is denoted by f whenever this abbreviation is sufficient to prevent misunderstanding. The frequency of correct response f_i is obtained by summing the raw scores in one column of the score matrix. The following expression shows clearly how the summation for an item over a number of individuals is made:

$$f_i = \sum_{j=1}^{N} X_{ji}. \tag{2–2}$$

Since the score matrix contains only ones and zeros, the frequency of correct response is obtained by counting the number of individuals who have solved the item correctly.

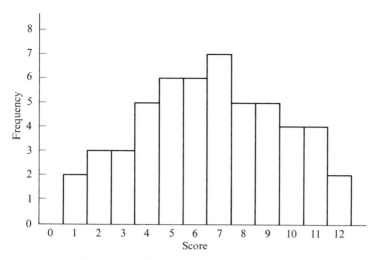

Fig. 2–1 A distribution of obtained scores.

2–2 VARIANCE

Variations (in ability, for example) expressed by differences in individuals' total scores can best be shown by means of a frequency distribution (see Fig. 2–1). We can tell from the distribution how many individuals solved correctly a given number of items and how many solved a greater or smaller number.

The variation of a distribution can be expressed in several different measures such as range, semi-interquartile range, and standard deviation. With distributions of test scores we most commonly use the square of the standard deviation (s^2), *the variance*, as an expression for the variation in the individuals' ability. Derivations are considerably simpler with this measure than with other measures of variability (see, e.g., Chapter 4).

Since the variance is the square of the standard deviation of the distribution, we obtain the equation

$$s_x^2 = \frac{\sum(X - M_x)^2}{N}.$$ (2–3)

The deviation from the mean of the distribution is computed for each individual. This result is squared and the sum of the squares of all individuals is computed. The mean of these squares is the variance. The variance is thus the area of the square which can be drawn with the standard deviation as side.

The variance is an expression for the extent to which the data differentiate among individuals. If there is no differentiation, everyone has the same score and the variance is zero. It should be pointed out that a large variance is not particularly desirable *per se*. What is important is to show that the differentiation is meaningful and reliable.

2–3   THE VARIANCE OF A SINGLE ITEM

Some conclusions, very important for test construction, can be arrived at by studying the variance of a distribution of individuals' performances on the test. We will approach the problem by studying the variance obtained when we test a number of individuals on only one item. The composition of the total test variance will then be dealt with in Chapter 4.

The scores for 20 individuals on a test consisting of 8 items are shown in a score matrix in Table 2–2.

Variations in scores on the whole test are based on variations in ability to solve each individual item. If performance on each item can be rated only

Table 2–2 Score matrix for a test consisting of 8 items administered to 20 individuals

Individual	Item 1	2	3	4	5	6	7	8	t_j
1	1	0	0	0	0	0	0	0	1
2	1	1	1	1	0	0	1	1	6
3	1	0	1	0	0	0	0	0	2
4	1	1	1	1	1	1	1	0	7
5	1	1	1	1	0	0	0	0	4
6	1	1	0	0	0	0	0	0	2
7	1	0	1	1	1	1	0	0	5
8	1	1	1	0	0	0	0	0	3
9	1	1	1	0	1	1	1	0	6
10	1	0	0	1	1	1	0	0	4
11	1	1	1	1	1	1	0	1	7
12	1	1	0	1	1	0	1	0	5
13	1	1	1	1	1	1	0	0	6
14	0	1	1	1	1	0	0	0	4
15	1	1	1	0	0	0	0	0	3
16	1	1	1	0	1	0	0	0	4
17	1	1	0	1	0	0	0	0	3
18	1	1	1	1	1	1	1	1	8
19	1	1	1	1	0	1	0	0	5
20	1	1	1	1	1	0	0	0	5
f_i	19	16	15	13	11	8	5	3	90

$p_i =$ 0.95   0.80   0.75   0.65   0.55   0.40   0.25   0.15
$q_i =$ 0.05   0.20   0.25   0.35   0.45   0.60   0.75   0.85
$s_i^2 = p_i q_i =$ 0.0475 0.1600 0.1875 0.2275 0.2475 0.2400 0.1875 0.1275

$$M = \frac{90}{20} = 4.50, \qquad \sum p = 4.50$$

as right or wrong, then the distribution of frequencies of correct response will consist of only two categories (1 and 0) for each item. We can see from the score matrix that (for example) item 5 has been correctly solved by 11 individuals, while 9 have failed to solve it. The distribution for the item will therefore contain 9 individuals in category 0 and 11 individuals in category 1.

The 11 individuals who solved item 5 make up $\frac{11}{20}$ or $\frac{55}{100}$ of the total number who attempted to solve the item. We say that the proportion 0.55 have solved the item, or that the *frequency of correct response* expressed as a proportion is 0.55. The proportion of persons who have solved each item is given in row p beneath the score matrix.

If the frequency of correct response is given by p, the proportion of individuals who have not solved the item will be $1 - p$. It is usual to denote this value by q. It follows that $p + q = 1$.

We obtain p_i, the proportion who have solved the item, for any item i by dividing the number of correct solutions by the number of individuals tested. Thus,

$$p_i = \frac{\sum X_i}{N}, \tag{2-4}$$

where X can take only the values 1 or 0. It will be seen at once that the right-hand side of Eq. (2–4) is the expression for the arithmetic mean:

$$\sum X_i / N = M_i.$$

Thus

$$p_i = M_i. \tag{2-5}$$

This means that the value of the proportion of individuals who have solved the item is also an expression for the average performance of all the individuals on the item.

When the number of individuals tested is the same for every item, the average performance of all individuals on the test (M_t) will be the sum of the means on the individual items:

$$M_t = \sum M_i. \tag{2-6}$$

But $\sum M_i = \sum p_i$ (Eq. 2–5). Therefore

$$M_t = \sum p_i. \tag{2-7}$$

It can be seen from the score matrix that Eq. (2–7) is correct.

We can now derive from the equation for the standard deviation an expression for the variance of a single test item:

$$s_i^2 = \frac{\sum (X_i - M_i)^2}{N}. \tag{2-8}$$

But $M_i = p_i$, so that Eq. (2–8) can be expanded in the following way:

$$s_i^2 = \frac{\sum(X_i - p_i)^2}{N} = \frac{\sum X_i^2}{N} + \frac{\sum p_i^2}{N} - \frac{2p_i\sum X_i}{N}. \qquad (2\text{–}9)$$

The only values X can take are 1 and 0. Therefore, $X_i^2 = X_i$ and

$$\sum X_i^2/N = \sum X_i/N = p_i.$$

Since p_i has the same value in all N terms, we can write $\sum p_i^2/N$ as Np_i^2/N or p_i^2. We can now write Eq. (2–9) as follows:

$$s_i^2 = p_i + p_i^2 - 2p_i^2 = p_i - p_i^2 = p_i(1 - p_i) = p_iq_i. \qquad (2\text{–}10)$$

The variance of any single test item is thus the product of the proportion of individuals who solve the item and the proportion who fail to solve it. Since $p = 0.55$ and $q = 0.45$ for item 5 in the score matrix in Table 2–2, s^2 is $0.55 \times 0.45 = 0.2475$. The variance of every item has been computed in this way and inserted in Table 2–2.

Some examples are given in Fig. 2–2 of the relation between the variance and the frequency of solution for a given item. Figure 2–3 shows how the variance (s^2) of a single item varies with the frequency of correct response (p). The variance is dependent on the frequency of solution, i.e., the number of individuals who solve the item. Thus, $p = 0$ and the variance is zero when nobody solves the item. The variance increases as the frequency of solution increases, until p reaches the value 0.50. When p is 0.50, q is then also 0.50, and pq reaches its maximum value. The variance is thus greatest for test items which are solved by half of the individuals tested.

It should be observed that an item is useless for testing purposes when p equals 1 or 0, i.e., when everyone has either solved or failed to solve it. It does not discriminate among individuals, and gives a variance of zero.

The appearance of the score distribution is directly dependent on the difficulty of the individual items. An example will give a more concrete picture of the relation between the frequency of correct solution of individual items and the appearance of the distribution of scores. The score matrices for two tests administered to the same 20 individuals are shown in Tables 2–3 and 2–4, and the respective score distributions in Figs. 2–4 and 2–5.

It can be seen from Table 2–3 that the items in the first test are relatively easy. The frequency of correct solution is over 0.50 for six of the nine items. That the items are easy is also obvious if we look at the column for individual scores, or the distribution of scores in Fig. 2–4, where the scores are grouped at the right-hand side of the distribution. By choosing easy test items (items with high frequencies of correct solution) we have obtained a *negatively skewed* distribution of scores.

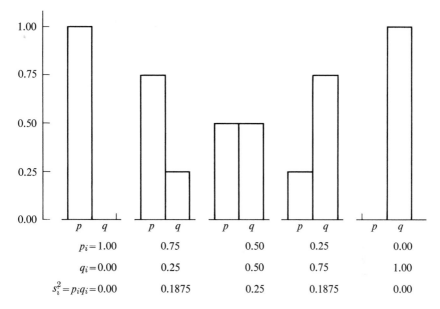

	$p_i = 1.00$	0.75	0.50	0.25	0.00
	$q_i = 0.00$	0.25	0.50	0.75	1.00
	$s_i^2 = p_i q_i = 0.00$	0.1875	0.25	0.1875	0.00

Fig. 2–2 The variance of items with varying frequency of correct response.

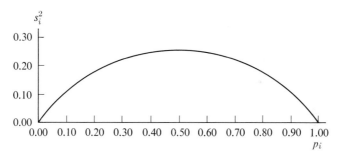

Fig. 2–3 The variance of a single item as a function of the frequencies of correct response.

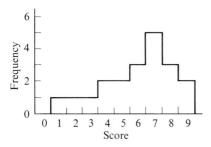

Fig. 2–4 A negatively skewed distribution.

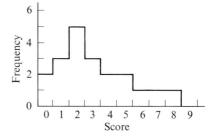

Fig. 2–5 A positively skewed distribution.

Table 2–3 Score matrix for a test administered to 20 individuals

					Item					
Individual	1	2	3	4	5	6	7	8	9	t_j
1	1	1	1	1	1	1	1	0	1	8
2	1	1	1	1	1	1	1	1	1	6
3	1	0	1	1	1	1	0	0	0	5
4	1	1	1	1	1	1	0	1	0	7
5	0	1	1	1	0	0	0	0	0	3
6	1	1	1	1	1	1	0	1	1	8
7	1	1	0	1	1	1	1	0	0	6
8	1	1	1	1	1	1	0	1	0	7
9	1	1	1	1	1	1	0	0	0	6
10	1	1	1	1	1	1	1	0	0	7
11	1	1	1	1	1	1	1	1	1	9
12	1	0	1	1	1	0	0	0	0	4
13	1	0	0	0	0	0	0	0	0	1
14	0	1	1	1	1	0	0	0	0	4
15	1	1	1	1	0	1	1	1	0	7
16	1	1	1	1	1	0	0	0	0	5
17	1	1	1	1	1	1	1	0	1	8
18	1	0	1	0	0	0	0	0	0	2
19	1	1	1	1	1	1	1	1	1	9
20	1	1	1	1	1	1	0	1	0	7
f_i	18	16	18	18	16	17	8	8	6	
p_i	0.90	0.80	0.90	0.90	0.80	0.70	0.40	0.40	0.30	

From Table 2–4 it can be seen that the items in the second test are relatively difficult. In this case the frequency of correct solution is over 0.50 for only three of the nine items. The difficulty of the items is also revealed by the column for individual scores, and by Fig. 2–5, in which the scores are grouped in the lower half of the distribution. By choosing difficult items (items with low frequencies of correct solution) we have obtained a *positively skewed* distribution of scores.

Intercorrelations between items are relatively high for both score matrices. Individuals who have solved items of a certain degree of difficulty have usually also solved items with higher frequencies of correct solution. We can establish that the score distributions in Figs. 2–4 and 2–5 have the same variance ($s_t^2 = 22.56$). On the whole, the two tests discriminate equally well among the individuals tested. However, the test whose score matrix is shown in Table 2–3 and which has given the negatively skewed distribution in Fig. 2–4 discriminates best among low-scoring individuals, while the test whose score matrix is shown in Table 2–4 and which has given the positively skewed distribution in Fig. 2–5 discriminates best among high-scoring individuals.

Table 2–4 Score matrix for a different test administered to the same 20 individuals

Individual	Item									t_j
	1	2	3	4	5	6	7	8	9	
1	1	1	0	0	0	0	0	0	0	2
2	1	0	1	1	1	1	0	0	0	5
3	1	1	0	1	0	0	0	0	0	3
4	1	1	1	0	0	0	0	0	0	3
5	1	1	1	1	1	1	0	1	0	7
6	1	1	0	0	0	0	0	0	0	2
7	1	1	1	0	1	0	0	0	0	4
8	1	0	0	0	0	0	0	0	0	1
9	1	1	0	1	1	0	0	0	0	4
10	1	1	1	1	1	1	1	0	1	8
11	1	0	1	0	0	0	0	0	0	2
12	1	0	0	0	0	0	0	0	0	1
13	1	1	0	0	0	0	0	0	0	2
14	1	1	1	1	0	1	0	0	0	5
15	0	0	0	0	0	0	0	0	0	0
16	1	0	0	0	0	0	0	0	0	1
17	0	0	0	0	0	0	0	0	0	0
18	1	1	1	1	1	1	0	0	0	6
19	1	1	0	0	0	0	0	0	0	2
20	1	1	1	0	0	0	0	0	0	3
f_i	18	14	9	7	6	5	1	1	1	
p_i	0.90	0.70	0.75	0.35	0.30	0.25	0.05	0.05	0.05	

PROBLEMS (Chapters 1 and 2)

1. In a test where the correct solution is denoted by 1 and the incorrect by 0, and where the items are homogeneous, item 1 has a frequency of correct solution $p = 0.50$. The distribution for this item is as follows.

0.50	0.50
0	1

Item 2 has $p = 0.80$. When $r_{12} = 1.00$, it is solved by all of the 50% who have solved the first item and by the best 30% of the remainder. The distribution of scores for items 1 and 2 is as follows.

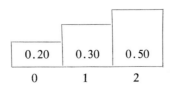

0.20	0.30	0.50
0	1	2

Draw the distribution for the entire test, where item 3 has $p = 0.90$, item 4 has $p = 0.70$, item 5 has $p = 0.60$, item 6 has $p = 0.10$, item 7 has $p = 0.20$, item 8 has $p = 0.30$, and item 9 has $p = 0.40$. What type of distribution is obtained?

2. Draw and describe the following distribution. Compare with Problem 1 (same assumptions as in Problem 1).

$$p_1 = 0.50 \qquad p_4 = 0.69 \qquad p_7 = 0.02$$
$$p_2 = 0.98 \qquad p_5 = 0.93 \qquad p_8 = 0.31$$
$$p_3 = 0.84 \qquad p_6 = 0.16 \qquad p_9 = 0.07$$

3. Ten items in a test have the following standard scores:

Item	1	2	3	4	5	6	7	8	9	10
Standard score	1.82	1.14	1.00	0.65	0.00	−0.48	−0.55	−0.75	−1.52	−1.77

Give for each item the frequency of correct solution expressed as (a) a proportion and (b) a percentage.

Item

Individual	1	2	3	4	5	6	7	8	9	10	11	12	13	14	15	16	17	18	19	20
1	1	1	1	1	1	1	1	1	1	1	1	1	1	1						
2	1	1	1	1	1	1	1	1	1	1	1	1	1	1	1	1	1			
3	1	1	1	1	1	1	1	1	1	1	1	1	1	1	1	1	1	1		
4	1	1	1																	
5	1	1	1	1	1	1	1	1	1	1	1									
6	1	1	1	1	1	1														
7	1	1	1	1	1	1	1	1	1	1	1	1	1	1	1	1	1	1	1	1
8	1																			
9	1	1	1	1	1	1	1	1	1	1	1									
10																				
11	1	1	1	1	1	1	1	1	1	1	1	1	1	1	1	1	1	1	1	
12	1	1	1	1	1	1	1	1	1	1	1	1	1	1	1	1				
13	1	1																		
14	1	1	1	1	1	1	1	1	1	1	1	1								
15	1	1	1	1	1	1	1													
16	1	1	1	1	1	1	1	1	1	1										
17	1	1	1	1																
18	1	1	1	1	1	1	1	1	1	1	1	1	1	1	1					
19	1	1	1	1	1	1	1	1												
20	1	1	1	1	1	1	1	1	1	1										

4. (a) Using Table B, p. 262, find the area to the left of z for the following z-values: -2.25, -1.75, -1.25, -0.75, -0.25, 0.25, 0.75, 1.25, 1.75, 2.25.

(b) Using the same z-table, find the area between the following z-scores: $-\infty$ and -2.25; -2.25 and -1.75; -1.75 and -1.25; -1.25 and -0.75; -0.75 and -0.25; -0.25 and 0.25; 0.25 and 0.75; 0.75 and 1.25; 1.25 and 1.75; 1.75 and 2.25; 2.25 and ∞.

5. Find the z-score corresponding to the p-value of each item in (a) Problem 1 and (b) Problem 2. Compare the relation between z-scores for the two sets of data.

6. (a) For the matrix on p. 30, construct a distribution of total scores with a class width of 2. (b) Compute f, p, and z for each item. (c) Select about 10 items to form a test which gives a normal distribution for 20 subjects. (d) Draw this distribution.

7. Do the following cells in the matrix have a value of 1 or 0: (a) $x_{3,8}$, (b) $x_{7,4}$, (c) $x_{2,19}$, (d) $x_{10,12}$, (e) $x_{3,10}$, (f) $x_{14,6}$?

8. Compute the variance of each of the items in the matrix.

9. Compute the variance of the distribution in Problem 6(a).

10. Compute the mean score for everyone tested using (a) $\sum X/N$ and (b) $\sum p$. Compare results.

CHAPTER 3

Correlation and Prediction

3-1 CORRELATION

A considerable number of methods have been devised for studying the
extent of those relationships which are important in differential psychology.
Consequently, only a very schematic and summary treatment of the problem
can be presented here. The reader is referred to Dixon and Massey (1957)
or Ezekiel and Fox (1959) for a more complete presentation of the concept
of correlation and its statistical significance. The main purpose of this
chapter is to make the concept of correlation easier to understand by explain-
ing the principles on which are founded the most common methods of
computing numerical values for psychological relationships. An attempt has
been made to do this with the aid of a minimum of statistical concepts and
definitions. The presentation is primarily intended for readers who have a
weak statistical background. The reader who has a good grasp of correlation
statistics may omit this chapter.

The relationship between variables is often referred to as correlation
between variables. The degree of correlation is expressed as a correlation
coefficient. A score is obtained for each of the two variables, the correlation
between which is to be studied. The correlation coefficient then gives the
extent to which the scores on one of the variables bear a systematic linear
relation to the scores on the other.

Let us take a practical example. Table 3-1 shows the results of an intelligence test and a school-achievement test for a class of 30 pupils.

We can see immediately from the scores in the table that there is a positive
relation between the results on the two tests. Those pupils who have high
scores on the intelligence test usually have high scores on the school-achievement test as well.

The relation between the two measurements can also be studied in a
rectangular coordinate system, where every individual's scores on both tests
are plotted.

In Fig. 3-1 every point on the graph expresses an individual's scores on
both tests. His score on the intelligence test can be read off on the x-axis

32

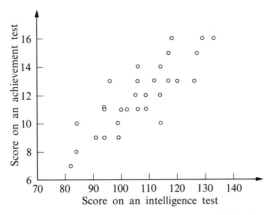

Fig. 3–1 Scatter diagram for the data in Table 3–1.

(the horizontal axis) by drawing a vertical line from his position on the graph to the x-axis. The individual's score on the school-achievement test can be read off on the y-axis by drawing a horizontal line from the point to this axis.

Figure 3–1 is an illustration of the relation between the scores on the two tests. We see that of 12 pupils with intelligence test scores above 110 only

Table 3–1 Obtained scores on an intelligence test (x) and a school-achievement test (y) for 30 girls

Intelligence test x	School-achievement test y	Intelligence test x	School-achievement test y
114	14	94	11
84	8	117	13
114	10	126	13
84	10	102	11
106	13	127	15
129	16	133	16
106	14	105	12
94	9	109	11
114	12	118	16
82	7	96	13
109	12	99	10
106	11	120	13
117	15	99	9
94	11	91	9
112	13	100	11

$$M_x = 106.700, \quad M_y = 11.933$$
$$s_x = 13.372, \quad s_y = 2.353$$

one has a score lower than 12 on the school-achievement test, but of 10 pupils with less than 100 on the intelligence test only one pupil has more than 12 on the school-achievement test.

In this way we can roughly establish that there is a positive relationship between the two measurements we have carried out, and we can also conclude that this relationship is relatively strong. For the present, however, we can merely make a subjective assessment of the extent of the relationship. This is of little use and by no means satisfactory as a measurement. An exact measurement is possible, however, if the relationship is expressed as a *coefficient of correlation*, which is generally denoted by r.

In the example based on the results of the 30 school children on an intelligence test and a school-achievement test, we saw that high scores on one usually corresponded to high scores on the other. This observation makes a prediction possible. If it can be verified that the relationship we have obtained in this class also holds in other classes, we may predict that if a pupil has a high score on the intelligence test he will probably have a high score on the school-achievement test. If another pupil obtains a low score on the intelligence test he will probably obtain a low score on the school-achievement test. In the immediately following section, the concept of correlation is seen primarily from the point of view of *prediction*. The most important problems connected with the interpretation of a correlation coefficient can be illustrated in this way.

3–2 THE REGRESSION LINE

Let us suppose that we are interested in the extent of the relation between scores on the intelligence test and the school-achievement test in order that we might on future occasions use the score on the intelligence test for a prediction about school performance.

The example illustrates in simplified form a situation which is very common in applied psychology. We first estimate the general relationship between scores on a prediction instrument, in this case the intelligence test, and a test of the accuracy of the prediction, in this case by giving the school-achievement test on a later occasion. It ought to be said right away, however, that in practical situations the prediction should be based on a considerably greater number of individuals than that used in our example.

We first study more closely the scores obtained on the school-achievement test by pupils with various scores on the intelligence test. We group the scores on the intelligence test into classes and compute the average school-achievement scores for each class interval on the intelligence test. The result is shown in Table 3–2 and, graphically, in Fig. 3–2. We see from the table that pupils who have scores in the class 75–84 on the intelligence test score an average of 8.33 on the school-achievement test, while pupils who have

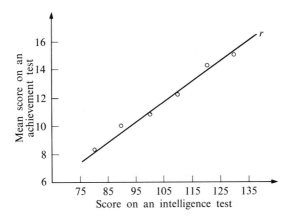

Fig. 3-2 Means of scores on the achievement test for pupils with various scores on the intelligence test (data in Table 3-2).

scores in the class 105–114 on the intelligence test have an average of 12.20 on the school-achievement test. However, each of the mean scores on the school-achievement test is based on a very small number of scores and is therefore unreliable. Some of the means would probably be different if we were to test some additional pupils. The greater the number of pupils in each class interval, the more reliable the mean scores on the school-achievement test.

Table 3-2 Mean scores on a school-achievement test for pupils with various intelligence quotients

I.Q.	75–84	85–94	95–104	105–114	115–124	125–134
M	8.33	10.00	10.80	12.20	14.25	15.00

If results from the two tests were available for a very large number of pupils, we should be able to use the mean scores on the school-achievement test as a best possible estimate of what score will be obtained on this test by any pupil whose I.Q. we know. With a sufficient number of pupils as a basis for computation of the means, we would of course be able to make the class intervals so small as to include only one intelligence score each. We should then obtain a mean score on the school-achievement test for every possible score on the intelligence test.

Those points which give the means of school-achievement scores (scores on the y-axis) for different class intervals on the intelligence test (scores on the x-axis) lie more or less in a straight line, as can be seen in Fig. 3-2. We assume for the present that deviations from such a straight line occur only as a result of the small number of individuals on which the computations are based. If we had access to scores for the whole population of pupils represented in Fig. 3–2 by a sample, the means of y-scores would, if the assumption is correct, lie along a straight line. This line is a regression line for the prediction of y-values when the object's x-values are known, in this case the prediction of pupils' scores on the school-achievement test when their scores on the intelligence test are known. The technical expression for it is the *regression line for the prediction of y on x.*

The points on this regression line give the best possible prediction of values on the y-axis from corresponding values on the x-axis. If we take a new individual from the same population and give him the intelligence test, the regression line gives for every intelligence test score obtained the best possible prediction of the score on the school-achievement test. This is true when certain conditions, which we shall return to later, are fulfilled. For the present we shall assume that they are satisfied. The exact position of the regression line can now be established for a given set of data. This is done by *the method of least squares* (cf., for example, Guilford, 1954, pp. 125–129). By this method the position of the line is determined so that the sum $[\sum(Y - Y')^2]$ of the squared deviations on the y-axis from the y-values which are given by the line is as small as possible. Only one line will satisfy this condition.

The equation of the straight line is written

$$y = a + bx. \tag{3–1}$$

The meaning of the symbols a and b is apparent from Figs. 3–3(a) and 3–3(b): a is the distance between the point where the straight line crosses the y-axis and the zero point, where the two axes meet; b is the tangent of the angle v, the angle between the x-axis and the straight line. The numerical

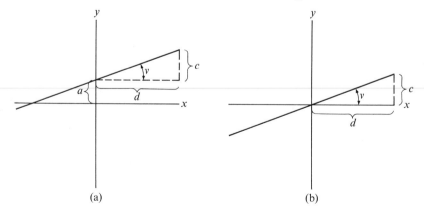

(a)   (b)

Fig. 3–3 The equation of a straight line in a rectangular coordinate system.

value of b is thus the ratio between the two distances denoted by the letters c and d in Fig. 3-3. That is, $b = c/d$.

Equation (3-1) expresses the linear relationship between observed values for the independent variable (x) and the best possible predictions of the dependent variable (y) for corresponding values of x. When we know an individual's observed score for the independent variable (his x-value) together with the position of the line which is given by the constants a and b, we can compute the score for the dependent variable (the y-value) which he is most likely to obtain. If the position of the straight line has been determined so that $a = 1.2$ and $b = 0.4$, the most likely y-value for an individual with an x-value of 1.5 will be $1.2 + 0.4 \times 1.5 = 1.8$.

Table 3-3 gives height in centimeters and body weight in kilograms for a group of 30 men, with the corresponding standard scores (z_x and z_y). For the values in this table the constants a and b have been calculated to be -63.08 and 0.772 for the straight line which has been computed by the method of least squares. This means, therefore, that the straight line crosses the y-axis (weight) at the value -63.08 on the weight scale. It should be observed that the computations are based on a sample of individuals. The values for a and b computed from this sample are thus an estimate of the values which

Table 3-3 Height in centimeters and body weight in kilograms for a group of 30 men

Height, cm	Standard score z_x	Weight, kg	Standard score z_y	Height, cm	Standard score z_x	Weight, kg	Standard score z_y
175	0.05	69	−0.54	168	−1.30	67	−0.91
171	−0.72	70	−0.35	180	−1.02	84	2.28
179	0.93	73	0.21	184	1.80	82	1.90
172	−0.53	65	−1.21	182	1.41	77	0.96
174	−0.14	68	−0.73	179	0.83	76	0.77
181	1.22	75	0.59	172	−0.53	74	0.40
169	−1.11	61	−2.04	171	−0.77	74	0.40
183	1.60	80	1.53	178	0.63	69	−0.54
167	−1.50	64	−1.48	177	0.44	70	−0.35
165	−1.89	65	−1.29	175	0.05	71	−0.16
170	−0.92	71	−0.16	176	0.25	74	0.40
173	−0.34	79	1.34	170	−0.92	68	−0.73
176	0.25	77	0.96	179	0.83	73	0.21
177	0.44	70	−0.35	175	0.05	67	−0.91
178	0.63	75	0.59				
166	−1.69	68	−0.73	$M_x = 174.73,$		$M_y = 71.87$	
				$s_x =$	5.16,	$s_y =$	5.33

hold for the whole population. We can now select a new individual from the population from which the 30 sample individuals were drawn. If we measure this individual's height, we can, with the help of the values computed for a and b, make a prediction about his body weight. If he is 180 cm tall his predicted weight according to Eq. (3–1) will be $-63.08 + 0.772 \times 180 = 75.88$ kg.

A situation of special interest for our discussion arises when the straight line passes through the meeting point of the coordinate axes, i.e., the zero point on the two axes. The position of the straight line under these circumstances is shown in Fig. 3–3(b). The value of a will then of course be zero and Eq. (3–1) will become

$$y = bx. \tag{3–2}$$

Thus, in this situation, the best possible prediction of the y-value for an individual with a given x-value is obtained by multiplying this x-value by the angle coefficient b.

It is apparent that every possible linear regression line will pass through the point of intersection of two straight lines that can now be drawn at 90° to each other through the means of the two distributions. The most probable y-value for someone who has an observed x-value which corresponds to the mean of the x-distribution will always be the mean of the y-distribution, no matter what relationship exists between the scores on the two distributions. We now let scores on both distributions be given as standard scores, so that the mean of both distributions is zero. The point of intersection of the two perpendicular axes through the means thus gives the zero point on both axes. Since every linear regression line passes through this point, the most probable value on the y-variable (under the given conditions expressed as a standard score, z'_y) for an individual with a given standard score on x will be obtained from the equation

$$z'_y = bz_x. \tag{3–3}$$

Thus, b is the multiple by which the standard score on x, which is our starting point, is to be multiplied in order to yield the most likely standard score on y which corresponds to this x-value. When every score is given as a standard score in the same units on both axes, then this angle coefficient is the same as the correlation coefficient for the relation between scores on distributions on the x- and y-axes and is denoted by r_{xy}.* Equation (3–3) can now be written

$$z'_y = r_{xy}z_x. \tag{3–4}$$

---

* Here the correlation coefficient is discussed only as an index of linear relationships (see also p. 43). It represents a special case of the more general regression function.

When we know an individual's observed standard score on x (z_x) and the correlation coefficient for the relation between scores on the x-distribution and scores on the y-distribution, we can obtain the best possible prediction of the individual's standard score on y by multiplying z_x by the correlation coefficient.

As has already been pointed out, b is the tangent of the angle between the x-axis and the straight line, the regression line, when prediction is made from the x-variable to the y-variable. Therefore, b is equal to the ratio between the y- and x-values for any point on the regression line, when values on both axes are given as standard scores. The highest positive value of b under these conditions will be 1.0 and the lowest negative value will be -1.0. When the regression line is parallel to the x-axis, as it is when the relation between the scores from two distributions is completely random, the angle coefficient will be zero.

It is perhaps worth pointing out here that the whole discussion so far has been based on the assumption that we wish to make a prediction from scores for the x-variable to scores for the y-variable. Exactly the same procedure can be used for predictions from scores for the y-variable to scores for the x-variable. In this case, b will be the multiple by which a standard score on y is to be multiplied in order to yield the corresponding score on x. This means that the regression line for prediction of x from y has a different slope from the regression line for prediction of y from x. The correlation coefficient will, however, be the same in both cases and the predicted x-value expressed as a standard score is obtained by multiplying the y-value from which the prediction is made by the correlation coefficient:

$$z_x' = r_{xy}z_y. \tag{3-5}$$

3–3   THE CORRELATION COEFFICIENT

Since $b = r$ under the conditions described in the previous section, what has been said about the value of b also holds for r, the correlation coefficient. Thus, r is the multiple by which a standard score on x is to be multiplied in order to give the corresponding standard score on y.

The correlation coefficient can have values between 1.0 and -1.0. The value 1.0 signifies that the agreement between the two sets of scores for which the correlation is computed is perfect and positive. Each individual has exactly the same position expressed as a standard score on both distributions. The value -1.0 signifies a perfect but negative relationship. In this case the individual's standard scores on the two distributions are the same, but have opposite signs. If there is no systematic linear relationship between the scores on the two distributions, the correlation coefficient is zero.

The correlation coefficient is thus a measure of the degree of linear relationship between two series of measurements. It can also be used in the same way as b, for making predictions from one variable to another. When we have expressed the degree of relationship between two variables as a correlation coefficient and know the value for a certain object for one of the variables, we can predict the most likely value for the other.

The accuracy with which a prediction can be made from one variable to the other increases with the degree of relationship between the scores: the greater the absolute magnitude of the correlation coefficient, the more certain the prediction becomes.

When the correlation coefficient is zero there is no systematic relationship between scores for the variables. The best we can do in this case, if we are forced to make a prediction of the most likely y-value from a known x-value, is to predict the mean of the y-distribution. The prediction would, of course, be exactly the same for all x-values. Thus, when the correlation is zero, it is impossible to make a meaningful prediction.

When the relationship is 1.0 the prediction can be made with perfect accuracy. The individual's standard scores are then the same for both variables. As soon as we know an individual's score on one distribution we know his score on the other. When the correlation coefficient is -1.0 we can make the prediction with the same accuracy.

The question of what degree of accuracy is possible for predictions based on correlation coefficients other than 1.0 and -1.0 will be dealt with more fully in Chapter 11. All that now remains is to derive an equation for the computation of the numerical value of the correlation coefficient.

The equation for the straight line which constitutes the regression line is $z'_y = r_{xy}z_x$. In a practical situation we know each individual's standard scores for the two variables whose relationship we wish to express as a correlation coefficient. The points which stand for these scores can be plotted in a coordinate system. Every point thus represents an individual. We then have to find the constant r in the equation for the straight line which best accommodates these points. By the method of least squares the position of the straight line is fixed so that, when the deviations of the individual scores (z_y) from the y-scores predicted by means of the regression line (z'_y) are squared, the sum of the squares will be as small as possible. This means that a value for r must be found which will give the expression $\sum(z_y - z'_y)^2$ the smallest possible numerical value. Since $z'_y = r_{xy}z_x$, the expression can be written $\sum(z_y - r_{xy}z_x)^2$. The x- and y-values are known for each term in this summation, and we have to find the value of r which gives the smallest sum of squares. Differentiating with respect to r, we find that the expression

$$r_{xy} = \frac{\sum z_x z_y}{N} \tag{3–6}$$

satisfies this condition. The constant r, the correlation coefficient, is thus equal to the mean of the products of the individual's standard scores for the two variables. (When making the derivation, we should note that

$\sum z_x^2 = N$, as is apparent when the equation for the standard deviation is expanded.)

In Table 3–4 the scores on the intelligence and the school-achievement tests for 30 girls, which were given in Table 3–1, are converted to standard scores. The product of standard scores on the two tests is computed for every girl. The mean of the sum of these products is the correlation coefficient, 0.832. Thus, we have to multiply an obtained standard score for one variable by 0.832 in order to make the best possible prediction of the standard score for the other.

We have now found the general equation for computing the *product moment coefficient*. Since computing scores for every individual on both variables in the form of z-scores is an unnecessarily tedious procedure, the equation is often written in another form. Since

$$z_x = \frac{X - M_x}{s_x} \quad \text{and} \quad z_y = \frac{Y - M_y}{s_y},$$

the general equation can be written

$$r_{xy} = \frac{\sum(X - M_x)(Y - M_y)}{N s_x s_y}. \tag{3-7}$$

Table 3–4 Standard scores for the results on an intelligence test and school-achievement test for 30 girls

Intelligence test z_x	Achievement test z_y	$z_x z_y$	Intelligence test z_x	Achievement test z_y	$z_x z_y$
0.546	0.880	0.4805	−0.950	−0.395	0.3753
−1.697	−1.670	2.8340	0.770	0.455	0.3504
0.546	−0.820	−0.4477	1.443	0.455	0.6566
−1.697	−0.820	1.3915	−0.351	−0.395	0.1386
−0.052	0.455	−0.0237	1.518	1.305	1.9810
1.668	1.730	2.8856	1.967	1.730	3.4029
−0.052	0.880	−0.0458	−0.127	0.030	−0.0038
−0.950	−1.245	1.1828	0.172	−0.395	−0.0679
0.546	0.030	0.0164	0.845	1.730	1.4619
−1.847	−2.095	3.8695	−0.800	0.455	−0.3640
0.172	0.030	0.0052	−0.576	−0.820	0.4723
−0.052	−0.395	0.0205	0.995	0.455	0.4527
0.770	1.305	1.0049	−0.576	−1.245	0.7171
−0.950	−0.395	0.3753	−1.174	−1.245	1.4616
0.396	0.455	0.1802	−0.501	−0.395	0.1979

$$\sum z_x z_y = 24.9618, \quad r = \frac{\sum z_x z_y}{N} = \frac{24.9618}{30} = 0.832$$

To find the correlation coefficient for the relation between two variables, we have to compute the product of the differences between raw score and mean on both distributions for every individual. We then add the products and divide the result by the number of products (individuals) in order to obtain the mean. The size of this mean is dependent on the scale on which the individual variables are measured. Since it is obvious that the relation between two variables should not be dependent on the scale used in establishing the individuals' scores, a correction is made for this by dividing the mean product by the standard deviations of the two distributions.

In practical situations Eq. (3–8), which is merely a different algebraic form of Eq. (3–7), can conveniently be computed directly from raw scores:

$$r_{xy} = \frac{\sum XY(\sum X \sum Y/N)}{\sqrt{[\sum X^2 - (\sum X)^2/N][\sum Y^2 - (\sum Y)^2/N]}}. \tag{3-8}$$

Some characteristic features of the correlation coefficient should be noted. It is the magnitude of the products, other things being equal, which determines that of the correlation coefficient. All products for points which lie in the upper right-hand or lower left-hand quadrants will be positive and will increase the sum of the products—since the products of the values have the same sign—while the products for points which lie in the other two quadrants will be negative and will reduce the sum. The sum of the products will be greatest when every individual's z-score is the same on both variables. The correlation between the variables is then perfect and positive and the correlation coefficient is 1.0. If the relation between the two variables is purely random, the points will be distributed randomly over the correlation field. The positive and negative product sums will then tend to cancel each other and the correlation coefficient will be zero.

3–4   THE REGRESSION COEFFICIENT

We saw previously that $r = b$ in the normal equation for a straight line if we express every individual's score as a standard score. We then obtained the equation $z_y' = r_{xy} z_x$. If, instead of expressing the individuals' positions on the distributions as standard scores, we express them as deviations from the means of the respective distributions ($y' = Y' - M_y$, and $x = X - M_x$), we obtain

$$\frac{y'}{s_y} = r_{xy}\frac{x}{s_x}.$$

Multiplying both sides by s_y we obtain

$$y' = r_{xy}\frac{s_y}{s_x}x. \tag{3-9}$$

If we express the individuals' scores as deviations from the means of the respective distributions, we then obtain the most likely y-score (y') for an individual with a given x-score by multiplying the x-score by the expression

$$r_{xy} \frac{s_y}{s_x}. \tag{3–10}$$

This is *the regression coefficient for prediction of y from x*. It is denoted by b_{yx}. It gives the slope of the regression line, regardless of whether we have the same units on the two axes. When we use the standard deviation of the distributions as a unit, i.e., express every score as a standard score, then $b_{yx} = r_{xy}$, as was previously explained.

The same reasoning can be used to derive *the regression coefficient for a prediction of x from y*. In this case, we obtain the equation

$$b_{xy} = r_{xy} \frac{s_x}{s_y}. \tag{3–11}$$

The most likely score for the x-variable for a given score for the y-variable is thus obtained by multiplying the y-score by the above expression (3–11). Thus,

$$x' = r_{xy} \frac{s_x}{s_y} y. \tag{3–12}$$

The expression for computing the most likely raw score for the y-variable for an individual with a given raw score for the x-variable is obtained by replacing y' by $Y' - M_y$ and x by $X - M_x$ in Eq. (3–9). Thus,

$$Y' = r_{xy} \frac{s_y}{s_x} (X - M_x) + M_y. \tag{3–13}$$

3–5   LINEARITY AND HOMOSCEDASTICITY

In the previous discussion we assumed that the points in the coordinate system which represent initial scores and predicted scores are grouped around a straight line, the regression line. When this is the case, we say that the relation between the distributions is *linear*. If we compute the mean of the y-values that correspond to each of the x-values obtained by a relatively limited number of individuals, we will probably find that these means do not lie exactly along a straight line. This is because of the limited number of individuals. We must tolerate a certain dispersion of these means around the regression line. The dispersion of these scores in every column is reduced as the number of subjects increases. The magnitude of deviation we can tolerate in a linear relationship can be computed when we know the number of individuals included in the distributions. If linearity is not apparent, this does not mean that there is no systematic relationship between the scores

Table 3-5 The variances of the score distributions on the school-achievement test (y-values) within each class interval

I.Q.	75–84	85–94	95–104	105–114	115–124	125–134
s^2	1.61	1.00	1.76	1.56	1.69	1.50

on the two distributions. The results can be perfectly correlated on the basis of nonlinear relationships with equally good opportunities for prediction. Such relationships are, however, relatively uncommon. To compute the degree of relationship between the results on distributions between which linearity does not exist, one must apply methods other than those discussed here (see, e.g., McNemar, 1962, pp. 202–203, 272–281).

Table 3–2 and Fig. 3–2 showed the means of the scores obtained on the school-achievement test by pupils with various scores on the intelligence test. The scores on which each mean is based (i.e., the achievement-test scores corresponding to each interval on the x-axis) are dispersed around the mean for the interval. This can be seen in Fig. 3–1.

For each of the intervals on the x-axis, it is possible to obtain a distribution of those y-values which correspond to the respective intervals on the x-axis. Table 3–5 shows the variances of these distributions of obtained scores on the school-achievement test for each class interval on the intelligence test.

We can see that the variance values for different intervals do not differ to any great extent. Since each value is based on a very small number of observations, we could expect relatively large differences among variance values, even if they had been the same for every interval for the total population of girls from which our 30 girls have been selected. A condition of one of the most important applications of the correlation coefficient (to be discussed in more detail in Chapter 11) is that the variances of the distributions of scores around the regression line—in the columns when we are predicting from x to y, and in the rows when we are predicting from y to x— do not vary more than can be explained in terms of sample size. If this condition is satisfied, the relation is *homoscedastic*.

Whenever the relation is homoscedastic, the variance of the distribution of scores for the variable to which the prediction is being made will thus be the same, no matter which score on the predictor variable the prediction is based on. This means that the size of the probable deviation (from the predicted score) in the variable to which the prediction is made is always the same, regardless of the size of the score on which the prediction is based. As the above discussion has already shown, we cannot expect equal variances in a limited sample, even when we have homoscedasticity. How much deviation we can tolerate depends on the number of individuals in the sample and can be estimated (cf. Ferguson, 1959, pp. 140–142).

3–6   THE ϕ-COEFFICIENT*

When treating data in differential psychology we must often compute the correlation between variables where there are scores in only two categories for each variable, e.g., 0 and 1. In such cases the degree of relationship between the variables can be expressed as a ϕ-*coefficient*. One of the uses of the ϕ-coefficient is to express the correlation between two test items.

Let us select two items, items 5 and 6, from the score matrix in Table 2–2 as an example (see Table 3–6).

Table 3–6

Individual

Item	1 2 3 4 5 6 7 8 9 10 11 12 13 14 15 16 17 18 19 20	p	q
5	0 0 0 1 0 0 1 0 1 1 1 1 1 1 0 1 0 1 0 1	0.55	0.45
6	0 0 0 1 0 0 1 0 1 1 1 0 1 0 0 0 0 1 1 0	0.40	0.60

The scores of every individual for both variables can now be summarized in a fourfold table (Table 3–7). As can be seen from this table, four individuals solved item 5 but failed to solve item 6, seven individuals solved both items, and eight failed on both items, while one individual failed to solve item 5 but managed to solve item 6.

Table 3–7 A fourfold table

Item 6

Item 5	$-$	$+$	Σ
$+$	4	7	11
$-$	8	1	9
Σ	12	8	20

At this stage we can immediately draw certain parallels with the product moment coefficient. The degree of relationship, as expressed by the correlation coefficient, indicates the degree of accuracy with which it is possible to predict from one of the two distributions to the other. Here, a perfectly accurate prediction could be made if each score were to be found in the upper right-hand quadrant and the lower left-hand quadrant or in the upper left-hand quadrant and the lower right. This would be the result if everyone who solved item 5 also solved item 6, and if everyone who failed on one also failed on the other. If we then knew an individual's result on item 5, we could predict his result on item 6 with complete confidence. Under these conditions the correlation coefficient should be 1.0.

---

* The symbol ϕ is the Greek letter phi. As a subscript it will be written r_{phi}.

Table 3–8

Item k

Item i	−	+	Σ
+	A a	B b	$a + b = p_i$
−	C c	D d	$c + d = q_i$
Σ	$a + c = q_k$	$b + d = p_k$	1.0

With the help of the symbols in Table 3–8 above, we can now derive the general equation for computing the ϕ-coefficient. Capital letters (A, B, C, D) denote frequencies of raw scores in each cell. Small letters (a, b, c, d) represent the proportions of the individuals tested which are to be found in the respective cells. This means that $a + b + c + d = 1.0$.

The usual equation for a product moment coefficient has already been given (Eq. 3–6). The correlation between items i and k can thus be written

$$r_{ik} = \frac{\Sigma(X_i - M_i)(X_k - M_k)}{Ns_i s_k} .$$

Expanding the right-hand side and ignoring the standard deviations, we arrive at the following:

$$\frac{\Sigma X_i X_k}{N} - \frac{M_k \Sigma X_i}{N} - \frac{M_i \Sigma X_k}{N} + \frac{\Sigma M_i M_k}{N} .$$

But

$$\Sigma X_i X_k / N = p_{ik}.$$

The expression p_{ik} is the proportion of the total number of individuals who solved both items, i.e., the proportion b in Table 3–8. All other products included in the summation in the first term will be zero:

$$\frac{\Sigma X_i}{N} = M_i \quad \text{and} \quad \frac{\Sigma X_k}{N} = M_k.$$

There are as many summations of the constant product $M_i M_k$ as there are individuals, so that the last term can be written

$$NM_i M_k / N = M_i M_k.$$

The whole equation can now be simplified to

$$p_{ik} - M_i M_k - M_i M_k + M_i M_k = p_{ik} - M_i M_k.$$

But $M_i = p_i$ and $M_k = p_k$ (Eq. 2–5), and we are left with the expression $p_{ik} - p_i p_k$. If we replace the expression we abstracted from the general equation for the product moment coefficient with the expression we have now derived, we obtain

$$r_{ik} = \frac{p_{ik} - p_i p_k}{s_i s_k}.$$ (3–14)

We found previously that the standard deviation of the distribution of scores from an item i was $\sqrt{p_i q_i}$ (Eq. 2–10).

We can now obtain the final equation for a ϕ-coefficient:

$$r_{phi} = \frac{p_{ik} - p_i p_k}{\sqrt{p_i q_i p_k q_k}},$$ (3–15)

where p_{ik} is the proportion of those tested who have solved both items. In the example which we used previously, r_{phi} for the correlation between items 5 and 6 would thus be

$$r_{phi} = \frac{\frac{7}{20} - 0.55 \times 0.40}{\sqrt{0.55 \times 0.45 \times 0.40 \times 0.60}} = \frac{0.35 - 0.22}{\sqrt{0.0594}} = 0.53.$$

In certain situations it can be an unnecessarily tedious procedure to compute p- and q-values when calculating the ϕ-coefficient. In these cases, one can compute r_{phi} directly from the frequencies of the fourfold table (Table 3–7) by means of the equation

$$r_{phi} = \frac{BC - AD}{\sqrt{(A + B)(C + D)(A + C)(B + D)}}.$$ (3–16)

From this equation, the correlation coefficient for the relation between items 5 and 6 is

$$r_{phi} = \frac{7 \times 8 - 4 \times 1}{\sqrt{11 \times 9 \times 12 \times 8}} = \frac{56 - 4}{\sqrt{9504}} = 0.53.$$

The product moment coefficient computed by Eq. (3–7) can have values between -1.0 and 1.0. It is, however, only under special conditions that the ϕ-coefficient has these extreme values. The maximum ϕ-coefficient will be 1.0 only when $p_i = p_k$, that is, when both dichotomous distributions have exactly the same form. It is also obvious that the prediction from one distribution to the other can be completely accurate only when everyone who belongs to the one category in distribution i belongs to the same category in distribution k. The ϕ-coefficient has the maximum negative value of -1.0 only when $p_i = q_k$, that is, when the two distributions are mirror images of each other. Under all other conditions, the maximum value of the ϕ-coefficient will be less than 1.0 and dependent upon the relationship p_i/p_k. The size of r_{phi} is thus systematically dependent upon the relationship p_i/q_i. A comparison between ϕ-coefficients which have been obtained from distributions of differing appearance ought to take this fact into account.

3–7   STANDARD ERROR OF CORRELATION COEFFICIENTS

As we have already said, when the correlation coefficient is zero the regression line, when we are predicting from x to y, is horizontal and passes through the mean of the y-distribution. This means that when the correlation is zero the angle coefficient is also zero, i.e., the regression line is parallel to the x-axis. This statement is likely to hold for an infinite number of individuals if we assume that there is no systematic relationship between the variables. We could then say that the "true" correlation, written ρ, between the variables is zero. If we select a number of individuals at random from a certain population and compute the correlation between the variables for this sample, we must expect random deviations from the horizontal regression line. These deviations can occur in either direction and can thus give positive or negative coefficients. If we compute the correlation between two variables for a great number of sufficiently large samples drawn from a total population for which no systematic relationship exists between the variables, i.e., for which the "true" correlation is zero, we will probably obtain a normal distribution of coefficients with zero as the mean. The smaller the number of individuals included in a sample, the greater the probability of a deviation from zero for the coefficient. It follows that the determination of the position of the straight line becomes more and more uncertain, the smaller the number of scores on which it is based.

The standard deviation of the sampling distribution of correlation coefficients—the standard error of the correlation coefficient—depends therefore on the number of individuals on which the computation is based.

If the standard error of the correlation coefficients is given, we can compute a confidence interval to establish whether a coefficient of a certain magnitude may have arisen although the "true" correlation is in fact zero.

The size of the standard error depends on the number of individuals in the sample (N). But it is also dependent on the size of ρ, as can be seen from the equation for the standard error of the product moment coefficient:

$$s_r = \frac{1 - \rho^2}{\sqrt{N - 1}}. \tag{3–17}$$

When we are judging the significance of correlation coefficients the given equation is used mainly for testing the null hypothesis, i.e., the assumption that $\rho = 0$. There are two reasons why the equation cannot be used for testing the significance of other values of the correlation coefficient.

First, the random distribution is not symmetric when ρ has values other than zero. For positive values it is negatively skewed, and for negative values it is positively skewed. The skewness increases with the size of the mean, i.e., the more ρ deviates from zero. It is possible to test the statistical significance of coefficients other than zero by means of a method developed by Fisher (cf. Edwards, 1959, pp. 126–128). Here one converts r to z_r, the so-called Fisher's z, in order to distinguish it from the z which is used to denote standard scores. The sampling distribution of Fisher's z is approximately normal, and its standard error depends only on the size of the sample.

Second, the r-value which is to be used in the numerator is one of the values in the distribution whose standard error is to be computed. We use this value as an estimate of ρ. But, since the size of the standard error depends on the size of ρ, the obtained value will be correct only if this estimate is correct.

For these reasons, the given equation for the standard error is used mainly for testing the null hypothesis. This done we then determine the limits for different confidence intervals with the help of the standard error. Equation (3–17) thus takes the form*

$$s_r = 1/\sqrt{N - 1}. \qquad (3\text{–}18)$$

Since $\rho = 0$ under these conditions, the standard error depends only on the number of individuals included in the sample. Let us take a practical example. We can compute s_r for three random distributions of correlation coefficients, where the coefficients are computed from samples of the following sizes: $N_a = 400$, $N_b = 100$, $N_c = 50$. The standard errors for coefficients computed from groups with this number of individuals will then be: $s_{r_1} = 0.05$, $s_{r_2} = 0.10$, $s_{r_3} = 0.14$. The sampling distributions are shown in Fig. 3–4. A correlation coefficient which lies outside $\pm 1.96 s_r$ in the random distribution will be obtained for approximately 5% of the coefficients which can be computed, even if $\rho = 0$. Thus, when we have a

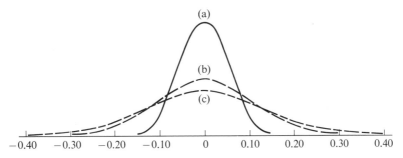

Fig. 3–4 Sampling distributions of correlation coefficients for samples of various sizes when the correlation in the population is zero.

---

* The equation ought to be used only when $N > 30$. The standard error for r of different sizes can be obtained directly from available tables. It should be observed that the number of degrees of freedom (Df) is $N - 2$.

sample of 50 individuals and the "true" correlation is zero, about 5% of all coefficients will be randomly greater than 0.28 in a positive or negative direction. The random probability of obtaining a correlation of 0.28 or greater (i.e., only in the positive direction) is half as great, or about 2.5%.

PROBLEMS

1. Twenty-eight pupils in fourth grade are given a verbal test. In their final examination in English at the end of the year the same pupils obtained the results shown in the table below. Grades on the final examination are from zero to 10.

Test scores	25	30	42	38	31	22	26	35	29	31	27	39	21	32
Final grades	3.5	4.5	7.5	6.5	5.0	4.0	4.0	6.5	5.0	5.5	5.0	7.0	2.0	4.0

Test scores	26	28	35	33	25	36	32	27	29	30	33	18	40	20
Final grades	3.0	3.0	5.0	5.5	4.0	6.0	5.0	4.0	4.5	5.0	6.0	2.0	7.0	3.0

(a) Plot the score of each pupil in a scatter diagram with test scores as the independent variable on the x-axis.

(b) Using the normal equations below, compute the constants a and b for the straight line and insert it in the diagram:

$$a = \frac{\sum Y - b\sum X}{N}, \qquad b = \frac{\sum XY - \sum X \sum Y/N}{\sum X^2 - (\sum X)^2/N}.$$

2. (a) Construct the frequency distribution of scores for the test and the final examination.

(b) Compute the standard deviation of each of the distributions and convert raw scores to standard scores in the respective distributions. Record the position of every individual as a standard score in a new scatter diagram.

(c) Compute the constant b for the straight line and draw this line on the scatter diagram.

3. Using Eq. (3–6), compute the correlation coefficient for the relation between the standard scores on the two distributions. Compare the size of the coefficient with the value of b in Problem 2(c).

4. Group the test scores into five classes and compute the mean of the final examination results (as a standard score) for each class. Using the regression line in Problem 2(c), compare the values obtained in this way with the prediction of the size of the y-values which can be made for every class of scores.

5. Using Eq. (3–8), compute the correlation between the raw scores of the distributions.

6. Distribution x has standard deviation $s_x = 2$ and $M_x = 15$; y has standard deviation $s_y = 10$ and $M_y = 50$. Draw both regression lines when (a) $r = 0.30$, (b) $r = 0.60$, and (c) $r = 0.90$. Use Eqs. (3–10) and (3–11).

7. The following scores have been obtained for the x- and y-variables in a test.

	x						
y	10	11	12	13	14	15	16
106				2	6	14	26
105		1	2	10	16	25	5
104	1	1	7	20	30	9	3
103	2	7	20	28	15	1	1
102	6	25	15	6	1		
101	20	15	8	1			

(a) Draw the two distributions in histogram form.   Discuss the shape of the distribution.

(b) For each column compute the mean of the y-scores for that group.

(c) Make predictions from x-scores to y-scores.

(d) Fit a straight line to these points (the means) by determining the size of b_{yx} (Eq. 3–7). Compare with Problem 1.

(e) Make the same predictions as in (c) and compare.

8. Using standard scores on both distributions, draw the regression lines in a coordinate system for the following correlation coefficients: 0.90, 0.75, 0.60, 0.45, 0.30, 0.15.

9. Plot the following points in a scatter diagram and draw both regression lines (without any arithmetic computations).   Read off b_{xy} and b_{yx}.   Is r a suitable measure of the relationship?

x	7 6 3 7 5 4 2 3 6 2 5 1 6 4 5 1 4 1 4 5 6 3 4 3
y	6 4 2 7 6 2 4 4 6 2 3 3 5 5 5 2 4 3 2 3 7 4 4 3

10. The following scores have been obtained for twelve individuals tested on five items:

Individual	Item 1	2	3	4	5	Individual	Item 1	2	3	4	5
1	1	1	1	1		7	1		1	1	
2	1	1		1		8	1	1	1	1	1
3	1		1		1	9	1	1	1	1	1
4	1	1	1	1	1	10	1	1			1
5	1	1	1	1		11	1	1	1	1	1
6			1			12	1	1	1	1	1

(a) Compute r_{phi} for the correlation between every pair of items.

(b) With the aid of r_{phi}, rank the items according to their ability to discriminate between the best 42% and the poorest 58% of the individuals.

11. The following scores were obtained when two groups were tested:

Score	Group I	Group II
1	3	1
2	5	3
3	9	3
4	11	7
5	7	6
6	9	8
7	5	10
8	4	10
9	2	8
10	6	5
11	3	2
12	5	4
13	1	1
14	0	2
15	1	1

By splitting the score distribution into two parts (a) at the score 3.5, (b) at the score 6.5, (c) at the score 11.5, compute the ϕ-coefficient for the correlation between group membership and the variable measured. Discuss differences in results.

12. From a sample of 225 individuals a value of 0.16 is obtained for r as a measure of the correlation between two variables x and y. Test for significance.

13. When $N = 75$, how large must a product-moment coefficient be for it to be significant at the 5% level? Use the normal distribution table (Table B, p. 262).

14. When $N = 75$, how large must a positive correlation coefficient be for it to be significant at the 5% level?

REFERENCES

DIXON, W. J., and F. J. MASSEY (1957). *Introduction to statistical analysis.* New York: McGraw-Hill.

EDWARDS, A. L. (1959). *Experimental design in psychological research.* New York: Rinehart & Co.

EZEKIEL, M., and K. A. FOX (1959). *Methods of correlation and regression analysis.* New York: Wiley.

FERGUSON, G. A. (1959). *Statistical analysis in psychology and education.* New York: Wiley.

GUILFORD, J. P. (1954). *Psychometric methods* (2nd ed.). New York: McGraw-Hill.

MCNEMAR, Q. (1962). *Psychological statistics.* New York: Wiley.

CHAPTER 4

Total Test Variance; Covariance

4-1   THE VARIANCE OF A DISTRIBUTION OF COMPOSITE SCORES

In Chapter 2 we found the equation for computing the variance of a distribution when testing with only one item and placing each response in one of two categories (Eq. 2–10). The frequency distribution of scores from a test composed of several items is dependent in appearance and size on the properties of the individual items included in the test. We shall now derive an equation for computing the variance of a test distribution and examine the properties of the individual items which affect its size.

We wish first to obtain an expression for the variance of a distribution of raw scores for a test consisting of *two* items i and k. The score of each individual on each of the items is expressed as a deviation from the mean of the item distribution:

$$x_i = X_i - M_i, \qquad x_k = X_k - M_k. \tag{4-1}$$

The result of this procedure is that the means of the distributions are chosen as zero points. The score of each individual on the composite distribution, expressed as a deviation from the mean of the distribution, will be made up of the sum of the deviations of the individual on the two distributions:

$$\begin{aligned}
x_{i+k} &= X_{i+k} - M_{i+k} \\
&= X_i + X_k - (M_i + M_k) \\
&= X_i - M_i + X_k - M_k \\
&= x_i + x_k.
\end{aligned} \tag{4-2}$$

Since $x_i + x_k$ is a deviation of $X_i + X_k$ from M_{i+k}, the variance of the composite distribution can now be written as

$$s_{i+k}^2 = \frac{\sum(x_i + x_k)^2}{N}, \tag{4-3}$$

where s_{i+k}^2 is the variance of a test with two items i and k,

$$s_{i+k}^2 = \frac{\sum(x_i + x_k)^2}{N} = \frac{\sum x_i^2}{N} + \frac{\sum x_k^2}{N} + \frac{2\sum x_i x_k}{N}$$

$$\frac{\sum x_i^2}{N} = s_i^2,$$

$$\frac{\sum x_k^2}{N} = s_k^2.$$

But $r_{ik} = \sum x_i x_k / N s_i s_k$. Therefore $\sum x_i x_k / N = r_{ik} s_i s_k$, and hence

$$s_{i+k}^2 = s_i^2 + s_k^2 + 2r_{ik} s_i s_k, \qquad (4\text{-}4)$$

where $r_{ik} s_i s_k$ is a covariance term. In the following section the concept of covariance will be treated in more detail.

The variance of a test consisting of two items is thus made up of the sum of the variances of the two items, together with twice the covariance (Eq. 4–4).

Table 4–1 shows scores from two tests (I and II), each consisting of two items. Both tests have been given to 12 subjects. The table can be used as an illustration of the effect of the two factors on the variance of a test with two items.

Table 4–1 Scores from two tests, each consisting of two items and administered to 12 subjects

Test	I		II	
Item	1	2	1	2
1	1	0	1	1
2	1	0	0	0
3	1	0	1	1
4	0	1	1	1
5	0	1	1	1
6	0	1	0	0
7	0	0	0	0
8	0	0	0	0
9	0	0	1	1
10	1	1	0	0
11	1	1	1	1
12	1	1	0	0
p	0.50	0.50	0.50	0.50
q	0.50	0.50	0.50	0.50
r_{phi}	0		1.0	

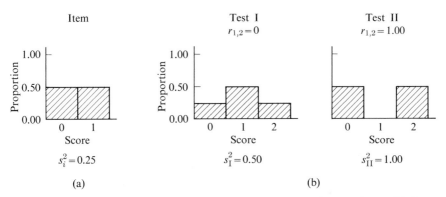

Fig. 4–1 Probability distribution of scores (a) for a test with one item, (b) for a test with two items for zero correlation (Test I) and for positive correlation between the items (Test II).

It is easily seen that r_{phi} for the two items making up Test I will be zero. The four cells in a fourfold table will all have equal frequencies, and no prediction will be possible from one item to the other. For the two items making up Test II, r_{phi} must be 1.0, since those individuals who solved the first item also solved the second. Predictions from one item to the other can therefore be made with complete certainty.

The frequency distribution of one of the items is shown in Fig. 4–1(a). The distribution of each of the items has the same form and the same variance. For each of the four items, p and q are 0.50 and $s^2 = pq = 0.25$. If we now compute the variance of the two tests I and II—each composed of two items with the same variance—we obtain

$$s_{\text{I}}^2 = s_1^2 + s_2^2 + 2r_{12}s_1s_2 = 0.25 + 0.25 = 0.50$$

and

$$s_{\text{II}}^2 = s_1^2 + s_2^2 + 2r_{12}s_1s_2 = 0.25 + 0.25 + 2 \times 1.0 \times 0.25 = 1.0.$$

The correlation between the items is zero in Test I, so that the last term is also zero. In Test II, $s_1 = s_2$, so that $s_1 s_2 = s_1^2$.

Figure 4–1(b) shows the shape of the two test distributions. The most probable distribution is *binomial* (see Fig. 1–2) when the correlation between the items is zero (Test I), and *bimodal* when the correlation is 1.0 (Test II).

In general, the variance of a test composed of n items is

$$s_t^2 = s_1^2 + s_2^2 + s_3^2 + \cdots + s_i^2 + \cdots + s_n^2 + 2r_{12}s_1s_2 + \cdots + 2r_{1i}s_1s_i$$
$$+ \cdots + 2r_{1n}s_1s_n + \cdots + 2r_{(n-1)n}s_{n-1}s_n.$$

When simplified this can be written as

$$s_t^2 = \sum s_i^2 + 2\sum r_{ik}s_is_k, \qquad i > k \tag{4-5}$$

where $\sum s_i^2$ is the sum of the variances of the individual items, and $2\sum r_{ik}s_is_k$ is the sum of all $n(n-1)$ covariance terms.

The size of the total test distribution is therefore determined by two factors: (1) the frequency of correct response on the individual items ($s_i^2 = p_iq_i$) and (2) the correlations between the individual items (r_{ik}).

The following conclusions, which are important for all test construction work, can be drawn from the formula for the total test variance:

1. The test variance is determined entirely by the variance of the individual items and their intercorrelations.

2. The test variance will be greatest, other things being equal, when the variance of the individual items is greatest, i.e., when $p_i = q_i$ and $s_i^2 = 0.25$.

3. The test variance will be greatest, other things being equal, when the intercorrelations between the items are greatest (see Fig. 4–1b).

4–2   COVARIANCE

The equation for the variance of a test composed of n items (Eq. 4–5) includes a summation of terms of the type $r_{ik}s_is_k$. The term is a covariance and is written as C_{ik}.

The usual equation for the product moment coefficient between items i and k is written in the following way:

$$r_{ik} = \sum x_i x_k / N s_i s_k.$$

On multiplying both sides by s_is_k we obtain an expression for the covariance:

$$C_{ik} = r_{ik}s_is_k = \sum x_ix_k/N. \qquad (4\text{–}6)$$

The covariance is thus the mean of the products of the deviations from the means of the two distributions. When computing the coefficient for the correlation, we relate this mean product to the standard deviations of the distributions to ensure that the size of the correlation coefficient will be independent of the scale on which we have chosen to express the individual values. The size of the covariance will, however, be dependent on the properties of the scale chosen. It will therefore vary if one or both of the distributions are subject to a linear transformation (see p. 233).

The correlation between items (r_{ik} in Eq. 4–4) should be computed as a ϕ-coefficient (see Eq. 3–15). Since $s_i = \sqrt{p_iq_i}$ and $s_k = \sqrt{p_kq_k}$, the equation for the covariance can be simplified and the following expression obtained:

$$C_{ik} = p_{ik} - p_ip_k, \qquad (4\text{–}7)$$

where p_{ik} is the proportion of individuals tested who have solved both item i and item k correctly.

The last expression in Eq. (4–6) reminds one of the expression for the variance of a single item. The variance of item i may be written as $\sum x_i x_i / N$ and the variance of item k as $\sum x_k x_k / N$. If the correlation between items i and k is 1.0, then x_i is equal to x_k for each individual. This assumes that $p_i = p_k$ in the case of ϕ-coefficients, i.e., that the standard deviations of the items are equal. We thus obtain

$$\sum x_i x_k / N = \sum x_i x_i / N = \sum x_k x_k / N.$$

The entire variance of an item is a common variance when the correlation between items is 1.0.

4–3　THE VARIANCE-COVARIANCE MATRIX

It can be seen from Eq. (4–5) that each item contributes two types of terms to the total test variance: (a) *one* term consisting of the variance of the item (s_i^2) and (b) $n - 1$ covariance terms, where the covariance with each of the other items is computed. The number of covariance terms is obviously $n - 1$, since $i \neq k$. The variance of the composite test will therefore be made up of n variance terms and $n(n - 1)$ covariance terms, i.e., the sum of all cell scores in a variance-covariance matrix.

Table 4–2 Variance-covariance matrix

				Item			
Item	1	2	3	$\cdots$	i	$\cdots$	n
1	s_1^2	C_{12}	C_{13}	$\cdots$	C_{1i}	$\cdots$	C_{1n}
2	C_{21}	s_2^2	C_{23}	$\cdots$	C_{2i}	$\cdots$	C_{2n}
3	C_{31}	C_{32}	s_3^2	$\cdots$	C_{3i}	$\cdots$	C_{3n}
$\vdots$	$\vdots$						$\vdots$
i	C_{i1}	C_{i2}	C_{i3}	$\cdots$	s_i^2	$\cdots$	C_{in}
$\vdots$	$\vdots$						$\vdots$
n	C_{n1}	C_{n2}	C_{n3}	$\cdots$	C_{ni}	$\cdots$	s_n^2

It can be seen from Table 4–2 that, as the number of items is increased (other conditions remaining unchanged), the sum of the covariance terms will make up an increasing share of the sum of the total matrix and thus of the total test variance as well.

The equations derived and presented in this chapter are important for understanding the composition of the variance of a test. However, unless the calculations are performed by machine, it is tedious to apply these equations in practice for computation of the total test variance. The number of covariance terms to be computed increases rapidly with the number of test items. The total variance can, however, be computed directly from the individual scores on the whole test. The variance of the scores in the column of the score matrix which contains the number of correct solutions for each individual is computed in the usual way. The result of such a computation is numerically the same as it would be if the test variance had been computed by summing over every cell score in the complete variance-covariance matrix.

PROBLEMS

1. Construct a frequency distribution of obtained scores for the individuals in Problem 10 (Chapter 3).
2. Construct the complete variance-covariance matrix for the items in Problem 10 (Chapter 3). Use the ϕ-coefficients which were computed in this question.
3. Compute the variance of the distribution of obtained scores from the matrix in Problem 10 (Chapter 3), (a) using the values in the complete variance-covariance matrix, (b) using the usual equation for computing variance.
4. Using Eq. (4–5) determine the total variance in a test of 10 items, if for every item $p = 0.50$ and for every pair of items (a) $r_{ik} = 0.30$, (b) $r_{ik} = 1.00$, (c) $r_{ik} = 0.00$.

Suggested reading

GULLIKSEN, H. (1950). *Theory of mental tests*. New York: Wiley.
HORST, P. (1963). *Matrix algebra for social scientists*. New York: Holt, Rinehart & Winston.

CHAPTER 5

Reliability

5-1 TWO ASPECTS OF MEASUREMENT DEPENDABILITY

Certain conditions must be fulfilled before the data which we obtain from different types of measuring instruments can be used in practical situations. First, the measuring instrument which is used on a given occasion and for a given purpose must really measure the trait it is intended to measure. Second, the instrument must give a reliable measurement, so that we obtain the same result if we remeasure the trait under similar conditions for the object or individual concerned. Data should thus be dependable from two points of view—they should be meaningful and they should be reproducible.

The first requirement imposed on the measuring instrument, that the results really refer to the trait intended to be measured, appears obvious. It presents no problems when the physical properties of objects are measured. It is completely obvious that if we use a measuring tape in the correct way, we measure the length of an object. This is not so obvious when we use a questionnaire of a certain type in order to measure the degree of an individual's neuroticism. We cannot be convinced immediately that data obtained from this instrument really express the individual's degree of neuroticism. In differential psychology instruments have often been constructed for measuring a certain trait and used for that purpose, but have later been discredited when careful testing has revealed that it was in fact other variables which determined the individual results. It is, therefore, necessary to test empirically whether the instrument measures the variable it is intended to measure in every specific case. This procedure is called investigating the *validity* of the instrument, and is an important stage in the work of constructing new instruments in differential psychology. Knowledge of the degree of its validity is necessary before data obtained from the instrument can be used meaningfully.

The second requirement of measuring instruments given at the beginning of this section was that the result obtained from the instrument on a certain occasion under certain conditions should be reproducible; i.e., the result should be the same if we remeasure the same trait under identical conditions on another occasion. This aspect of the accuracy of a measuring instrument is its *reliability* in the technical sense of this term. Here reliability is the accuracy of the measurement, irrespective of whether one is really measuring what one intended to measure. For instance, if one tests the reliability of a school-readiness test, the measure which one obtains from empirical testing of the reliability is a measure of the test's ability to give the same result on repeated testings, regardless of whether or not this result has anything to do with a child's readiness for school.

As was the case for validity, reliability must be empirically investigated for each test instrument. Knowledge of the reliability is necessary if data from differential psychology instruments are to be used correctly.

5-2   RELIABILITY; RELIABILITY COEFFICIENT

Reliability problems are thus concerned with the accuracy with which a measuring instrument, e.g., a test, measures whatever it measures. Knowing its reliability, we can interpret data from the instrument with some known degree of certainty.

If we measure a certain distance a number of times with a steel measuring tape, we shall probably obtain almost identical results throughout the operation. This will be true whether or not the same individual carries out every measurement. The data we obtain have a high degree of reliability. Let us assume instead that the measurement is carried out with a measuring tape of elastic material. On repeated measurement of the same distance we would not, in this case, obtain the same result every time. Instead, we would have a distribution of values with a certain amount of dispersion. This would be true whether or not the same individual carried out all the measurements. If a number of measurements of the same distance were carried out by different individuals, the dispersion of obtained values would probably be greater than if the same number of measurements were carried out by one individual. The data we obtain from the measurements with the elastic measuring tape have a lower degree of reliability than those obtained with the steel measuring tape. The dispersion of values obtained from repeated measurements of the same distance under similar conditions can be taken as an expression for unreliability. The greater the difference between measurements of the same trait on repeated occasions, the lower the reliability.

The values obtained with the elastic measuring tape will be affected not only by the distance measured, but by other factors as well. In this case the measuring instrument is sensitive to, and expresses, intraindividual fluctuations and interindividual differences in the extension of the measuring tape on different occasions. Unreliability is a result of an instrument's sensitivity to the very factors which do not affect the size of the measurement systematically but change from one measurement situation to the next. A later chapter will deal with the nature of the error factors which we must consider when we make measurements in differential psychology.

The extent of the agreement between measurements on different occasions can be computed by means of correlation methods. The correlation coefficient for the agreement between repeated measurements under similar conditions constitutes the numerical value of the reliability of the data which can be obtained with a given instrument. This correlation coefficient is called the *reliability coefficient*. It can take values between 0 and 1 but cannot be negative (see also p. 62). If the instrument is insensitive to random factors, the individual's scores on successive measurements will be identical, their positions on the distributions which we can draw for every measurement occasion will be the same, and the correlation between the distributions will be 1.0. The measurements which can be made with such an instrument are completely reliable.

When measuring the characteristics of objects with the aid of physical instruments—measuring tapes, balances, etc.—one can as a rule remeasure the same object with the same instrument in order to obtain values on two distributions, as is necessary when we want to establish the reliability of an instrument. This can be done so long as the magnitude of the trait being measured does not change for the object in question (e.g., as a result of applying the measuring instrument to the object), and so long as the value whose magnitude is to be estimated remains unchanged.

When psychological variables are measured by methods used in differential psychology it is often difficult to obtain an estimate of the instrument's reliability in this way. One reason is that the individuals who take part in the testing are affected by the first testing procedure. This effect is somewhat different for different individuals. As a result, the individuals' relative values for the variable measured on the first occasion will be somewhat different on the second measuring occasion, simply because the material has already been presented once. If there is a time lapse between the two testings, the individuals may have developed in different ways. This also leads to the measurement of changed objective values. It is not necessary, however, to make repeated measurements with the same instrument in order to estimate its reliability. Instead, we can use equivalent measuring instruments, so-called *parallel tests*.

What is described above is the classical theory of reliability. The most complete presentation of this theory has been given by Gulliksen in his basic and well-known book, *Theory of Mental Tests* (1950).

According to the classical reliability theory, parallel tests should be constructed so that one testing with two parallel tests will give the same correlation between the two distributions of scores as two testings with one of the tests. This condition is based on the assumption that we could remove all traces of the first testing on the second occasion. Items corresponding to each other in the parallel tests should be so similar in content and difficulty that measurement with both of them gives the same result as remeasurement with one of them. When constructing parallel tests according to this definition, we should make sure that the items in the one test correspond to the items in the other with respect to content, instructions, response type, etc. In theory, parallel tests have equal means, equal variances, and equal intercorrelations. If the conditions are entirely satisfied, the tests will be completely parallel. However, in practice it is not possible to achieve this.

Our treatment of basic reliability theory will be based on the above definition of reliability as the correlation between parallel tests. The measurements can be made either by means of repeated administration of the instrument whose reliability we are testing (if we assume that every trace of the first administration can be erased), or by means of two parallel tests which are constructed to satisfy the conditions for such tests. Henceforth, the term "parallel tests" refers to such measurements.

The correlation between two parallel tests which satisfy the above conditions gives us an expression for the accuracy with which the specific items we have chosen for the test measure a given variable. However, in many situations we are interested in the accuracy with which this type of item measures the trait measured in the first test. Parallel tests have, therefore, also been defined as tests consisting of items randomly selected from the same "population" of items. Parallel tests of this type are referred to in the following text as *random parallel tests*. The consequences of this definition of parallel tests will be discussed in this and following chapters.

The interested reader is referred to Cronbach, Rajaratnam, and Gleser (1963) for a more detailed study of an important question in reliability theory —that of reliability as an expression of the possibilities of generalizing from an array of observations to a specified universe of observations.

5–3   OBSERVED SCORE; TRUE SCORE; ERROR SCORE

The theory of reliability is based upon an assumption, already presented by Spearman (1910), that an obtained score t for an individual j (that is, t_j) can be regarded as being made up of two components: T_j (a *true score*) and e_j (an *error score*):

$$t_j = T_j + e_j. \tag{5–1}$$

The trait measured by a certain performance test can be represented by a latent continuum, an ability scale, on which every individual takes up a certain position. The position an individual takes up on this ability scale determines with perfect but nonlinear correlation his *true score* on the test, his position on a true-score scale.

In classical reliability theory, the true score which can be predicted with complete certainty from the latent continuum is the same for every individual from one parallel test to the other (see Fig. 5–1).

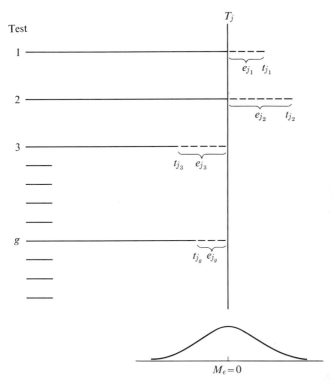

Fig. 5–1 A number of parallel tests 1, 2, 3, . . . , g, all with the same true score (T_j) but with varying error scores, e_{j_1}, e_{j_2}, etc., independent of each other, for the individual j.

When, using equivalent measuring instruments to estimate the individual's true scores, we obtain different values for a certain trait, this may be taken to be the result of the presence of error scores, which can be characterized as chance errors or random errors. They arise because of the instrument's sensitivity to those factors whose effect varies from occasion to occasion, i.e., factors other than those which determine the individual's true scores. These can be individual factors, such as whether or not the individual is tired, has just eaten, has just taken part in physical exertion, is in a state of anxiety, etc. They can also be environmental factors, such as the presence of external disturbances which distract the individual. These factors change from one measurement occasion to another and to a certain extent change the performance ability of the individual.

The error score for an individual on a certain measurement is made up of the difference between observed score and true score:

$$e_j = t_j - T_j. \tag{5-2}$$

Some properties of errors are usually defined by the following equations:

$$M_e = 0, \tag{5-3}$$

$$r_{ee} = 0, \tag{5-4}$$

$$r_{eT} = 0. \tag{5-5}$$

Equation (5-3) states that the mean of error scores is zero. This is true (a) for an infinite number of individuals on the same test, regardless of their true scores, and (b) for one individual's error scores on an infinite number of parallel tests (see Fig. 5-1).

Equation (5-4) states that the correlation between error scores from different testing occasions is zero for an infinite number of individuals. This is reasonable if error scores are considered as random errors.

Equation (5-5) states that the correlation between true scores and error scores is zero. There has been considerable discussion about this assumption. It will be dealt with in more detail in the next chapter. It should, however, be observed that one implication of the assumption of zero correlation between error and true scores—namely, that the direction of the errors is independent of the size of the true scores for an infinite number of individuals—holds in the deductions immediately following. One result of this is that a summation over a number of individuals of products of the type $T_j e_j$, where T_j and e_j are deviations from the means of the distributions of true and error scores respectively, will be equal to zero for an infinite number of products.

It should be observed that the definition of errors as random errors means that so-called *constant errors*, for example, the error involved when a measuring tape always gives a result which is 2 in. too long or 10% too short, are not included in error scores (see, e.g., Andreas, 1960, pp. 107–108).

Assuming that error scores have an expected mean value of zero, we can define an individual's true score as the mean of scores from an infinite number of parallel tests. The greater the number of parallel tests we administer, the greater the chances are that the random errors will cancel each other out. The sum of the error scores will be zero for an infinite number of parallel tests.

A frequency distribution of scores, in which every individual's score is included, can be drawn after a number of individuals have been given a

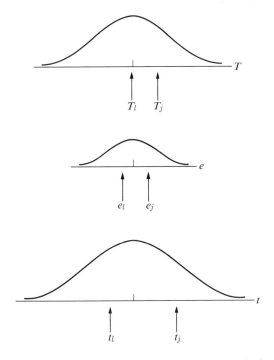

Fig. 5–2 Distributions of true scores (T), error scores (e), and obtained scores (t) for the same data population.

certain test. This distribution (t in Fig. 5–2), has been obtained by combining the T- and e-distributions, i.e., the distributions which could be drawn for true scores and error scores. Each individual included in the t-distribution, e.g., individuals j and l, is also included in each of the T- and e-distributions. Using the assumptions made previously, we can write the variance of the t-distribution as the sum of the variance of the two subdistributions. The correlation between true and error scores is assumed to be zero, so that the covariance term, which should have been included on the right-hand side, is also zero:

$$s_t^2 = s_T^2 + s_e^2. \tag{5–6}$$

The total test variance (s_t^2) is equal for parallel tests. The variance of true scores (s_T^2) is also equal for parallel tests, since each individual contributes exactly the same score to the various distributions of true scores. It follows that the error distribution also has the same variance for parallel tests. But, whereas the individuals have the same scores in the various true-score distributions, the size and direction of their error scores will vary randomly from one parallel test to the other.

5–4   THE STATISTICAL DEFINITION OF RELIABILITY

Returning now to the question of estimating a test's reliability, we begin from the definition of reliability as the correlation between the given test and a parallel test.

The scores of an individual j on two parallel tests are denoted by t_{j_1} and t_{j_2}. These scores give the individual's results as deviations from the means of the distributions. We thus obtain

$$t_{j_1} = T_j + e_{j_1} \quad \text{and} \quad t_{j_2} = T_j + e_{j_2},$$

where e_{j_1} is the error component of the individual's score on test 1, and e_{j_2} is the error component of the individual's score on test 2. Note that the true score for a given individual is the same for parallel tests.

From the equation which defines a correlation coefficient (Eq. 3–6), we obtain the following expression for the correlation between the two parallel tests:

$$r_{t_1 t_2} = \frac{\sum(T_j + e_{j_1})(T_j + e_{j_2})}{Ns_{t_1}s_{t_2}}$$

$$= \frac{\sum T_j^2}{Ns_{t_1}s_{t_2}} + \frac{\sum T_j e_{j_2}}{Ns_{t_1}s_{t_2}} + \frac{\sum e_{j_1} T_j}{Ns_{t_1}s_{t_2}} + \frac{\sum e_{j_1} e_{j_2}}{Ns_{t_1}s_{t_2}}.$$

The second and third terms will be zero (see p. 64), since the directions of true and error scores can be assumed to be independent of each other. The fourth term is also zero, since in agreement with the assumptions made, the errors are uncorrelated with each other.

The two tests were assumed to be parallel. One result of this is that the standard deviations of test scores are equal:

$$s_{t_1} = s_{t_2} = s_t.$$

The first term can now be written $\sum T_j^2/Ns_t^2$, where T_j expresses the individuals' deviations from the mean of the distribution of true scores, and $\sum T_j^2/N$ is thus the expression for the variance of the true scores (s_T^2). The first term can now be written s_T^2/s_t^2. We thus obtain

$$r_{tt} = s_T^2/s_t^2. \tag{5–7}$$

But $s_T^2 = s_t^2 - s_e^2$, so that Eq. (5–7) can be written

$$r_{tt} = 1 - s_e^2/s_t^2. \tag{5–8}$$

With the classical assumptions we have made, reliability can thus be defined as the ratio of true to total variance. The reliability coefficient for the relation between two parallel tests gives the numerical value of the ratio of the variance of the distribution of true scores to the variance of the distribution of obtained test scores.

We can now return to Fig. 5–2. When the variance of the total distribution (t) has a given size, the reliability is determined by the magnitude of the true-score variance. If every individual's score on the total distribution is the same as his true score, then the variance of the total distribution will be the same as the variance of the true scores and the reliability will be 1.0. If this is the case, the measurement has exactly expressed every individual's true score, and the error variance is zero.

Equation (5–8) is the basis of the previously unsubstantiated statement that the correlation coefficient, which expresses the relation between measurements on parallel tests and is thus a reliability coefficient, can take only positive values. When the error variance is a maximum, it is equal to the total test variance, which gives the value zero for the reliability coefficient. This occurs when the entire score obtained by each individual is an error score. The test is then completely unreliable. It should, however, be observed that, when the computations are based on a small sample of individuals, and the reliability coefficient is (for instance) zero for the population, one may obtain negative coefficients.   (See the discussion of standard errors of correlation coefficients, p. 48.)

The definitions of reliability discussed in this chapter can now be summed up as follows. Reliability is the certainty with which the instrument measures true scores. This certainty is expressed by the relation between the results of two parallel measurements of the same trait under the same conditions. The coefficient for this relationship is the reliability coefficient for one of the tests. It gives the proportion of the total test variance for one of the tests which is made up of the variance of the true-score distribution.

5–5 CORRELATION BETWEEN TRUE AND OBTAINED SCORES

It is perhaps of value for the following discussion to present the relation between observed and true scores in the form of an equation. If this relationship is denoted by r_{tT} and if T, e, and t still represent deviations from the means of the respective distributions, we obtain the following expression:

$$r_{tT} = \sum(T + e)T/Ns_t s_T. \tag{5–9}$$

Expanding the right-hand side in Eq. (5–9), we have

$$\sum T^2/Ns_t s_T + \sum eT/Ns_t s_T. \tag{5–10}$$

But $\sum T^2/N = s_T^2$, so that the first term in Eq. (5–10) can be written s_T/s_t. The sum of the products eT is zero, so that the second term will also be zero. We now obtain

$$r_{tT} = s_T/s_t. \tag{5–11}$$

But from Eq. (5–7) $s_T^2/s_t^2 = r_{tt}.$ (5–12)

From Eqs. (5–11) and (5–12) we thus obtain

$$r_{tT} = \sqrt{r_{tt}}.$$ (5–13)

The square root of the reliability coefficient thus gives the correlation between observed and true scores for the test. This value is usually called the test's *reliability index*.

5–6   RELIABILITY AND TEST LENGTH

The reliability of test scores is a function of the number of items included in the test. This can easily be seen by studying Fig. 5–1. A test of a certain length gives a random error of a certain size and direction when a given individual is tested. If several parallel tests (1, 2, 3, . . . , *g*) are then given in addition, the error scores on the various subtests will have different signs and magnitudes and, if we combine the parallel tests into one total test, the greater the number of subtests included in the total test, the more of them will cancel each other. We will gradually approach the true score for each individual. Since reliability can be defined as the certainty with which a test estimates true scores, the reliability will increase as we increase the number of parallel tests included in the total test. With the addition of an infinite number of parallel tests we approach the true score for every individual and the reliability value 1.0 for the total test's scores.

We shall examine more closely the influence of test length on reliability. Test length is assumed to be a linear function of the number of items. The problem can best be made clear by reference to what has been said about the array of terms in a variance-covariance matrix (p. 57). Let us examine how the total variance, the true variance, and the error variance are affected when the length of the test is changed.

A. Total test variance

Let us first see what happens to the variance of observed scores when the test is doubled in length by the addition of an equal number of new items. These items are assumed to be parallel to the items in the original test. The variances of the two test halves are therefore equal:

$$s_{t_1}^2 = s_{t_2}^2.$$

The variance of the distribution we obtain by combining the scores from the two subtest distributions (s_{2t}^2) can then be written

$$2s_{2t}^2 = s_{t_1}^2 + s_{t_2}^2 + 2r_{t_1 t_2}s_{t_1}s_{t_2}.$$

The variance of the two tests is the same and the correlation between the two parallel test halves gives the reliability coefficient for either of them. This leads to the following expression for the variance of a test after the number of items is doubled:

$$s_{2t}^2 = 2s_t^2(1 + r_{tt}). \tag{5–14}$$

Equation (5–14) is a special case of a more general equation for the increase in the variance of observed scores which occurs when the test length is increased in accordance with the above conditions. The general equation can be derived most easily from the variance-covariance matrix.

We let n strictly parallel tests, each with a variance of s_t^2, make up the raw scores in rows and columns, where g and h denote any two tests in the matrix. For every row, i.e., for every test, we then obtain the variance terms shown in Table 5–1. The total variance is also shown for the test consisting of n parallel subtests.

The total variance of a test composed of n parallel tests (s_{nt}^2) is thus $\sum s_t^2 + \sum\sum r_{t_g t_h} s_{t_g} s_{t_h}$. All of the terms included in the first summation are of equal size, since variances are equal for parallel tests. Since we have n of these terms, we obtain

$$\sum s_t^2 = n s_{t_g}^2.$$

The correlation $r_{t_g t_h}$, which is included in every term in the second summation, is the correlation coefficient for the relation between parallel tests

Table 5–1 Variance-covariance matrix for observed scores on parallel tests

Test (row in the variance-covariance matrix)	Sum of variance terms	
1	$s_{t_1}^2 + \sum r_{t_1 t_g} s_{t_1} s_{t_g}$	$(g \neq 1)$
2	$s_{t_2}^2 + \sum r_{t_2 t_g} s_{t_2} s_{t_g}$	$(g \neq 2)$
3	$s_{t_3}^2 + \sum r_{t_3 t_g} s_{t_3} s_{t_g}$	$(g \neq 3)$
$\vdots$		
g	$s_{t_g}^2 + \sum r_{t_g t_h} s_{t_g} s_{t_h}$	$(g \neq h)$
$\vdots$		
n	$s_{t_n}^2 + \sum r_{t_n t_g} s_{t_n} s_{t_g}$	$(g \neq n)$
Total sum of variance terms:	$\sum s_t^2 + \sum\sum r_{t_g t_h} s_{t_g} s_{t_h}$	$(g \neq h)$ $\quad$ (5–15)

(r_{tt}) and is the same for every subterm. Standard deviations are equal for parallel tests $(s_{t_g} = s_{t_h})$. Since we have in the second summation $n(n - 1)$ terms, all of which are equal, we obtain

$$\sum\sum r_{t_g t_h} s_{t_g} s_{t_n} = n(n - 1) r_{tt} s_t^2.$$

The total test variance for a test composed of n parallel tests (s_{nt}^2) can now be written

$$s_{nt}^2 = n s_t^2 + n(n - 1) r_{tt} s_t^2 = n s_t^2 [1 + (n - 1) r_{tt}]. \qquad (5\text{–}16)$$

B. True variance

Let us also examine here what happens to the true variance when the number of items is doubled. The variance of the distribution of true scores, which we obtain by combining individual true scores in the subdistributions, can be written

$$s_{2T}^2 = s_{T_1}^2 + s_{T_2}^2 + 2 r_{T_1 T_2} s_{T_1} s_{T_2}.$$

The variance of true scores is equal for parallel tests. True scores on parallel tests are assumed to be equal for every individual. Thus, s_{T_1} will be equal to s_{T_2} and $r_{T_1 T_2}$ will be 1.0. The true variance after the number of items is doubled can then be written

$$s_{2T}^2 = 4 s_T^2. \qquad (5\text{–}17)$$

When the test length is doubled, the true-score variance will be four times as great as in the original test.

Equation (5–17) is a special case of a more general equation for the increase in the variance of the distribution of true scores when the number of items in the test is increased.

In the same way as for the total variance, we can group together in a variance-covariance matrix the different variance terms for the true variance in n parallel tests. Table 5–2 shows the sum of variance terms for each row, i.e., for each parallel test, together with the total true variance for n parallel tests. Since the true variance is equal for parallel tests, we obtain

$$\sum s_T^2 = n s_{T_g}^2.$$

The correlation between true scores on parallel tests is 1.0. All correlation terms of the type $r_{T_g T_h}$ will then also be 1.0. Since the standard deviations of the true scores are the same for parallel tests, the products $s_{T_g} s_{T_h}$ will be constants and can be written as $s_{T_g}^2$. We have $n(n - 1)$ terms in the second summation and obtain

$$\sum\sum r_{T_g T_h} s_{T_h} s_{T_h} = n(n - 1) s_{T_g}^2.$$

Table 5–2 Variance-covariance terms for true scores on n parallel tests

Test (row in the variance-covariance matrix)	Sum of variance terms	
1	$s_{T_1}^2 + \sum r_{T_1 T_g} s_{T_1} s_{T_g}$	$(g \neq 1)$
2	$s_{T_2}^2 + \sum r_{T_2 T_g} s_{T_2} s_{T_g}$	$(g \neq 2)$
3	$s_{T_3}^2 + \sum r_{T_3 T_g} s_{T_3} s_{T_g}$	$(g \neq 3)$
$\vdots$		
g	$s_{T_g}^2 + \sum r_{T_g T_h} s_{T_g} s_{T_h}$	$(g \neq h)$
$\vdots$		
n	$s_{T_n}^2 + \sum r_{T_n T_g} s_{T_n} s_{T_g}$	$(g \neq n)$

Total sum of variance terms:	$\sum s_T^2 + \sum\sum r_{T_g T_h} s_{T_g} s_{T_h}$	$(g \neq h)$	(5–18)

The total sum of the true variance for a test consisting of n parallel tests (s_{nT}^2) can then be written $s_{nT}^2 = ns_T^2 + n(n-1)s_T^2$ and we obtain

$$s_{nT}^2 = n^2 s_T^2. \tag{5–19}$$

In general, the true variance increases as the square of n when the length of the test is increased n times.

We have assumed here that the additional tests have been parallel to the original test, and that there have been (a) a correlation of 1.0 for true scores and (b) equal variances of true scores on the parallel tests which make up the total test.

C. Error variance

When the number of items in the test is doubled, the effect on the error variance is:

$$s_{2e}^2 = s_{e_1}^2 + s_{e_2}^2 + 2r_{e_1 e_2} s_{e_1} s_{e_2}.$$

Error distributions in parallel tests have equal variances, and error scores can be assumed to be uncorrelated. Thus s_{e_1} is equal to s_{e_2}, $r_{e_1 e_2}$ is zero, and the error variance after doubling the number of items can be written

$$s_{2e}^2 = 2s_e^2. \tag{5–20}$$

When the number of items is doubled, so is the variance of the distribution of error scores.

Equation (5–20) is merely a special case of a general equation for the increase in size of the error variance when the number of items is increased.

In the same way as for the total variance and the true variance, we can obtain the total variance for error scores (s_{ne}^2) from a variance-covariance matrix of error scores for n parallel tests:

$$s_{ne}^2 = \sum s_e^2 + \sum \sum r_{e_g e_h} s_{e_g} s_{e_h}. \tag{5–21}$$

The variance of error scores for parallel tests is the same, so that s_e^2 is a constant for n parallel tests:

$$\sum s_e^2 = n s_e^2.$$

The correlation between error scores for parallel tests is zero. Every correlation in the second summation will therefore be zero and every term included in the sum will also be zero. We obtain the following expression for the increase in the error variance when the length of a test is increased n times:

$$s_{ne}^2 = n s_e^2. \tag{5–22}$$

The increase in the error variance when the test is increased in length is therefore, in general, directly proportional to the number of times the test is increased in length. The only assumption made here is that there is no systematic relationship between error scores for parallel tests.

Reliability has previously been defined as that part of the total variance which is made up of the variance of the true score distribution. It can be seen from Eqs. (5–19) and (5–22) that, when the test is lengthened, the true variance increases at a faster rate than the error variance. While the true variance increases as the square of the number of times the test is increased in length, the increase in the error variance is directly proportional to the increase in test length. This means that, when the test increases in length, the true variance represents a greater share of the total variance. This in turn means that the test will become more reliable.

An example should make the situation clearer. Reliability is determined by the proportion of the total variance which is made up of the true score variance. If s_t^2 is made equal to 1.0, the true score variance will give the numerical value of the reliability coefficient directly. We assume a test with $r_{tt} = 0.50$, which means that both the true variance and the error variance are 0.50. If we double the test length, the true variance will be $4 \times 0.50 = 2.00$, the error variance will be $2 \times 0.50 = 1.00$, and the total variance will be $2.00 + 1.00 = 3.00$. The ratio of true variance to total variance is $2.00/3.00 = 0.67$, which is thus the reliability coefficient of the doubled test. If we double the test length again, the result will be as follows: $s_T^2 =$

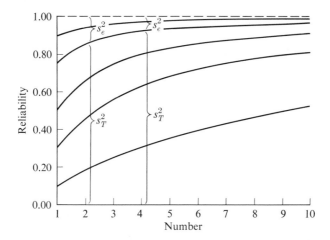

Fig. 5–3 Reliability as a function of increasing test length.

$4 \times 0.67 = 2.68$; $s_e^2 = 2 \times 0.33 = 0.66$; $s_t^2 = 2.68 + 0.66 = 3.34$. The reliability coefficient after this new doubling of the test length will thus be $2.68/3.34 = 0.80$, which is the same value we would have obtained if we had increased the length of the initial test with $r_{tt} = 0.50$ four times. In the same way we can compute the function for the relation between test length and reliability for original tests of any given reliability. The function is given in Fig. 5–3 for a number of tests with various reliabilities in the initial test.

This procedure is clumsy in practice. A general equation can be derived for computing the reliability of a test whose length is increased n times (r_{tt_n}).

We begin from the definition of reliability as the relation between true variance and total variance. The reliability of a test whose length is increased n times can then be written

$$r_{tt_n} = s_{nT}^2/s_{nt}^2.$$

From Eqs. (5–19) and (5–16) we obtain

$$r_{tt_n} = \frac{n^2 s_T^2}{n s_t^2[1 + (n - 1)r_{tt}]}.$$

But $s_T^2/s_t^2 = r_{tt}$. We then obtain

$$r_{tt_n} = \frac{n r_{tt}}{1 + (n - 1)r_{tt}}, \qquad (5\text{–}23)$$

where n is the number of times the test is increased in length, r_{tt_n} is the reliability on increasing the length of the test n times, and r_{tt} is the reliability of the initial test.

We can now see that the same results are obtained from Eq. (5–23) as from our previous computations of what the reliability coefficient would be when an initial test with the reliability coefficient 0.50 was made two and four times as long. On increasing the test length to twice that of the initial test ($n = 2$), the reliability coefficient will become $(2 \times 0.50)/(1 + 0.50) = 0.67$, and on increasing it to four times that of the initial test ($n = 4$), it will become $(4 \times 0.50)/(1 + 3 \times 0.50) = 0.80$. In both cases the result agrees with that obtained previously.

Equation (5–23) is the so-called Spearman-Brown prophecy formula, which can be used to compute the effect of an increase in test length on reliability. In the common case where the test length is doubled, i.e., where $n = 2$, the formula has the following appearance:

$$r_{tt_2} = \frac{2r_{tt}}{1 + r_{tt}}. \tag{5–24}$$

The derivation of the Spearman-Brown formula (Eq. 5–23) assumes that the items added to the original test are similar to the initial items in difficulty, intercorrelations, and content, i.e., that additional test parts can be considered to be parallel to those included in the original test. Application of the equation thus assumes that these conditions are satisfied.

When constructing a test, one sometimes wishes to obtain reliability of a previously determined magnitude. If one has a preliminary version of a newly constructed test with known reliability, the practical question will be by how many items this version must be increased to yield the desired reliability. Figure 5–3 can also be used in this case for computing n. We find the desired reliability on the vertical axis. Then, from the function for the test whose original reliability is known, we read off on the horizontal axis the value which corresponds to the desired reliability, i.e., the number of times the test must be increased in length.

The general equation for computing n is obtained by solving Eq. (5–23) for n:

$$n = \frac{r_{tt_n}(1 - r_{tt})}{r_{tt}(1 - r_{tt_n})}, \tag{5–25}$$

where r_{tt_n} is the desired reliability after the test is increased in length n times, and r_{tt} is the reliability of the initial test.

If the reliability coefficient for a trial version of a new test is calculated to be 0.75 and the designer of the test is not satisfied with a reliability coefficient smaller than 0.90 for the final test, it is obvious that he should make the test $0.90(1 - 0.75)/0.75(1 - 0.90) = 3$ times as long.

5–7 THE RELIABILITY COEFFICIENT AND THE HOMOGENEITY OF THE SAMPLE

For a specific variable the variance of true scores varies from sample to sample of individuals. The error variance, however, depends on the inability of the test to measure individual true scores accurately, and is thus the same from sample to sample, even if the samples differ in the magnitude of the true-score variance. It follows from these two facts that the size of the reliability coefficient is dependent on the heterogeneity of the sample of true scores.

We begin with the reliability coefficient computed from the equation

$$r_{tt} = 1 - s_e^2/s_t^2$$

for a sample with known total variance. If we now test a more homogeneous sample of individuals, the variance of the distribution of true scores is less. The total variance will be reduced, while the error variance will remain unchanged. We immediately see the effect of this change in Eq. (5–8)— the reliability coefficient will be reduced. Assuming the same error variance at different levels of the test, we can derive an equation for computing the reliability of a test when it is to be used on a sample with a total variance other than that of the sample on which the original reliability coefficient has been computed. If we denote the sample for which the reliability is to be estimated by u, we obtain the following expression for the test's reliability in this group:

$$r_{uu} = 1 - s_e^2/s_u^2. \tag{5–26}$$

From Eq. (5–8) the variance of the error distribution can be written

$$s_e^2 = s_t^2 (1 - r_{tt}).$$

But the error distribution has the same variance in the sample of different heterogeneity. We can therefore replace s_e^2 in Eq. (5–26) by $s_t^2 (1 - r_{tt})$.

Assuming that the total variance of the sample u is known, we obtain the following expression, which can be used for estimating the test's reliability in this sample:

$$r_{uu} = 1 - \frac{s_t^2(1 - r_{tt})}{s_u^2}, \tag{5–27}$$

where r_{uu} is the estimated reliability of sample u, s_t^2 is the variance of the sample for which the known reliability coefficient has been computed, r_{tt} is the known reliability of sample t, and s_u^2 is the variance of the sample for which the reliability is estimated.

The dependence of the reliability coefficient on the total dispersion of obtained scores can be shown by an example. What is the reliability of a test in a sample with $s = 10$, if the reliability coefficient is 0.90 in a sample with $s = 15$? In this case, $s_t = 15$, $r_{tt} = 0.90$, and $s_u = 10$. Inserting these values in Eq. (5–27), we obtain

$$r_{uu} = 1 - \frac{225(1 - 0.90)}{100} = 0.775.$$

It should be observed that the error variance (s_e^2) has a lower limit. The error variance and the total variance will be equal, and the reliability zero, when the homogeneity of the sample being tested is perfect, i.e., when everyone tested has the same true score. The error variance can never be greater than the total variance, and the reliability can never be less than zero.

As was pointed out previously, it is only the size of the reliability coefficient which is affected by differences in the sample's homogeneity. The certainty with which the individual's true score can be estimated from a certain test is independent of the group of individuals in which he is included.

PROBLEMS

1. What is the reliability of a test when the proportion of the total variance which consists of true variance is (a) 0.45, (b) 0.71, (c) 0.66?

2. What is the reliability of a test when the proportion of the total variance which consists of error variance is (a) 0.42, (b) 0.22, (c) 0.56?

3. For a given test, $s_T^2 = 3$ and $s_e^2 = 3$. What is the reliability?

4. For the test in Problem 3 compute (a) true variance, (b) error variance, (c) reliability, after the length is increased 3 times. Compare with the reliability in Problem 3 before the length is increased.

5. (a) Compute by how many hundredths the reliability coefficient rises when the length is doubled at different levels. Draw the function when r rises from 0 to +1.

    (b) Make the same computation when the test is increased in length 4 times.

6. A test with reliability 0.94 contains 80 items.

    (a) What will the reliability be if the number of items is reduced by half?

    (b) How many of the original items will need to be retained if a reliability of 0.90 is considered sufficient?

7. A test containing 40 items with a reliability of 0.64 is to be expanded so as to give a reliability of 0.80. How many new items of the same type as the original ones must be added?

8. What will the reliability of a test with $r_{tt} = 0.70$ be after the length is increased (a) 2 times, (b) 3 times, (c) 4 times, (d) 5 times?

9. How many times must a test with $r_{tt} = 0.80$ be increased in length in order to give a reliability of (a) 0.90, (b) 0.95?

10. In a given situation a group of 10 raters have interrater reliability of 0.30. Using the Spearman-Brown equation calculate the number of raters required to give a reliability of 0.90. Discuss the feasibility of this action.

11. A test has true variance $s_T^2 = 3$ and error variance $s_e^2 = 2$. Compute the reliability index.

12. A test has $r_{tt} = 0.92$. Compute the reliability it will have when used on a selected group whose standard deviation on the variable is only 71% of that of the population.

13. A newly constructed test has the values $s = 10$ and $r_{tt} = 0.93$ for a normal group. The test is then used for college students and a reliability coefficient of 0.82 is obtained. Find the standard deviation of the distribution of obtained scores for the student group.

REFERENCES

ANDREAS, B. G. (1960). *Experimental psychology*. New York: Wiley.

CRONBACH, L. J., N. RAJARATNAM, and G. C. GLESER (1963). Theory of generalizability: a liberalization of reliability theory. *Brit. J. Stat. Psychol.*, **16**, 137–163.

GULLIKSEN, H. (1950). *Theory of mental tests*. New York: Wiley.

SPEARMAN, C. (1910). Correlation calculated from faulty data. *Brit. J. Psychol.*, **3**, 271–295.

Suggested reading

GHISELLI, E. E. (1964). *Theory of psychological measurement*. New York: McGraw-Hill.

LORD, F. M. (1959). An approach to mental test theory. *Psychometrika*, **24**, 283–302.

——— (1960). Inferring the examinee's score. In I. H. GULLIKSEN and S. MESSICK (Eds.) *Psychological scaling*. New York: Wiley.

THORNDIKE, R. L. (1951). Reliability. In E. F. LINDQUIST (Ed.) *Educational measurement*. Washington D.C.: Am. Council on Educ.

WOODBURY, M. A. (1963). The stochastical model of mental testing theory and an application. *Psychometrika*, **28**, 391–394.

CHAPTER 6

Standard Error of Measurement

In this chapter we shall discuss procedures for obtaining an empirical measure of the error variance around a single true score. We do this in order to estimate the size of the error we make when we use an obtained score as an estimate of the individual's true score. We shall first present a solution of the problem which uses the classical assumptions made in the previous section, and then we shall present a solution for random parallel tests without assuming equal error variances for different true scores.

6-1 EQUAL STANDARD ERRORS FOR DIFFERENT TRUE SCORES

When testing an individual on any given occasion, we wish to know how accurate our estimate of the individual's true score is. Beginning from the classical assumptions about errors, we can derive an equation for computing the scale interval within which we can find the individual's true score with some known degree of certainty, when we have the individual's obtained score.

In Fig. 5–1 we see the scores on a number of parallel tests for individual j. Since error scores have been defined as random scores, they will give a normal distribution with M_e equal to zero. It thus follows that the individual's true score is equal to the mean of scores on an infinite number of parallel tests (see p. 68). What we now need, in order to compute the confidence interval which is sought for individual j, is the standard deviation of the distribution of error components for j.

The size of the error distribution is the same for parallel tests. According to the previously mentioned assumption (which is debatable and has been much discussed), the size of this error distribution is independent of the individual's true score and is the same for all individuals. It thus follows that the error distribution on test g for an infinite number of individuals with

78

true score T_j will be the same as the error distribution for individual j on an infinite number of parallel tests (the e-distribution in Fig. 5–2). The probability of a given error for an individual on a given occasion can be seen from this distribution and is the same for all individuals.

What we now need is the standard deviation of the error distribution (s_e) for every individual on a given test occasion. An equation for computing s_e is derived from the reliability equation (Eq. 5–8):

$$r_{tt} = 1 - s_e^2/s_t^2;$$
$$s_e^2 = s_t^2(1 - r_{tt}); \tag{6–1}$$

$$s_e = s_t\sqrt{1 - r_{tt}}. \tag{6–2}$$

Equation (6–2) is the equation for computing the *standard error of measurement;* s_e gives the standard deviation of the distribution of errors we make, if we allow a certain individual's obtained score on every one of an infinite number of parallel tests to represent his true score. According to the assumptions which were presented previously and on which the derivation of Eq. (6–2) is based, this standard deviation is the same for every individual who takes the test, and is independent of the true scores. The probability of an error of a given size arriving from a measurement performed with a certain instrument is then the same for every individual, regardless of his true score. The reliability of a test was calculated to be 0.84 for a certain group of individuals with standard deviation 10 on the distribution of observed scores. Inserting these values in Eq. (6–2), we see that the standard deviation is 4.0 on the distribution of scores we would obtain if we tested any one of the individuals with an infinite number of parallel tests.

Since the measurement errors are assumed to be independent of the true score they represent, independent of each other, and normally distributed, the standard deviation can be used for computing confidence intervals and can be interpreted in the same way as any other standard error.

The estimate of the standard deviation of the error distribution [obtained from Eq. (6–2)] can be used for calculating, with a known degree of certainty, the limits within which the observed scores for individuals with a given true score will lie. The probability of obtaining on a given occasion a score in the interval 40 ± 4, i.e., the interval 36–44, for an individual with true score 40 is about 0.68, and the probability that a score will be obtained in the interval 32–48 is about 0.95.

We do not, however, know the true score for this or any other individual. In practical situations, we have instead an obtained score from which we wish to estimate the limits within which the true score lies with, say, 95% certainty.

We do not have a known probability distribution for the true scores which have given rise to the obtained score. We can, however, estimate, with the

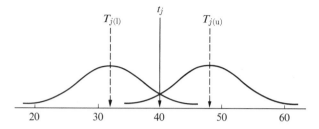

Fig. 6–1 An illustration of the method of establishing a confidence limit around an observed score by means of error distributions for two given true scores.

desired degree of certainty, the interval within which the true scores capable of giving the obtained score will be found. Consider Fig. 6–1.

The probable distribution of obtained scores is assumed to be the same for any true score. The location of $T_{j(1)}$ is such that its distance from t_j is 1.96 standard deviations: $t_j - T_{j(1)} = 1.96s_e$. If we go down the scale from the score t_j obtained for a certain individual, we will gradually approach the true score $T_{j(1)}$. The probability that individuals with true score $T_{j(1)}$ will attain a score as high as or higher than t_j is 0.025. Going up the scale we now find the score $T_{j(u)}$, which is also $1.96s_e$ from t_j. The probability that individuals with this true score will obtain a score as low as or lower than t_j is 0.025. The probability is thus less than 2.5% that true scores lower than $T_{j(1)}$ will have given the obtained score t_j, and the probability is equally small that true scores higher than $T_{j(u)}$ will have given the obtained score t_j. The probability that scores outside $T_{j(1)}$ and $T_{j(u)}$ will have yielded the score t_j is thus less than 0.05. The true score which has given rise to the obtained score t_j will thus be found, with about 95% certainty, within the interval $T_{j(1)} - T_{j(u)}$. The scores $T_{j(1)}$ and $T_{j(u)}$ are $t_j - 1.96s_e$ and $t_j + 1.96s_e$ respectively. Thus, directly from the standard error of measurement, we can obtain the interval within which, with a known degree of certainty, we can expect the true score to be found.

We can therefore expect, with approximately 68% certainty, that the true score for a certain individual lies within a distance of $\pm 1s_e$ from his obtained score. With approximately 95% certainty we can expect his true score to be within a distance of $\pm 1.96s_e$ from his obtained score.

An example: When given the Stanford-Binet test a child was found to have an I.Q. of 115. Within what limits can we expect the child's true score to lie, with 95% certainty, if the reliability of the test is 0.95 and the standard deviation is 16 units? Inserting these values in Eq. (6–2) we obtain $s_e = 16\sqrt{1 - 0.95} = 3.5$. The required interval has thus the limits $115 \pm 1.96 \times 3.5$. Thus, the true score with 95% certainty lies between 108 and 122.

The problem can take another form, perhaps at least as common in practical situations as the above example. Let us assume that we have obtained an I.Q. of 90 with the Stanford-Binet test for a child of the same age as in the previous example. We want to find an answer to the question: What is the probability that a child with a true score of 100 will be found to have the obtained I.Q.? We have already computed the size of the standard deviation of the distribution of obtained scores for individuals with a given true score; it is this standard deviation which is the standard error of measurement. Below the position -1.96×3.5 in the distribution of obtained I.Q.'s for individuals with the true score 100 (i.e., below 93) we find approximately 2.5% of the obtained I.Q.'s. The probability that a child with the true score 100 will be found to have an I.Q. of 90 or lower is thus less than 2.5% under the given conditions.

Equation (6–2) shows the circumstance discussed previously, namely, that the magnitude of the standard error of measurement is a function of the magnitude of the reliability coefficient. The latter is one way of expressing the uncertainty with which an instrument measures—by giving the proportion of the total variation which is made up of true variance. The reliability coefficient can, however, give a deceptive impression of certainty. The standard error of measurement gives a more realistic indication of how uncertain the estimate of the true score is, even with relatively high reliability coefficients. In the example given above, the distribution of obtained scores has standard deviation 10. With a reliability coefficient of 0.84, the standard deviation of the distribution of obtained scores around a given true score (i.e., the standard error of measurement) will be 4, or 40% of the standard deviation of the distribution of obtained scores. For a reliability coefficient of 0.91, the standard error of measurement will be 3, or 30% of the standard deviation of the distribution of obtained scores. Thus, even with relatively high reliability coefficients, we obtain a rather uncertain estimate of the single true score. Figure 6–2 shows, for different values of the reliability coefficient, the percentage of the total standard deviation which consists of the standard deviation of the distribution around a single true score.

Both the derivation of Eq. (6–2) and the given application of the equation for estimating the standard error of measurement presuppose that the distribution of errors around the individual's true score is normal, and that the size of the standard error is independent of the size of the true score for which the estimate is intended. Both assumptions have been subjects of frequent discussion. The latter, that the error scores are independent of the true score, has been especially criticized. An equation for the standard error without this assumption will be presented in the next section. The obtained standard error must be interpreted with caution when the standard error of measurement is computed by means of Eq. (6–2) and used for judging the certainty of an obtained score. It is merely an estimate of the average value of the standard error for individuals, independent of their true scores.

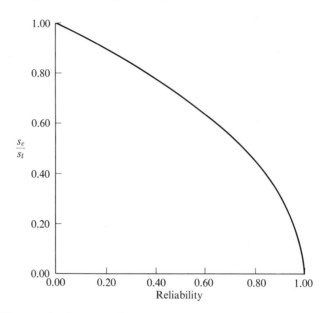

Fig. 6–2 The standard error of measurement (s_e) in relation to the obtained standard deviations (s_t) as a function of the reliability coefficient.

It is only the magnitude of the reliability coefficient which is affected by changes in the sample's homogeneity, as was pointed out previously. (See p. 75.) The magnitude of the standard error of measurement does not, however, depend on this. The measurement of a variable for a single individual takes place with a certainty which is independent of the homogeneity of the sample in which he is included. This implies that the standard error of measurement is in many situations a better and more applicable measure of the instrument's reliability than the reliability coefficient.

6–2 DIFFERENT STANDARD ERRORS FOR DIFFERENT TRUE SCORES

As was mentioned previously, the assumption of equal variance of error distributions for true scores of varying magnitudes has been criticized. It is necessary for the derivation and application of Eq. (6–2). Lord, however, has derived a different equation for computing the uncertainty of an obtained score without using this classical assumption (cf. Lord, 1955).

Lord assumes that the test can be considered as a randomly selected sample of items from an item population. A number of such tests with the same number of items, drawn from the same item population, are randomly parallel forms or randomly parallel tests.

It is assumed that every individual can in fact solve a certain number of items in the population from which the particular sample of items is chosen, and that this number is constant under all normal conditions. The proportion (out of the total number of items) which this number of items represents for a given individual j is also the probability that items which he can solve will be included when the selection of items for the test is made. Let us call this proportion p_j. The true score which we wish to estimate by means of the test for individual j is therefore np_j, where n is the number of items in the test:

$$T_j = np_j. \tag{6–3}$$

We now wish to obtain the standard deviation of the distribution of observed scores for the true score np_j, so that we will be able to estimate the magnitude of the error we make when we use an observed score (i.e., the number of correctly solved items on one of the tests) as an expression for the individual's true score (T_j).

Randomly parallel tests will give a binomial distribution of scores for individual j. The standard deviation for a binomial distribution can be computed from the simple equation

$$s = \sqrt{npq}. \tag{6–4}$$

In general, Eq. (6–4) gives the standard deviation for the number of successful attempts from a total number of n attempts, when the probability of success is p. In this case, p gives the probability that, when an item is selected for the test, it will be one that individual j can solve. As has been said before, this p-value is equal to the proportion of the total number of items which j can in fact solve; q is the probability that we get an item which j is unable to solve. The value q is the same as the proportion of items in the population which j is unable to solve, and can also be written $1 - p$. The standard deviation of the distribution of obtained scores for randomly parallel tests for individual j can now be written

$$s_e(t_j) = \sqrt{np_jq_j}. \tag{6–5}$$

But $np_j = T_j$ (Eq. 6–3) and $q_j = 1 - p_j$, so that Eq. (6–5) can also be written

$$s_e(t_j) = \sqrt{T_j(1 - p_j)}. \tag{6–6}$$

In order to obtain an unbiased estimate of the population's standard error, we must multiply the right-hand side of Eq. (6–6) by $\sqrt{n/(n - 1)}$ (see, e.g., Dixon and Massey, 1957, p. 51). We obtain

$$s_e(t_j) = \sqrt{t_j(n - t_j)/(n - 1)}. \tag{6–7}$$

The standard error of measurement expressed by Eq. (6–7) is thus an estimate of the standard deviation of the distribution of scores that results from testing an individual with an infinite number of randomly parallel tests.

An example will be given to illustrate the practical applications of the equation for computing $s_e(t_j)$.

Let us assume that individual j can in fact solve 80% of the items in the population from which the items for a 50-item test were selected. His true score on the test is thus 40, and $s_e(t_j)$ computed from Eq. (6–6) will then be 2.83. This value is not, however, of any use, since we are unable to measure T_j, and $s_e(t_j)$ is dependent on the value of j inserted in Eq. (6–5). Let us assume instead that the individual has obtained a score of 40 on the test, and that we wish to estimate the limits within which his true score lies. We are not yet able to compute $s_e(t_j)$ for an n-value of 50 and a T_j-value of 40, and use this value as an expression for the confidence interval within which we can find his true score with some known degree of certainty. The probability that he has obtained the score 40 when his true score is 42 is less than the probability that he has obtained 40 when his true score is 38. The standard error is greater for the true score 38 than for the true score 42.

It is possible, however, to compute the score which, when reduced by $1.96s_e(t_j)$, gives the obtained score 40. We thus obtain the upper limit t_u of the confidence interval for 95% certainty. This value is equal to the obtained score plus 1.96 times the standard error for the required true score t_u:

$$t_u = t_j + 1.96\sqrt{t_u(n - t_u)/(n - 1)}. \qquad (6\text{–}8)$$

We know t_j and n and obtain $t_u = 40 + 1.96\sqrt{t_u(50 - t_u)/49}$. The equation can now be solved for t_u and we obtain the value 44.4. For the true score 44.4, $s_e(t_j)$ is 2.231. If the standard error is multiplied by 1.96, we obtain the difference $44.4 - 40.0$. The probability that the true score for individual j in this case is 44.4 or more is therefore approximately 2.5%.

In the same way we obtain a lower limit t_l by solving Eq. (6–9) for t_l:

$$t_l = t_j - 1.96\sqrt{t_l(n - t_l)/(n - 1)}. \qquad (6\text{–}9)$$

We obtain $t_l = 33.5$. The standard error for this true score is 3.326. If the standard error is multiplied by 1.96, the difference $40 - 33.5$ is obtained. The probability that the true score for individual j is 33.5 or less is therefore 2.5%. [Both Eqs. (6–8) and (6–9) give the same roots when we solve the second-degree equation. These roots give t_u and t_l.]

We have just found the limits for the confidence interval within which the true score lies with 95% certainty for individual j who has solved 40 items on a 50-item test. The limits are 44.4 and 33.5. We can also express this by saying that the number of items which j can in fact solve lies with 95% certainty between 67% and 89% of the total number of items in the population from which the test items are drawn.

It can be seen from Eq. (6–5) that the numerical value of $s_e(t_j)$ is a function of the number of test items and the proportion of the total number of test items in the population which the individual can solve.

When n is constant, $s_e(t_j)$ varies as p, that is, as the proportion of the number of items which the individual can solve. The value will be greatest when p and q are equal, i.e., when the individual can solve half the items. It will become smaller for increasing or decreasing values of p and will finally be zero when p is 1 or 0. The standard error computed with $s_e(t_j)$ is thus greatest for true scores in the middle of the distribution. The more extreme the value taken by the true score, the smaller the standard error computed with $s_e(t_j)$.

Figure 6–3 shows how $s_e(t_j)$ and $1.96 s_e(t_j)$ vary with the value of the true score for a test containing 100 items.

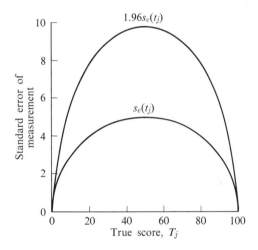

Fig. 6–3 The standard error of measurement $[s_e(t_j)]$ as a function of the size of true scores.

The fact that $s_e(t_j)$ is a function only of the number of items in the test and the number of these which the individual can solve has several consequences. One of them is that the standard deviation, according to this equation, is independent of the items' content, frequency of correct solution, and intercorrelations. This means that tests which have the same number of items should have the same average standard error, regardless of the nature of the tests. Lord has presented empirical data which support this conclusion for cognitive tests (cf. Lord, 1957, 1959).

Certain facts should be borne in mind when the standard error of measurement computed from the equation for $s_e(t_j)$ is to be used and interpreted.

The derivation of $s_e(t_j)$ is based upon the assumption of randomly parallel tests. The test which is used for measuring a certain trait is considered to be one of a series of randomly parallel tests. It is assumed that the number of items which the single individual can solve varies from one test to the other. The "true" score on a single test is different from the "true" score on another test from the same population. The derivation of s_e (Eq. 6–2), on the other hand, assumes that any two measurements for a given individual, obtained from parallel tests, have exactly the same true score. The difference is that Lord assumes for every one of the items in the population from which the random parallel tests are drawn that it either can or cannot be solved by a single individual and, furthermore, that every item which can be solved by the individual under all normal circumstances gives a score of 1. Thus he does not take into account such sources of error as lack of agreement between different raters of a given response.

The assumption that the items are considered to be randomly drawn from a population means that the standard error of measurement cannot be computed from $s_e(t_j)$ for tests with a time limit.

When deriving the usual equation for the standard error of measurement (s_e) we assume that the parallel tests measure exactly the same true score. When we construct parallel tests in practice, we attempt to make the tests as similar as possible. This is achieved in some instances by matching the items. Traditional parallel tests cannot usually be taken to be composed of items randomly drawn from the same population. The standard error we obtain from these tests will be less than that estimated by $s_e(t_j)$.

From the previous discussion it should be apparent that the two standard errors, s_e from Eq. (6–2) and $s_e(t_j)$ from Eq. (6–7), are two completely different measures. The former, s_e, is the standard deviation of the distribution of errors around a true score, which is always the same for the parallel tests which have given the error dispersion. The latter, $s_e(t_j)$, is the standard deviation of the distribution of true scores for an individual around the true score which holds for the population of items from which the unmatched parallel tests are drawn. The fact that $s_e(t_j)$ varies with the true score in the manner shown in Fig. 6–3 cannot, therefore, be taken as support for the rejection of the assumptions on which the application of s_e is based. Even though there are other reasons for questioning these assumptions, it is scarcely likely that s_e varies with the true score in exactly the same way as $s_e(t_j)$.

6–3   A PRACTICAL APPLICATION

The standard error of measurement is used in so-called *multiple-stage methods* for estimating the positions of individuals on a continuum. An individual's test score is obtained from a number of items in a test or from a series of tests in (for example) a test battery. The usual administrative procedure is to let every subject attempt each item on the single test and each subtest in the test battery. Another principle is used in multiple-stage methods. When the standard error of measurement for the single test is known, a gradual narrowing down of possibilities for each particular individual takes place on successive testings with different subtests. The area within which a particular true score ought to be found can be limited once one subtest (or, as in the common Stanford-Binet test for children, once a small number of items) has been completed. All individuals do not then attempt the same test in the second round of testing. We choose tests for each individual which are especially sensitive within the area in which we can now expect to find his true score. This procedure can be repeated as long as every new round of testing makes a more accurate measurement at reasonable cost. The multiple-stage methodology has obvious advantages, in (for instance) diagnostic situations. We can begin the examination with multidimensional tests of relatively low reliability; even with low reliabilities we can exclude a number of possibilities at an early stage and deal with those which remain. Repeated testing with items so chosen that they measure more and more accurately within a critical zone for more specific variables leads to smaller and smaller standard errors and a more certain diagnosis. However, test strategy makes special demands with regard to the situations where this method can be applied and the construction of the instruments to be used. A basic treatment of the problems connected with test construction and the practical application of the multiple-stage methodology is given by Cronbach and Gleser (1964).

PROBLEMS

1. Compute the standard error of measurement for tests with the following standard deviations and reliability coefficients.

Test	s_t	r_{tt}
a	10	0.90
b	15	0.95
c	2	0.85

2. An individual has obtained the following scores on the three subtests in Problem 1: (a) 55, (b) 60, (c) 6. Between which scores is his true score located with 95% certainty on the three variables measured?

3. The manual for a given test reports a reliability of 0.84 and mean and standard score distributions of 130 and 12.5 respectively. What is the probability that an individual with true score 130 will obtain a score of 146 or more?

4. What is the probability that individuals with true scores (a) 119, (b) 115, (c) 110 will obtain the score 124 or more on the test described in Problem 3?

5. Individuals A, B, and C have the same true score 50 for a test with mean 50, standard deviation 10, and reliability coefficient 0.84. What is the probability that each of them will obtain a score of 46, 42, and 39 or less respectively?

6. Individuals A and B have true scores of 100 and 80 respectively on a test with mean 100, standard deviation 15, and reliability 0.875. What is the probability that A will obtain a score of 90 or less and that B will obtain a score of 90 or more?

7. Individual C has obtained a score of 90 on the test described in Problem 6. Within what limits can we expect C's true score to be located with 95% certainty?

8. The standard error of measurement for a given test has been found to be 5. What will the reliability of the test be when applied to groups with the following characteristics?

Group	Mean	Standard deviation
I	50	10
II	50	15
III	60	10
IV	60	15

9. (a) A certain individual is considered to be able to solve (a) 20%, (b) 50%, (c) 90% of the items in an item population. Compute the standard error of measurement, $s_e(t_j)$, for a test consisting of 50 items drawn randomly from the population. Investigate how the standard error varies for different frequencies of correct solution.

(b) Compute the reliability at the different levels if the test variance is 7.

10. An individual has obtained a score of 30 on a test consisting of 50 items. Estimate with $s_e(t_j)$ the confidence interval within which his true score can be expected to be located with 95% certainty.

11. Compute for Problem 10 the percentage of the total number of items which the individual with 95% certainty can in fact solve.

12. Estimate the standard error of measurement $[s_e(t_j)]$ for the upper and lower limits respectively of a 95% confidence interval for obtained scores of (a) 8, (b) 29, (c) 42 for a test with 50 items.

13. A test consists of 65 items randomly drawn from an item population.

(a) Compute the standard error $s_e(t_j)$ for the true scores $T_j = 0$, $T_j = 5$, $T_j = 10$, $T_j = 15$.

(b) Draw the function describing the relation between the magnitude of the standard error and test scores.

REFERENCES

CRONBACH, L. J., and G. C. GLESER (1964). *Psychological tests and personnel decisions.* Urbana: University of Illinois Press.

DIXON, W. J., and F. J. MASSEY (1957). *Introduction to statistical analysis.* New York: McGraw-Hill.

LORD, F. M. (1955).   Estimating test reliability.   *Educ. Psychol. Measmt.*, **15,** 325–336.

—— (1957).   Do tests of the same length have the same standard error of measurement? *Educ. Psychol. Measmt.*, **17,** 510–521.

—— (1959).   Tests of the same length *do* have the same standard error of measurement. *Educ. Psychol. Measmt.*, **19,** 233–239.

Suggested reading

GHISELLI, E. E. (1964).   *Theory of psychological measurement.* New York: McGraw-Hill.

GULLIKSEN, H. (1950).   *Theory of mental tests.* New York: Wiley.

LORD, F. M. (1964).   Nominally and rigorously parallel test forms. *Psychometrika,* **29,** 335–345.

TRYON, R. (1957).   Reliability and behavior domain validity: a reformulation and historical critique. *Psychol. Bull.,* **54,** 229–249.

CHAPTER 7

The Reliability
of Difference Scores

7-1 THE STANDARD ERROR OF DIFFERENCES
BETWEEN SINGLE SCORES

The reliability of differences is an important matter for both intraindividual and interindividual comparison. When working with intraindividual differences we want to know whether an obtained difference between scores for the same individual with respect to different variables is reliable. If so, it can, for example, be used for predicting relative success in different courses of education. In interindividual comparison we want to know whether the obtained differences between scores for different individuals with respect to different variables are sufficiently reliable that a choice between job applicants, for example, can be based on them.

A. Intraindividual differences

We begin by assuming that the comparison is intraindividual in order to derive an expression for computing confidence intervals for differences between test scores. When testing for clinical diagnoses or vocational guidance, one often presents the result in the form of a *profile* (Fig. 7–1). All subtest distributions are converted to the same scale, so that the profile will be easier to interpret. Figure 7–1 shows the score for an individual on every subtest, expressed on a T-scale ($M = 50$, $s = 10$). The same relative position on the various subdistributions will always correspond to the same score. The profile thus gives a direct expression for the relationship between the individual's positions on the subdistributions.

As a result of the unreliability of the two subtests, we will always obtain random differences in both directions between scores for an individual on different subdistributions. We are interested in knowing how great a difference in a certain direction must be to ensure that the probability of its arising as a result of measurement error will be so small that we are confident in using it, for example, as a basis for prediction purposes.

We begin by assuming the null hypothesis (i.e., that there is no difference between the individual's true scores on the parallel tests g and h), and then we calculate the difference for every pair of parallel tests. These differences will be distributed randomly around zero: in some cases, the difference $g_j - h_j$ will be positive; in others, negative. We now need the standard deviation of this distribution.

The equation for the variance of the sum of two scores has already been derived (Eq. 4–4). The variance of a distribution of differences can be derived in the same way—we need only change the sign in the initial equation. We thus obtain, for the variance of a difference between two scores on subtests g and h,

$$s_{g-h}^2 = s_g^2 + s_h^2 - 2r_{gh}s_g s_h. \tag{7-1}$$

The equation contains the same numerical expressions as the equation for the variance of a sum. The only difference is the sign of the covariance terms.

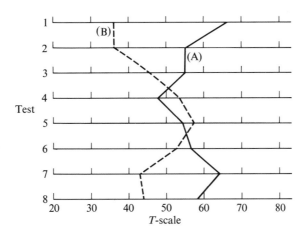

Fig. 7–1 Profiles for two individuals (A and B) for 8 subtests with scores given on the T-scale ($M = 50$, $s = 10$).

In the example given for testing the null hypothesis, the whole of the obtained distribution of differences is made up of differences which are the result of measurement errors. The variance of the distribution of these error differences ($s_{e_{g-h}}^2$, henceforth written $s_{e_d}^2$) can now be written in the following way:

$$s_{e_d}^2 = s_{e_g}^2 + s_{e_h}^2 - 2r_{e_g e_h} s_{e_g} s_{e_h}. \tag{7-2}$$

Since the errors in the tests g and h can be assumed to be uncorrelated ($r_{e_g e_h} = 0$), the covariance terms will be zero. Thus, the variance of the distribution of random differences can be written as the sum of the variance of the distribution of errors on the one test and the variance of the distribution of errors on the other test:

$$s_{e_d}^2 = s_{e_g}^2 + s_{e_h}^2. \tag{7-3}$$

It is also clear that the magnitude of the random differences is dependent on the magnitude of the measurement errors on each of the subtests.

An expression for the error variance of a single score has already been derived (Eq. 6-1). The error variance of each of the subtests g and h can be written in the form of $s_{e_g}^2 = s_g^2(1 - r_{gg})$ and $s_{e_h}^2 = s_h^2(1 - r_{hh})$, where r_{gg} is the reliability of subtest g, and r_{hh} is the reliability of subtest h. The variance of the distribution of random differences can now be written

$$s_{e_d}^2 = s_g^2(1 - r_{gg}) + s_h^2 (1 - r_{hh}).$$

The variances are equal ($s_g^2 = s_h^2$), since the test distributions in a profile are converted to the same scale. The standard deviation of the distribution of random differences can thus be simplified to

$$s_{e_d} = s_g\sqrt{2 - r_{gg} - r_{hh}}; \tag{7-4}$$

or, if $r_{gg} = r_{hh}$,

$$s_{e_d} = s_g\sqrt{2(1 - r_{gg})}. \tag{7-5}$$

We can now calculate how large the difference between two scores in a certain direction must be in order to be significant at a given level.

The scores on two subtests I and II have been transformed to a T-scale with $M = 50$ and $s = 10$. The reliability of the subtests is 0.80 and 0.90 respectively. Inserting these values in Eq. (7-4), we obtain

$$s_{e_{I-II}} = 10\sqrt{2 - 0.80 - 0.90} = 5.5.$$

The result means that a difference between scores on subtests I and II in a given direction of 11 points (two standard deviations) or more will arise as a result of errors in measurement of the true scores in only 2.5% of a very large number of testings. Note that the probability is calculated for a one-tailed hypothesis, since we are interested not only in the magnitude of the difference but also in its direction.

B. Interindividual differences

Exactly the same reasoning as was used in the previous section can be applied to the difference between two scores for the same test, i.e., the difference one obtains from an interindividual comparison. Let us assume that the comparison is made for two individuals A and B on Test 2 in Fig. 7-1. For a large number of tests parallel to Test 2 we would obtain a distribution of differences between scores for A and B. This distribution of difference scores has arisen merely as a result of the inability of the test to measure the true scores for A and B and is thus a distribution of errors. Since the reliability will be the same for the scores for A and B (they have been obtained with the same test), the equation for the standard deviation of the distribution can be written in an analogous form to Eq. (7–5):

$$s_{e_{A-B}} = s_t\sqrt{2(1 - r_{tt})}. \qquad (7\text{–}6)$$

Note that this is the equation for computing the standard deviation of the distribution of randomly obtained differences between two scores on the same test. The equation is used for testing the significance of obtained differences in the same way as Eq. (7–5) was used for testing the reliability of a difference between scores on two different tests.

7–2   THE RELIABILITY OF DIFFERENCES

The reliability of intraindividual difference scores can also be expressed generally in a reliability coefficient. This can be derived from equations which are already known. The reliability of a distribution's score can be obtained when the variance of error scores and the variance of observed scores are known (see p. 66). To compute the reliability coefficient for differences, we require, therefore, (a) the variance of the error distribution of the differences, and (b) the variance of the distribution of obtained differences. The expression for the variance of the error distribution is obtained from Eq. (7–5). Equation (7–1) gives an expression for the variance of the distribution of obtained difference scores. From this we can proceed as follows.

Since profile scores are given on the same scale for every test, $s_g = s_h$ and $s_g^2 = s_h^2$. If s_{g-h}^2 is written s_d^2, we obtain

$$s_d^2 = 2s_g^2 - 2r_{gh}s_g^2 = 2s_g^2(1 - r_{gh}). \qquad (7\text{–}7)$$

The variance of a distribution of differences depends, therefore, partly on the scale on which the difference scores are computed, and partly on the correlation between the scores with which the differences are computed. It is also obvious that the higher this correlation between scores becomes, the smaller the distribution of differences will be. When $r_{gh} = 1.0$, every individual will have the same obtained score on both variables and every difference will be zero. [Compare the variance of the distribution of random differences—Eq. (7–5).] The reliability of the differences between individuals' scores on tests g and h can now be written and explained in the following way:

$$r_{dd} = 1 - \frac{s_{e_d}^2}{s_d^2} = 1 - \frac{2s_g^2(1 - \bar{r}_{gg})}{2s_g^2(1 - r_{gh})} = \frac{1 - r_{gh} - 1 + \bar{r}_{gg}}{1 - r_{gh}};$$

$$r_{dd} = \frac{\bar{r}_{gg} - r_{gh}}{1 - r_{gh}}, \qquad (7\text{–}8)$$

where $\bar{r}_{gg}$ is the mean of r_{gg} and r_{hh}.

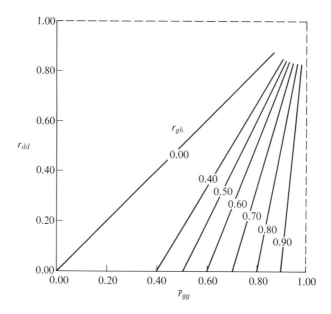

Fig. 7–2 The reliability of difference scores (r_{dd}) as a function of the mean reliability of the subtests ($\bar{r}_{gg}$) for different correlations between the subtests (r_{gh}).

It can be seen from Eq. (7–8) that the reliability of difference scores depends partly upon the reliability of each of the tests on which the difference computations are based (r_{gg} and r_{hh}), and partly upon the extent to which the two tests vary jointly.

The coefficient of reliability for difference scores increases as the size of the mean of the reliability coefficients of the tests, when the correlation is constant. This is shown in Fig. 7–2 for different values of the intercorrelation (r_{gh}). When the reliability coefficients of both tests are 1.0, the reliability of difference scores is also 1.0 for all values of r_{gh}. When both tests measure true scores with complete certainty, all differences will be true differences and their reliability will be 1.0. When the intercorrelation between the tests increases, the reliability of the difference scores is reduced, the average reliability of the tests remaining unchanged. This is illustrated in Fig. 7–3 for different values of $\bar{r}_{gg}$. The higher the intercorrelation between the tests, the greater the extent to which they measure the same true scores. Thus, the higher the intercorrelation between the tests, the smaller will be the proportion of the distribution of obtained differences (which are also reduced) that will be made up of true difference scores. The error distribution of differences remains, of course, unchanged as long as the reliabilities of the tests are unchanged. When the proportion of true variance in the difference distribution is reduced, the reliability of the difference scores is also reduced.

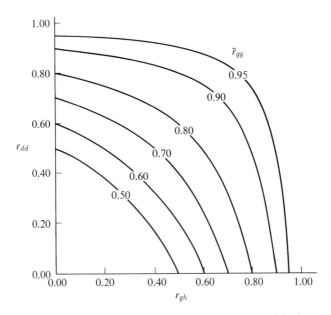

Fig. 7-3 The reliability of difference scores (r_{dd}) as a function of the intercorrelation between subtests (r_{gh}) for different sizes of the mean reliability of the subtests ($\bar{r}_{gg}$).

7-3 SUMMARY AND APPLICATION

In the first section of this chapter, we derived the expression for the standard deviation of interindividual differences obtained purely as a result of the tests' inability to measure true scores. With this we can compute how large the difference in a given direction must be, if we are to consider the probability of its arising as a result of measurement errors so small that we are prepared to use it as a basis for various types of practical application. An example showed that the probability of a difference of 11 units or more arising by chance is 2.5%, if the reliabilities of the two tests on which the difference scores are computed are 0.90 and 0.80 respectively and the scores on both the tests are expressed on a T-scale ($M = 50, s = 10$). We should not, therefore, use differences of less than 11 units if, when using the difference scores, we do not wish to run a risk greater than that given above. This result at first glance seems to imply that only a very small number of the differences we can obtain, and might wish to use for the tests in question, can in fact be used. Let us examine this problem a little more closely.

The first and most important thing we wish to know about a difference is whether its direction is certain. Let us assume that individual A has T-score 57 on subtest I and T-score 48 on subtest II. The first question then is, How reliable is the direction of the difference $57 - 48$, i.e., how certain is it that A's true position is higher on the continuum measured by Test I than on that

Table 7–1

		$\bar{r}_{gg}$	r_{gh}						
			0.10	0.20	0.30	0.40	0.50	0.60	0.70
	s_d	0.90	13.4	12.6	11.8	11.0	10.0	8.9	7.7
		0.80	13.4	12.6	11.8	11.0	10.0	8.9	7.7
	r_{dd}	0.90	0.89	0.88	0.86	0.83	0.80	0.75	0.67
		0.80	0.78	0.75	0.71	0.67	0.60	0.50	0.33
	s_{e_d}	0.90	4.42	4.42	4.42	4.42	4.42	4.42	4.42
		0.80	6.30	6.30	6.30	6.30	6.30	6.30	6.30
Percentage of obtained differences which can be used with a risk of 5% and 10% respectively	5%	0.90	58	56	53	51	47	41	34
		0.80	44	40	38	34	30	24	18
	10%	0.90	67	65	62	60	57	52	46
		0.80	55	54	50	46	42	36	29

measured by Test II? Let us choose various levels of risk of using differences which may possibly be the result of measurement error, and find the percentage of the total number of individuals for which we can establish the direction of the differences, assuming that the average reliability coefficients of the two subtests are 0.90 and 0.80 respectively.

We begin by evaluating the standard deviation of the distribution of obtained differences. This is computed with the aid of Eq. (7–7). Its size depends on the standard deviation of the distribution of scores on each of the subtests (s_g), and on the extent of the intercorrelation between the scores on the two distributions (r_{gh}). The standard deviation of the distribution of differences on a T-scale is given in Table 7–1. It can be seen that the standard deviation of the difference distribution decreases as the intercorrelation increases, and that its size is independent of the reliability of the subtests.

Table 7–1 also confirms the previously mentioned circumstance, that the reliability of obtained difference scores is dependent on the reliability of the subtests and decreases as the intercorrelation between the subtests increases.

With the usual equation for the standard error of measurement, we obtain

$$s_{e_d} = s_d\sqrt{1 - r_{dd}}. \tag{7–9}$$

The standard deviation of the distribution of random differences has been computed from Eq. (7–9). This gives the same numerical value as Eq. (7–5), as can easily be seen by inserting empirical values. This standard deviation is the same for different values of the intercorrelation coefficient, but is dependent upon the reliability of the subtests.

Let us assume that we want to use as many differences as possible without taking a risk greater than 5% that any difference is a result of measurement error and not, therefore, an expression for a genuine difference between true scores in the given direction. Consequently, we wish to use every obtained positive difference which is equal to or greater than the positive value on the distribution of random differences which separates the highest 5% from the rest of the distribution. Of obtained negative differences, we wish to use those that are equal to or greater than the negative value on the distribution of random differences which separates the lowest 5% from the rest of the distribution. The standard score on a normal distribution which separates the highest 5% from the rest of the distribution is 1.65. Computing the standard deviation of random differences to be 4.42 when the reliability of the two subtests is 0.90, we can now find the position on the random distribution which divides it in the proportion 5/95. To do this, we multiply the standard deviation of random differences by 1.65, thus obtaining $1.65 \times 4.42 = 7.29$. We can thus conclude that, under the given conditions, a positive difference of 7.29 or more will be obtained randomly in 5% of all cases, and also that a negative difference of the same size or greater will be obtained in 5% of all cases. We can now, with the aid of the difference distribution for obtained scores on variables whose intercorrelation is 0.40, find out how large a proportion of the composite distribution of these differences lies outside ±7.29 units on a T-scale. The value 7.29 is 0.663 of the standard deviation of the obtained difference distribution, which is equal to 11.0 when $r_{gh} = 0.40$. From a normal distribution table it can be seen that 25.4% of the total distribution lies above the standard score 0.663. We can, therefore, with a 5% risk of error, use the obtained differences for 25.4% of the total number of individuals for whom differences have been computed, as an expression for genuine differences in true scores, when the true score for these individuals is higher on test g than on test h (i.e., when the difference $g - h$ is positive). The obtained differences can also be used (again with a 5% risk of error) for an equal number of individuals, as an expression of genuine differences in true scores, when the true score for these individuals is lower on test g than on test h (i.e., when the difference $g - h$ is negative). We can, therefore, for 50.8% of all individuals establish with reasonable certainty on which of the two variables measured the individuals have their higher true scores; 60% of all obtained differences can be used if a 10% error risk is taken instead of 5%.

The proportion of the total number of differences which can be used for different sizes of the intercorrelation, with average reliabilities of 0.80 and 0.90, when the error risks are 5% and 10% respectively, can be computed as above. The result of these computations is shown in Table 7–1.

PROBLEMS

1. The reliability of three subtests a, b, and c is 0.95, 0.91, and 0.84 respectively. How large a difference in a given direction on a T-scale ($M = 50$, $s = 10$) must there be between the scores on the respective subtests for it to be obtained with 97.5% certainty?

2. Individuals A, B, and C have obtained scores of 46, 42, and 39 respectively on a test where the scores have been transformed to a T-scale. The reliability of the test is 0.84. Calculate the probability that, if A, B, and C had the same true score, they would obtain these or greater differences in the same direction.

3. In a given test, $r_{tt} = 0.875$, $M = 100$, and $s = 15$. What is the probability that the same individual will obtain scores which differ by 15 units or more when tested twice under similar conditions?

4. See Problem 3. What is the probability that the individual will obtain a score on the second testing which is 8 units better than that obtained on the first?

5. On Test 1, an individual has obtained a score of 60 on a T-scale distribution. On Test 2 he has obtained a score of 124 on an I.Q. scale ($M = 100$, $s = 16$).

   (a) Which score is the better performance?

   (b) Calculate the probability that the individual's true score will be higher on Test 2 than on Test 1 if the reliability of Test 1 is 0.90 and that of Test 2 is 0.85.

6. Variables a ($r_{tt} = 0.91$), b ($r_{tt} = 0.92$), and c ($r_{tt} = 0.94$) are included in a test battery used for vocational guidance. Scores are given on a T-scale. How large must the differences between the different test scores be in order for the direction of the difference to be certain at the 95% and 99% levels respectively?

7. Test 1 has reliability 0.80; Test 2 has reliability 0.70. The correlation between Tests 1 and 2 is 0.45. Compute the reliability of differences between individuals' scores on the two tests.

8. See Table 7–1. Compute the values of s_d, r_{dd}, s_{e_d}, etc., for $\bar{r}_{gg} = 0.70$. (Values are given in the table for $\bar{r}_{gg} = 0.90$ and 0.80.)

Suggested reading

Bass, A. R., and F. E. Fiedler (1959). *Interpersonal perception scores: a comparison of D scores and their components*. Urbana: University of Illinois Press.

Cronbach, L. J., and G. C. Gleser (1953). Assessing similarity between profiles. *Psychol. Bull.*, **50**, 456–473.

Cronbach, L. J. (1958). Proposals leading to analytic treatment of social perception scores. In R. Tagiuri and L. Petrullo (Eds.) *Person perception and inter-personal behavior*. Stanford: Stanford University Press.

Gulliksen, H. (1950). *Theory of mental tests*. New York: Wiley.

Harris, C. W. (Ed.) (1963). *Problems in measuring change*. Madison: University of Wisconsin Press.

Lord, F. M. (1958). The utilization of reliable difference scores. *J. Educ. Psychol.*, **49**, 150–152.

MITRA, S. K., and D. W. FISKE (1956). Intraindividual variability as related to test score and item. *Educ. Psychol. Measmt.*, **16**, 3–12.

MOSIER, C. I. (1951). Batteries and profiles. In E. F. LINDQUIST (Ed.) *Educational measurement*. Washington D.C.: Am. Council on Educ.

NUNNALLY, J. (1962). The analysis of profile data. *Psychol. Bull.*, **59**, 311–359.

CHAPTER 8

Error Variance in
Estimations of Reliability

8-1 INTRODUCTION

The reliability coefficient was previously defined by the expression $1 - s_e^2/s_t^2$. When computing the size of the reliability coefficient in a practical example, we can obtain an exact numerical expression for s_t^2 (the variance of the distribution of obtained scores). We do not, however, know the size of s_e^2 (the variance of the distribution of the error components), and this must be estimated. There are a number of methods used for making this estimate.

Every individual score has so far been regarded as the sum of two components, a true score (T_j) and an error score (e_j). Every individual contributes with these two components to the true-score distribution and the error-score distribution respectively. The error component for a certain individual can now be considered as the sum of a number of error components which are the result of a number of specific sources of error. It is reasonable to suppose that these error factors are independent of each other, so that the different parts of the error component which are derived from different error sources are uncorrelated with each other. For a number of individuals we can now let the error component from a given source of error form a distribution. The variance of the distribution in which every individual's total error component is included will then be made up of the sum of the distributions from each of the error sources.

Computation of the reliability coefficient was based upon the estimate of the variance of the distribution of total error components (s_e^2). It is, however, an important fact that different practical methods give different estimates of the size of this variance. This is because the estimates of the error variance, as obtained by different methods, are affected by different sources. In some methods, a true component is included in the estimate of the total error component. As a result of this procedure, s_e^2 is overestimated; this in turn means that the reliability is underestimated. In others, a part of the error component serves as true score—a procedure which leads to an underestimate of error variance and an overestimate of reliability. For a correct assessment of a given reliability coefficient, it is therefore important to know by which

100

method it has been obtained and what variance the particular method includes in the error variance. This chapter is concerned with the variance terms for different methods. In the next chapter we shall consider the most common practical methods for estimating reliability.

8–2   MEASUREMENT ERRORS

This heading refers to errors produced by factors which result in individual scores differing from one parallel test to the other, even though the true scores are the same. Errors which are the result of such factors are genuine measurement errors.

Measurement errors can in principle arise as a result of the following factors: (a) the administration of the test, (b) guessing, and (c) scoring.

A. Administration of the test

The test administrator doubtless plays a decisive part in the measurement errors which can arise during the actual administration. In recent years, two aspects have attracted considerable attention: (a) the role of the test administrator in different types of testing and (b) the important effect that the unavoidable interaction between the individuals testing and those being tested (in certain test situations especially) has on the performance and behavior of the individuals tested. Since the effect of this interaction is dependent on both parties, it is often important, when judging the significance of the result, to know who administered the test. This factor probably varies in importance with different types of method and with different types of test situation—for example, it might be more important in an individual than in a group test. When testing individually, the test administrator has greater opportunities to make conditions conducive to an optimal performance by adapting his behavior to the individual being tested, an adaptation which is difficult to make in a group test situation. Some individuals, on the other hand, are easily affected and inhibited by the intimate personal contact in individual test situations.

Other factors in the test administration itself which can influence the scores are the surroundings in which the testing is carried out, the extent of outside disturbance, etc. One especially important aspect is the instructions given to the individuals tested, which can also be a source of error. If the formulation of the items, the possible responses, the requirements placed on a response, etc., are ambiguous, there is a possibility that the individuals will not interpret the items in the same way from one occasion to the next. Some error variance may thus be caused by lack of clarity in the instructions.

The variance of the distribution of measurement errors which is a result of a change, from one test occasion to another, of administrator and/or milieu will be denoted by $s_{e(\mathrm{adm})}^2$.

B. Guessing

In so-called multiple-choice methods responses are given in the form of a number of alternatives, one of which is correct. If the individual tested is unable to solve such an item, he can make a guess. He will give a correct guess with a certain probability for each single item, and for a test with a given number of items he will give a number of correct responses by guessing without knowing the correct solution. Because of guessing he will, therefore, obtain ones in the score matrix where he should in fact have zeros; this effect is a pure measurement error. (The possibilities of correcting for the effect of guessing are dealt with in Chapter 15.) In certain circumstances, we must also expect guessing to result in correct solutions in other than multiple-choice tests.

The variance which arises from guessing is therefore an error variance and is denoted by $s_{e(\mathrm{g})}^2$.

C. Scoring

The person who rates the responses, i.e., who decides whether a response is right or wrong, plays an important part in the production of measurement errors. If we define *objectivity* as agreement between different judges, lack of objectivity in scoring will produce an error variance. Different judges will arrive at different conclusions about what is right or wrong with reference to doubtful responses. In most group tests this error factor is of little importance. The correction of the test is often so objective that it can be carried out by machine. The objectivity obtained here is a result of the limited number of possible responses and the fact that every alternative is given. The scoring instructions can cover every conceivable response. In many individual tests, however, it is not possible to give scoring rules for every conceivable response alternative. Whenever an individual has given a response which has not been foreseen or completely covered by the rules with which the test is standardized, the score depends on the raters' skill and judgment.

Error variance which arises because of subjectivity in scoring will be denoted by $s_{e(\mathrm{subj})}^2$.

8–3 LACK OF AGREEMENT BETWEEN PARALLEL MEASUREMENTS OF TRUE SCORES

Chapter 5 presented two different ways of obtaining parallel measurements. We can, first, consider reliability to be the agreement between parallel tests, assuming that the parallel tests measure exactly the same true score for each individual. Second, we can consider reliability to be the agreement between random parallel tests, which are taken to be composed of items drawn from the same population of items.

Reliability as the correlation between parallel tests which measure exactly the same true score for each individual gives the accuracy with which the items included in the test in question measure whatever they measure. The coefficient we obtain is an expression for the error variance, which assumes its minimum value when every condition for parallel tests is completely satisfied. This coefficient has been called a *coefficient of precision* (cf. Coombs, 1950). It can be regarded as a purely theoretical value, for reasons presented in the following discussion.

Reliability as the correlation between random parallel tests gives the degree of certainty with which one can measure, with a test consisting of items randomly drawn from a certain item population, the trait which is measured by that population. We can select a large number of random parallel tests from this population and thus obtain an array of correlation coefficients. Their mean is the most likely value of a correlation coefficient for the relationship between random parallel tests of this length. This mean is a function of (a) the number of items in each test and (b) the homogeneity of the population of items, i.e., the extent to which the items measure the same variable. A coefficient for the relationship between random parallel tests is an *internal consistency coefficient*.

When constructing tests for parallel measurements we normally attempt to make the tests as similar to one another as possible. In this way we approach the conditions for strictly parallel tests. In practice, however, it is impossible to satisfy completely the theoretical requirements for such tests. The tests which we use will in fact measure somewhat different true scores for each individual. On the whole, they measure the same true score. There will thus be a positive correlation between the tests. But each of the tests will also measure something which is a true score on one test but is not measured by the other. The latter measures, instead, a true component which is specific to it and is not measured by the first test.

The specific true component which is measured by one of the parallel tests but not by the other will not contribute to the correlation between the tests (i.e., to the reliability coefficient), despite the fact that it is true components which contribute to the total true variance of each of the tests. When estimating reliability as the correlation between parallel tests, this specific true variance will be treated as error variance—in the following text denoted by $s^2_{T(\text{equ})}$.

A coefficient obtained when estimating the correlation between parallel tests is usually called a *coefficient of equivalence*. The effect of treating $s^2_{T(\text{equ})}$ as error variance when computing equivalence coefficients is that the coefficient we obtain underestimates the precision coefficient (see above).

The true variance, which we treat as error variance when computing equivalence coefficients, will be greatest when nothing is done to make the tests for which the coefficient is computed more similar than they are when randomly constructed from items drawn from the same population.

Normally, we attempt to make the tests as similar to one another as possible, which means that we attempt to make the value $s^2_{T(\text{equ})}$ as small as possible. The equivalence coefficient obtained for these tests thus over-estimates the coefficient which we should obtain for random parallel tests.

8–4 FLUCTUATION IN THE INDIVIDUALS' TRUE SCORES

The correlation between parallel tests as an expression for the reliability of each of the tests assumes that the true scores are the same on both tests for each particular individual. One can, however, assume that the true score changes from situation to situation, where the extent of the change is related to a time lapse between the two occasions. If a completely reliable test is applied on two separate occasions, the correlation between the results on the two occasions for a large number of individuals will not necessarily be 1.0, since each single measurement gives the individuals' true scores on one specific occasion. The true variance on one occasion which does not correlate with the true variance on the other will thus be treated as error variance. It is as a result of fluctuations in the individuals' true positions on the continuum and has nothing to do with the test's ability to measure true scores accurately. If, when computing the test's reliability, we include this variance in the total error variance, we will underestimate the ability of the test to measure true scores. This variance will be denoted by $s^2_{T(\text{fl})}$.

8–5 MEMORY EFFECTS

The two preceding sections of this chapter deal with true variance which is included in the error variance and which thus leads to the overestimating of the latter. We must, at the same time, include a factor present in certain situations which gives rise to a superficially true variance. We are dealing here with memory effects which can arise on repeated administration of a test.

Memory effects from the first administration will affect the result of the second if the same test is administered on two successive occasions. The individuals need only remember the response given on the first occasion and make the same response on the second, for us to obtain complete agreement between the results of the two measurements. We will obtain an agreement which affects the correlation between repeated measurements but which is not an expression of the method's reliability. That component of the score obtained on the first occasion which reappears on the second occasion will in part do so, not because the tests measure the same true score, but as the result of memory. A conceivable case is that which arises when every score on the first administration of the test is an error score but the correlation with scores from the second occasion is nevertheless relatively high because of this factor. If the superficially true variance arising in this way is denoted by $s_{e(m)}^2$, the reliability in this case will incorrectly be estimated to be $s_{e(m)}^2/s_t^2$.

It follows that, when we compute the correlation between repeated measurements of a variable with the same test, the error variance due to memory will be treated as true variance and will therefore contribute to an overestimate of the test's ability to measure true scores, and hence an overestimate of its reliability.

REFERENCE

COOMBS, C. H. (1950). The concepts of reliability and homogeneity. *Educ. Psychol. Measmt.*, **10**, 43–56.

Suggested reading

THORNDIKE, R. L. (1951). Reliability. In E. F. LINDQUIST (Ed.) *Educational Measurement*. Washington D.C.: Am. Council on Educ.

CHAPTER 9

Practical Methods for Estimating Reliability

A number of different methods are available for estimating reliability. Only the most common ones will be discussed here. The reliability estimates usually found in test manuals are as a rule obtained by one of these methods.

Four methods will be presented:

1. the test-retest method;   2. the parallel-test method;
3. split-half methods;   4. the Kuder-Richardson method.

9-1   THE TEST-RETEST METHOD

This method involves administering the same test twice. Using the notation given previously for different variance terms and assuming that the terms are uncorrelated, the composition of the total test variance for the retest method can now be written as follows:

$$s_t^2 = s_T^2 + s_{e(m)}^2 + s_{e(adm)}^2 + s_{e(g)}^2 + s_{e(subj)}^2 + s_{T(fl)}^2, \qquad (9-1)$$

where s_t^2 is the total test variance, s_T^2 is the true variance, $s_{e(m)}^2$ is the error variance due to memory, $s_{e(adm)}^2$ is the error variance due to administration effects, $s_{e(g)}^2$ is the error variance due to guessing, $s_{e(subj)}^2$ is the error variance due to lack of agreement between scorers or raters, and $s_{T(fl)}^2$ is the variance due to fluctuation in true scores from one occasion to the next.

The variance, treated as error variance when we compute the correlation between scores on the two test occasions, will be

$$s_e^2 = s_{e(adm)}^2 + s_{e(g)}^2 + s_{e(subj)}^2 + s_{T(fl)}^2.$$

This means that the true variance will include both s_T^2 (the true variance which appears on both test occasions) and $s_{e(m)}^2$ (the error variance due to memory).

The reliability coefficient will then be obtained as follows:

$$r_{tt} = 1 - \frac{s^2_{e(\text{adm})} + s^2_{e(g)} + s^2_{e(\text{subj})} + s^2_{T(\text{fl})}}{s^2_t}. \tag{9-2}$$

The term $s^2_{e(\text{adm})}$ perhaps requires some comment. If factors in the administration of a test affect the individuals' performances on a given occasion without appearing systematically on the retest occasion, this effect will give an error variance, which will be treated as such when the reliability coefficient is computed. If, however, one or the other of these factors, say the interaction effect between the tester and the individual tested, systematically recurs (e.g., because the same tester administers the test on both occasions), the result can be an illusory true variance similar to that described previously for the effects of memory. In these circumstances, this error variance will not be included in the total error variance when the reliability coefficient is computed.

If the variance which results from fluctuation in true scores is treated as error variance, the result will be an underestimate of the test's reliability; on the other hand, if the variance which arises as a result of memory is treated as true variance, the opposite effect will be produced. The former increases as the time interval between the testings increases; the latter is reduced. Since both can be regarded as undesirable variance terms in reliability computations, the length of the interval should be chosen so that the combined effect will be as small as possible.

Some theorists believe that fluctuation in individuals' true scores between test occasions should be regarded as error variance when a test's reliability is assessed. It seems desirable, however, to distinguish between (a) a test's ability to measure the magnitude of a trait and (b) the stability of this trait for the objects or individuals measured. It is quite natural to consider a measuring tape completely reliable despite the fact that it gives different results for an individual's broad-jump performance on different occasions.

9–2 PARALLEL TESTS

In the classical form of this method two tests are constructed, in which one attempts, as far as possible, to satisfy the conditions for strict parallelism. The two tests are administered within a given time interval, and the reliability is computed as the correlation between the results of the two measurements. The reliability coefficient obtained is usually called an equivalence coefficient.

The total variance for one of the two tests can now be written

$$s^2_t = s^2_T + s^2_{e(m)} + s^2_{T(\text{equ})} + s^2_{e(\text{adm})} + s^2_{e(g)} + s^2_{e(\text{subj})} + s^2_{T(\text{fl})}. \tag{9-3}$$

The terms included in the error variance when reliability is computed with the method of parallel tests can be seen from the expression for the reliability:

$$r_{tt} = 1 - \frac{s^2_{T(equ)} + s^2_{e(adm)} + s^2_{e(g)} + s^2_{e(subj)} + s^2_{T(fl)}}{s^2_t}. \qquad (9\text{–}4)$$

What was said about the term $s^2_{e(adm)}$ in connection with the retest method also applies here. In the parallel-test method, there is also the same problem concerning the choice of a time interval that will minimize the effect of fluctuation in true scores.

Those who consider that fluctuation in true scores between test occasions is a relevant error variance when one is estimating a test's reliability regard the parallel-test coefficient to be the best expression for the test's reliability.

9–3 SPLIT-HALF METHODS

Parallel-test methods have certain disadvantages. One difficulty is the effect that the first test has on the scores of the second. Furthermore, two tests must be constructed, of which often only one will be put to practical use.

The two difficulties mentioned above can easily be solved in the following way. Two parallel tests are constructed. To test reliability, they are administered on the same occasion with an item chosen from each test alternately. The score for each individual on Test 1 is obtained by counting the number of odd-numbered items answered correctly, and the score on Test 2 is obtained by counting the number of even-numbered items answered correctly. The correlation between the two parallel tests can be computed and gives the reliability of each of the tests. We can now make use of both tests by combining them. Since the combined tests are parallel, the Spearman-Brown formula for reliability when test length is doubled can be used for estimating the reliability of the new test.

It is in principle this procedure and its underlying assumptions which are used in split-half methods. For reasons given below, it is also the best procedure to employ when one wishes to use split-half methodology in computing a test's reliability. However, the procedure is often not carried out exactly in the way described. One does not construct two parallel tests but obtains parallel measurements by dividing a test into halves, the two halves constituting the parallel tests. This is usually done in the following way. After scoring the test, the items are placed in the score matrix in order of frequency of correct solution. One parallel test is then made up of even-numbered items and the other of odd-numbered items. The object of this is, of course, to make the two tests equally difficult and equally differentiating, or (to use statistical terms) to give the test distributions equal means and variances. This will be the approximate result, even if we must take into account the systematic effect on the size of the means of the two distributions which results from always placing the more difficult item in each pair in the same test. We shall, however, examine in more detail why such measures are often insufficient to achieve parallelism between two tests obtained by dividing up a single, previously administered test.

Split-half methodology is one procedure for estimating a test's precision coefficient (see p. 103). In this procedure the two parallel test halves are intended to measure, as far as possible, the same true scores. To achieve this, the test halves should be equally difficult and have the same standard deviation. They should also be similar in content, so that the correlation between the true scores measured by them approaches 1.0 as closely as possible. This second condition presents no problem so long as the tests whose reliability we are to estimate are homogeneous. Every item in the test then measures the same sort of true score. If we give the test halves the same mean and the same dispersion of scores in the manner described, then for homogeneous tests we will obtain an equivalence coefficient as the best estimate of the test's precision coefficient.

The situation is different when we wish to estimate the precision coefficient for a heterogeneous test by means of an equivalence coefficient. Heterogeneity means that the subitems in part measure different true scores. If, when we divide the items into two test halves, we take into account their difficulty alone, we then run the risk of grouping items of the same type in one of the test halves while items of another type are grouped in the other; i.e., we have no control over the way in which different types of items are grouped in the two test halves. We have made the mean and the variance of the tests equal but not the content. A split-half coefficient obtained by dividing a test into two halves only on the basis of frequencies of correct response is not, therefore, a satisfactory expression for a test's reliability in the sense of precision. Nor is it an adequate expression for the test's internal consistency. Better methods, which will be dealt with later, are available for this purpose.

In conclusion, we can state the following: Split-half methodology can be used for estimating a test's precision. The precision is empirically estimated by an equivalence coefficient. This can be computed for homogeneous tests between odd and even test items placed in random order or in order of difficulty. For heterogeneous tests the equivalence coefficient should be computed with matched test halves, in which the items have been matched with regard not only to difficulty but also to content.

A. The common split-half method

The most common split-half method of estimating a test's precision by an equivalence coefficient is the following, which is applied to two test halves obtained by one of the methods described previously.

Table 9–1 Split-half computation of the reliability of the scores in Table 2–2

Subjects	Odd x	Even y	x^2	y^2	xy
1	1	0	1	0	0
2	3	3	9	9	9
3	2	0	4	0	0
4	4	3	16	9	12
5	2	2	4	4	4
6	1	1	1	1	1
7	3	2	9	4	6
8	2	1	4	1	2
9	4	2	16	4	8
10	2	2	4	4	4
11	3	4	9	16	12
12	3	2	9	4	6
13	3	3	9	9	9
14	2	2	4	4	4
15	2	1	4	1	2
16	3	1	9	1	3
17	1	2	1	4	2
18	4	4	16	16	16
19	2	3	4	9	6
20	3	2	9	4	6
Σ	50	40	142	104	112

$$r_{xy} = \frac{112 - (50 \times 40)/20}{\sqrt{(142 - 50^2/20)(104 - 40^2/20)}} = 0.594$$

$$r_{tt} = \frac{2 \times 0.594}{1 + 0.594} = \frac{1.188}{1.594} = 0.745$$

We compute the correlation coefficient between the scores on the two test halves obtained from the administered test. This correlation coefficient can be regarded as the reliability coefficient for one of the test halves. We then assume that the two test halves are parallel tests and estimate the reliability coefficient for the whole test by means of the Spearman-Brown formula (Eq. 5–23).

A score matrix in which the items are already placed in order of difficulty is shown in Table 2–2. If we merely wish to make the test halves approximately equal with respect to mean and variance, items 1, 3, 5, and 7 should be placed in one of the parallel tests and the remaining items in the other.

We can then obtain the score from each of the test halves for each of the individuals tested. These scores are shown in Table 9–1, where other computations of the reliability coefficient for the total test are also given.

B. The split-half method according to Rulon and Guttman

Rulon (1939) also starts with a division of the test into two halves, but his method does not necessarily assume equal variances on the subtests. What we require, of course, for estimating reliability is the size of the error variance. Rulon considers the variance of the distribution of differences of the test halves to be completely determined by the error variances of the subtests. Together they make up the error variance of the total test, so that with this approach the variance of the distribution of obtained differences can be used for estimating the total test's reliability by means of the equation

$$r_{tt} = 1 - s_d^2/s_t^2. \qquad (9\text{–}5)$$

Thus, for the matrix shown in Table 2–2, s_d^2 is equal to the variance of the differences which can be computed between x- and y-scores in Table 9–1. The complete computation of the reliability coefficient with Rulon's equation has been carried out in Table 9–2.

An equation which is sometimes simpler for computational purposes, and which gives results identical to those obtained from Rulon's equation, was derived by Guttman (1945). Reliability is estimated here by the equation

$$r_{tt} = 2[1 - (s_a^2 + s_b^2)/s_t^2], \qquad (9\text{–}6)$$

where a and b refer to the respective test halves.

By expanding the equation it can easily be shown that Eqs. (9–5) and (9–6) give the same result. Since $s_d^2 = s_a^2 + s_b^2 - 2r_{ab}s_a s_b$ and $s_t^2 = s_a^2 + s_b^2 + 2r_{ab}s_a s_b$, Eq. (9–5) can be written

$$r_{tt} = 4r_{ab}s_a s_b/s_t^2.$$

We arrive at the same result by expanding Eq. (9–6). Note that Eqs. (9–5) and (9–6) give the reliability coefficient for the whole test directly.

It can be shown that the reliability coefficient computed from Eq. (9–5) or (9–6) will be the same as the coefficient computed by the common split-half method when the variances of the test halves are equal ($s_a^2 = s_b^2$). When the variances of the test halves are not equal, the common split-half coefficient corrected by the Spearman-Brown formula will be systematically greater (cf. Gulliksen, 1950a, pp. 198–201). Compare the coefficients obtained in Table 9–1 and Table 9–2. Under normal conditions, however, the variation is small (see, e.g., Cronbach, 1951).

Table 9–2 Computation of reliability of scores in Table 2–2 using Rulon's method

Subjects	Odd x	Even y	d_j	d_j^2	t_j	t_j^2
1	1	0	1	1	1	1
2	3	3	0	0	6	36
3	2	0	2	4	2	4
4	4	3	1	1	7	49
5	2	2	0	0	4	16
6	1	1	0	0	2	4
7	3	2	1	1	5	25
8	2	1	1	1	3	9
9	4	2	2	4	6	36
10	2	2	0	0	4	16
11	3	4	−1	1	7	49
12	3	2	1	1	5	25
13	3	3	0	0	6	36
14	2	2	0	0	4	16
15	2	1	1	1	3	9
16	3	1	2	4	4	16
17	1	2	−1	1	3	9
18	4	4	0	0	8	64
19	2	3	−1	1	5	25
20	3	2	1	1	5	25
Σ	50	40	10	22	90	470

$$s_d^2 = \frac{22}{20} - \left(\frac{10}{20}\right)^2 = 1.10 - 0.25 = 0.85$$

$$s_t^2 = \frac{470}{20} - \left(\frac{90}{20}\right)^2 = 23.50 - 20.25 = 3.25$$

$$r_{tt} = 1 - \frac{0.85}{3.25} = 1 - 0.262 = 0.738$$

C. Total variance and error variance for split-half reliability

Let us examine the composition of the total variance of each of the test halves and the variance which will be regarded as error variance when estimating reliability by means of split-halves.

$$s_{t_1}^2 = s_T^2 + s_{T(\mathrm{equ})}^2 + s_{e(\mathrm{adm})}^2 + s_{e(\mathrm{g})}^2 + s_{e(\mathrm{subj})}^2, \qquad (9\text{–}7)$$

where t_1 is one of the test halves, and s_T^2 denotes here as before (see the parallel-test method) the true variance in Test 1 which is also measured by Test 2, while $s^2_{T(\text{equ})}$ is the true variance which is measured by one of the tests and not by the other.

The error variance will be made up of the last four variance terms:

$$r_{t_1 t_2} = 1 - \frac{s^2_{T(\text{equ})} + s^2_{e(\text{adm})} + s^2_{e(\text{g})} + s^2_{e(\text{subj})}}{s^2_{t_1}}. \qquad (9\text{–}8)$$

The size of the error variance with the split-half method is thus determined partly by the actual measurement errors—which are the only variance we wish to include as error variance—and partly by a less than 100% agreement between the test halves with respect to the measurement of true scores.

With split-half coefficients we will therefore underestimate the precision coefficient for the test, even if we attempt to make the test halves as similar as possible. We shall, however, under these conditions overestimate the average correlation between the possible combinations of parallel test halves, i.e., between random parallel test halves.

The agreement between test halves with respect to the measurement of true scores will be greatest if the total test is homogeneous, i.e., if the items in the test measure the same function. The more heterogeneous a test is, the greater is the chance that the halves obtained by splitting up the test will in part contain different types of items and thus measure somewhat different true scores. This leads to an increase in that part of the total true variance in each of the subtests which is not measured by the other [$s^2_{T(\text{equ})}$]. As was stated previously, the items in the test halves must therefore be matched with each other, even with respect to content, when an equivalence coefficient is to be computed for heterogeneous tests with split-half methods.

D. Split-half methods for estimating the reliability of tests with a time limit

A time limit is introduced as a factor which will affect an individual's score in most group tests and in some individual tests. Time limitation means that every individual does not have time to attempt to solve every item. As a result, a person who works slowly will have a smaller number of correct solutions than he would have obtained if he had had unlimited time at his disposal.

Tests in which time limits affect the individual's score are called *speed tests*, as opposed to *power tests* in which no time limit is introduced. The time limit can, of course, be varied so that its importance for the final result varies. A pure speed test consists of items which are so easy that every single item can be solved by everyone who is tested. The result on the test is thus determined not by the individual's ability to solve the items but by the speed with which he solves items of the type included in the test. Every individual will then solve every item up to a certain number, which will be a measure of his speed. In a pure power test every individual has time to attempt every item. Zeros will then appear among the ones for an individual in the score matrix. The variation in the distribution of obtained scores on a power test will be affected by differences in the individual's ability to solve items in the test, and will be independent of the speed of solution.

From the above description of the properties of speed and power tests, it should be obvious that split-half methods are not immediately applicable to estimating the reliability of measurements carried out with speed tests. In a pure speed test a speed measure is obtained from the number of completed items. Every item is solved correctly up to that stage. It is meaningless to split up this number of items into two parts, which must of course be equal, in order to investigate the reliability of the speed measure which the total number of items represents. The two measures obtained in this way would not be independent measures of the individual's speed in solving such items. A practical example will illustrate this situation. If we wanted to measure the running speed of a group of athletes with the type of speed test used in psychology, we would, instead of timing a given distance as is normally done, measure how far every individual can run in a certain time, e.g., 60 seconds. In order to determine the accuracy with which we have established the individuals' positions on the continuum measured (i.e., the reliability of the measurements we have carried out) we would not divide the distance every individual had run into two equal parts and then compute the correlation between these parts for every individual. The coefficient would obviously be 1.0 for this form of split-half correlation. We should instead let the athletes try a rerun with the same time limit. The correlation between the results of the two independent runs would give us the reliability coefficient of measurement of the individuals' speeds expressed by the number of yards per unit of time. Similarly, the reliability of a pure speed test must be computed by the correlation between two speed estimates obtained independently. This can be done either by the test-retest method or with parallel tests. In the latter case the two parallel tests can afterward be combined into one, for which the reliability can be estimated by the Spearman-Brown formula.

Split-half methods are thus not applicable when we are computing the reliability of pure speed tests. But even for tests which are not pure speed tests, but where there is a time limit and speed, consequently, is of some importance for the result—and these tests are certainly in the majority—the time limit has the effect that in reliability computations with split-half methods the test's reliability tends to be overestimated. In such cases reliability should, if possible, be computed by retest or with parallel tests. In many situations this can give rise to difficulties of another type (see the discussion of these methods earlier in this chapter). Gulliksen (1950b) derived three equations which can be used for correcting the effect of time limitation on the split-half coefficient in cases where the effect of the time limit can be considered small. A minimum value for reliability is obtained with the following equation, if every unattempted item at the end of the test is taken to be an incorrect solution:

$$r_{tt(\text{min})} = r_{tt} - s_o^2/s_e^2, \qquad (9\text{–}9)$$

where r_{tt} is the split-half coefficient, o represents unattempted items at the end of the test, and e represents incorrect solutions, test items which have been passed over, and unattempted items at the end of the test.

The correction term consists of the proportion of the total error variance in the test which is made up of the variance of the distribution of unattempted items. In a pure speed test we have no incorrect solutions or items which have been passed over. After correcting for the effect of the speed factor, we have $r_{tt} = 1.0$, the ratio $s_o^2/s_e^2 = 1.0$, and zero as the lower limit for reliability.

9–4   THE KUDER-RICHARDSON METHOD

Split-half methods are based upon two test parts which are treated as parallel tests. One can, of course, split up a test into more than two parts. By regarding a test as composed of as many parallel tests as the test has items, so that every item is treated as parallel to each of the other items, it is possible to derive some of the most common equations used for computing reliability coefficients. They were derived originally by Kuder and Richardson (1937), with the assumption that every item has the same mean and the same variance.

The equation for the variance of a test composed of n items was derived previously (Eq. 4–5):

$$s_t^2 = \sum s_i^2 + 2\sum r_{ik}s_is_k \qquad (i \neq k).$$

There are $n(n-1)$ covariance terms included in the second term on the right-hand side (see p. 57). We now begin the derivation by considering each item to be parallel to each of the other items. This means that every item is assumed to have the same frequency of correct response and the same intercorrelation with other items. We can then replace s_is_k by s_i^2, and the sum of the covariance terms can be written $n(n-1)\bar{r}_{ik}\bar{s}_i^2$. We thus obtain

$$s_t^2 = \sum s_i^2 + n(n-1)\bar{r}_{ik}\bar{s}_i^2. \qquad (9\text{–}10)$$

If we now solve this equation for $\bar{r}_{ik}$, with $n\bar{s}_i^2 = \sum s_i^2$, we obtain

$$\bar{r}_{ik} = \frac{s_t^2 - \sum s_i^2}{(n-1)\sum s_i^2}, \qquad (9\text{–}11)$$

which is an expression for the average correlation among the individual items in a test.

Since $\bar{r}_{ik}$ gives the correlation between an item and its parallel item, Eq. (9–11) also gives the reliability of a single item. With the general Spearman-Brown formula (Eq. 5–23) we can estimate the reliability of a test consisting of n items, where the reliability of one item is expressed by the right-hand side of Eq. (9–11):

$$
\begin{aligned}
r_{tt} &= \frac{n\bar{r}_{ik}}{1 + (n-1)\bar{r}_{ik}} \\
&= n\,\frac{s_t^2 - \sum s_i^2}{(n-1)\sum s_i^2}\;\frac{1}{1 + (n-1)[(s_t^2 - \sum s_i^2)/(n-1)\sum s_i^2]} \\
&= \frac{n}{n-1}\,\frac{s_t^2 - \sum s_i^2}{\sum s_i^2}\;\frac{1}{1 + (s_t^2/\sum s_i^2) - 1} = \frac{n}{n-1}\,\frac{s_t^2 - \sum s_i^2}{\sum s_i^2}\,\frac{\sum s_i^2}{s_t^2} \\
&= \frac{n}{n-1}\,\frac{s_t^2 - \sum s_i^2}{s_t^2}\,.
\end{aligned}
$$

The Kuder-Richardson formula for the reliability of a test with n items will thus be

$$
r_{tt} = \frac{n}{n-1}\,\frac{s_t^2 - \sum s_i^2}{s_t^2}\,, \tag{9–12}
$$

or

$$
r_{tt} = \frac{n}{n-1}\,\frac{s_t^2 - \sum pq}{s_t^2}\,. \tag{9–13}
$$

This is the Kuder-Richardson "Formula 20" for estimating reliability. In the following text it will be written KR_{20}.

Equation (9–13) is used for estimating the reliability of tests in which the items are scored as 1 or 0. Equation (9–12) is a special case of Cronbach's coefficient α, which can be used for estimating the reliability in tests or ratings where the items give weighted scores (cf. Cronbach, 1951).

In accordance with the assumption of equal frequencies of solution, p and q will be the same for every item and $\sum pq$ can be replaced by $n\bar{p}\bar{q}$. Equation (9–13) can then be simplified to

$$
r_{tt} = \frac{n}{n-1}\,\frac{s_t^2 - n\bar{p}\bar{q}}{s_t^2}\,. \tag{9–14}
$$

This is the Kuder-Richardson "Formula 21." In the following text it will be designated by KR_{21}. It can also be written in a form which is usually simpler for computational purposes:

$$
r_{tt} = \frac{n}{n-1}\left(1 - \frac{M_t - M_t^2/n}{s_t^2}\right). \tag{9–15}
$$

Here the derivation of the formulas is based on the original assumptions made by Kuder and Richardson. These assumptions permit a simple and easily understandable derivation. More recently, however, it has been shown in various situations that the derivations can be carried out with less restrictive assumptions (see, e.g., Jackson and Ferguson, 1941, and Gulliksen, 1950a). Jackson and Ferguson showed that KR_{20} could be derived by assuming only that the means of the covariances for items in each of two parallel tests are the same, and equal to the mean of the covariances for the items in the two tests ($\overline{C}_{ik} = \overline{C}_{i'k'} = \overline{C}_{ik'}$).

The formula KR_{20} is directly connected with the equations derived by Rulon and Guttman (see p. 111–112) for estimating reliability with split-half methods. For a test consisting of items whose solutions are independent of one another, there are many ways of splitting it into two parts. The number of possible divisions depends directly upon the number of items in the test. The reliability coefficient obtained with the split-half technique for a given set of data depends on which of the possible divisions we have made. It can now be shown that KR_{20} (Eq. 9–13) gives the mean of the split-half coefficients which can be computed by Rulon's or Guttman's equation for every possible division of the test into two parts (cf. Cronbach, 1951). Thus, KR_{20} is an internal consistency coefficient which gives the best measure of reliability expressed as the correlation between random parallel tests. The correlations we obtain for this sort of test with the split-half methods previously presented are estimates of the value obtained with KR_{20}.

The usual equation for the variance of a composite test (Eq. 4–5) can be expanded in the following way:

$$s_t^2 - \sum s_i^2 = n(n-1)\overline{C}_{ik}. \tag{9–16}$$

The terms on the left-hand side in Eq. (9–16) are included in the denominator in KR_{20} (see Eq. 9–12). They can now be replaced by the terms on the right-hand side, and Eq. (9–12) can be written

$$r_{tt} = \frac{n}{n-1}\left[\frac{n(n-1)\overline{C}_{ik}}{s_t^2}\right] = \frac{n^2\overline{C}_{ik}}{s_t^2}. \tag{9–17}$$

Equation (9–17) is in agreement with the variance-analysis method of computing reliability derived by Hoyt (cf. Hoyt, 1941, and Edwards, 1959). We can now examine Eq. (9–17) bearing in mind the definition of reliability as the proportion of the total test variance which is made up of true variance (Eq. 5–7). We then find, when computing reliability with KR_{20}, that the true variance is determined by the size of the covariance terms for a given number of items. The size of the covariance terms is in turn determined by the intercorrelations and standard deviations of the items. The internal consistency coefficient we obtain from KR_{20} will therefore be directly dependent on the correlations between the items in the test, i.e., on the extent to which the items measure the same variable. The more homogeneous the items are, the greater the numerical value of KR_{20} will be for a given number of items in the test. This is also true for KR_{21}.

It was mentioned previously that KR_{20} gives the mean of the distribution of coefficients we should obtain if we were to compute every possible split-half coefficient for the test. Thus, when computing the split-half reliability, we will find that random composition of the parts in the test halves gives coefficients higher than KR_{20} equally often as lower ones. As soon as we take steps to make the two test halves as equivalent as possible (e.g., by placing items in order of difficulty and then placing odd-numbered items in one test half and even-numbered items in the other) we will systematically obtain higher reliability coefficients with split-half methods than with KR_{20}. If we insert values from the score matrix in Table 2–2 in Eq. (9–12) we obtain

$$\frac{8}{7} \times \frac{3.25 - 1.425}{3.25} = 0.642.$$

This value should be compared with that obtained from Rulon's equation, namely, 0.738 (Table 9–2).

For computational purposes, KR_{21} (Eq. 9–14) is a simpler equation for estimating reliability with the assumption that every item has the same variance. Lord has shown that KR_{21} can be derived from the equation he has presented for the standard error of measurement (Eq. 6–7; cf. Lord, 1955). He considers the reliability coefficient obtained from KR_{21} to be a coefficient for the correlation between random parallel tests, and uses the mean of the squared individual standard errors for the test as an empirical expression of the error variance in the reliability equation $r_{tt} = 1 - s_e^2/s_t^2$.

The derivation of KR_{21} from Lord's standard error equation illustrates a point frequently remarked upon, namely, that KR_{21} gives systematically lower estimates of reliability than KR_{20}. As has been pointed out previously, Lord's standard error equation gives, on the average, a higher standard error for the test than the normal standard error equation (see p. 86). Since we use Lord's standard error when deriving KR_{21}, this equation will also give a systematically lower estimate of the test's reliability.

9–5 NEW TRENDS

The starting point of the classical reliability theory on which this presentation has so far been based is the assumption that every individual has a true score for every instrument on which he is tested. Another definition of true score has been given in Chapter 6, namely, that the individual's true score holds for the population from which the items for a given test are drawn. An expression for the accuracy with which the instrument measures true scores is required in order to assess the value of obtained data. We have established that different methods give different measures of reliability which vary in content. Different types of reliability express different things. It is not sufficient to say that an instrument has a reliability of a certain size; we must specify the reliability to which we are referring. There are several different aspects of the concept of reliability.

An attempt at a further definition of reliability which gives a general coverage of several aspects of the concept in a more precise way than that presented previously is given by Cronbach, Rajaratnam, and Gleser (1963). They attempt to derive various expressions for the possibilities of generalizing from an array of observations to other arrays which represent the same population. They distinguish between a generalizability study (*G*-study), which gives data for estimating the dependability of the instrument when generalizing, and a decision study (*D*-study), which gives a measure of the dependability of decisions which can be made about individuals or groups. In analysis of variance terms, the possibility of generalization can then be specified for the varying conditions under which the observations are made. This new interpretation of general reliability theory which Cronbach, Rajaratnam, and Gleser have presented is without doubt an important advance. It gives both a more meaningful and precise definition of the concept of reliability and more concise and applicable measures of reliability.

9–6 SUMMARY

From the above presentation of the most common methods of estimating a test's reliability, it should be apparent that one must take into account whether the items of the test are homogeneous or heterogeneous, and whether

Table 9–3 Methods for estimating the reliability of homogeneous tests and heterogeneous tests

Aspect of reliability	Homogeneous tests (parallel tests = random parallel tests)	Heterogeneous tests (parallel tests ≠ random parallel tests)
Precision	Split-half Guttman Rulon $KR_{20}(\alpha)$ KR_{21}	Matched split-half Parallel tests
Internal consistency	The same as for equivalence	$KR_{20}(\alpha)$
Precision and stability of true scores	Test-retest	Test-retest

the reliability computed is an estimate of the test's precision in the form of an equivalence coefficient or an estimate of the test's internal consistency. Table 9–3 shows what methods are recommended for various situations.

PROBLEMS

1. Eight raters independently gave the following ratings of 15 school pupils with respect to general adjustment.

Rater

Pupil	A	B	C	D	E	F	G	H
1	2	1	3	2	3	3	1	3
2	6	6	4	4	4	6	4	5
3	5	4	4	3	5	6	4	5
4	3	4	4	3	4	4	5	2
5	5	5	5	5	4	4	5	5
6	3	5	4	5	2	5	6	5
7	2	2	5	4	3	5	5	4
8	1	3	2	1	1	3	1	4
9	4	5	6	6	5	5	6	5
10	4	2	5	4	4	4	3	2
11	3	3	5	5	4	3	4	4
12	4	3	3	4	2	4	5	3
13	4	4	5	3	4	4	4	4
14	3	5	4	5	6	4	6	7
15	5	2	7	6	5	4	5	6

(a) Compute the reliability of the means of ratings with the common split-half method. (b) Compute the reliability of the means of ratings using the Kuder-Richardson method. (c) Compute the reliability of the ratings of a single rater, assuming that the raters can be regarded as "parallel raters."

2. Compute the reliability with the common split-half method after first ranking the items in order of difficulty. Compare the result with that in Problem 6.

3. Compute the reliability of the score matrix using (a) Rulon's method and (b) Guttman's method, first with the approach used in Problem 1 and second with that used in Problem 2. Compare the results obtained with Rulon's and Guttman's methods respectively, and the results of the two different approaches.

4. Compute the reliability of the score matrix using KR_{20} and KR_{21}. Compare these results with each other and with the values obtained by other methods.

5. The complete variance-covariance matrix was computed in Problem 2 (Chapter 4) for the items included in the score matrix in Problem 10 (Chapter 3). Use the covariance values in this matrix to check Eq. (9–17).

6.

Subject	1	2	3	4	5	6	7	8
A	1			1		1	1	
B		1	1			1	1	1
C	1					1	1	
D						1	1	
E					1	1	1	
F	1			1		1	1	1
G	1		1	1		1	1	1
H	1			1	1	1	1	1
J						1		
K	1		1	1	1	1	1	1

Compute the reliability with the common split-half method by assigning to each subtest every other item in the order in which the items appear in the matrix.

REFERENCES

CRONBACH, L. J. (1951). Coefficient alpha and the internal structure of tests. *Psychometrika*, **16**, 297–334.

CRONBACH, L. J., N. RAJARATNAM, and G. C. GLESER (1963). Theory of generalizability: a liberalization of reliability theory. *Brit. J. Stat. Psychol.*, **15**, 137–163.

EDWARDS, A. L. (1959). A note on Tryon's measure of reliability. *Psychometrika*, **24**, 257–260.

GULLIKSEN, H. (1950a). *Theory of mental tests.* New York: Wiley.

——— (1950b). The reliability of speed tests. *Psychometrika*, **15**, 259–269.

GUTTMAN, L. (1945). A basis for analyzing test-retest reliability. *Psychometrika*, **10**, 255–282.

HOYT, C. (1941). Test reliability obtained by analysis of variance. *Psychometrika*, **6**, 153–160.

JACKSON, R. W. B., and G. A. FERGUSON (1941). *Studies on the reliability of tests.* Bull. 12, Dept. of Ed. Res., University of Toronto.

KUDER, G. F., and M. W. RICHARDSON (1937). The theory of the estimation of test reliability. *Psychometrika*, **2**, 151–160.

LORD, F. M. (1955). Sampling fluctuations resulting from sampling of test items. *Psychometrika*, **20**, 1–22.

RULON, P. J. (1939). A simplified procedure for determining the reliability of a test by split-halves. *Harvard Educ. Rev.*, **9**, 99–103.

Suggested reading

CRONBACH, L. J., and W. G. WARRINGTON (1951). Time-limit tests: estimating their reliability and degree of speeding. *Psychometrika*, **16**, 167–188.

CRONBACH, L. J., P. SCHÖNEMAN, and D. McKIE (1965). Alpha coefficients for stratified parallel tests. *Educ. Psychol. Measmt.*, **25**, 291–312.

EBEL, R. L. (1951).   Estimation of the reliability of ratings. *Psychometrika*, **16,** 407–424.

GHISELLI, E. E. (1964). *Theory of psychological measurement.* New York: McGraw-Hill.

LAFORGE, R. (1965). Components of reliability. *Psychometrika*, **30,** 187–195.

LYERLY, S. B. (1958). The Kuder-Richardson formula 21 as a split-half coefficient, and some remarks on its basic assumption. *Psychometrika*, **23,** 267–270.

RAJARATNAM, N., L. J. CRONBACH, and G. C. GLESER (1965). Generalizability of stratified parallel tests. *Psychometrika*, **30,** 39–56.

TRYON, R. C. (1957). Reliability and behavior domain validity: reformulation and historical critique. *Psychol. Bull.*, **54,** 229–249.

WEBSTER, H. (1960). A generalization of Kuder-Richardson's reliability formula 21. *Educ. Psychol. Measmt.*, **20,** 131–138.

CHAPTER 10

Validity

10-1 INTRODUCTION

Chapters 5 through 9 dealt with one aspect of dependability in testing procedures—that of reliability. The second aspect of dependability—validity —will now be discussed. In general, the validity of a method is the accuracy with which meaningful and relevant measurements can be made with it, in the sense that it actually measures the traits it was intended to measure. If some trait is significant for success in a college course or the development of some mental illness, we construct a test for measuring this trait, and use it for counseling and selection or for diagnosis. Obviously we want the test to measure the trait which we have established as significant in the situation where the test is to be used, and not some other trait. So long as we were dealing with reliability, we were not interested in what the test measured, only in finding whether it gave the same results on repeated measurement. When testing validity, we investigate whether the test whose reliability is known measures what it has been constructed to measure.

The instrument's validity is seldom a problem when we are dealing with physical measurements such as length, weight, etc. It is obviously weight that is measured with a balance (provided the balance is functioning correctly). However, with methods used for measuring psychological variables, it is necessary to test empirically whether the instrument is valid in every case. When we construct a questionnaire to obtain a measure of psychosomatic disorders, we must show that the test scores really distinguish between degrees of psychosomatic disorders and not other differences. Sometimes it might appear obvious that a test measures some trait, while empirical testing shows that in fact it measures something entirely different. Many examples of this sort can be given.

The application of a psychological instrument must not be based on subjective confidence that the instrument works in practical situations. Empirical studies show that in clinical practice impressions of that type are very unreliable bases for judging the dependability of a given method (see, e.g., Magnusson, 1959, pp. 110–118). The requirement must be maintained that every method's validity has to be tested empirically in the different situations where it is to be used.

When we construct a test, we are primarily interested in whether it has high validity. Reliability is mainly of interest as a necessary condition for valid measurements.   It should be borne in mind that high reliability is a necessary but not sufficient requirement for high validity.   However, it happens occasionally that high reliability, for instance in the form of agreement among different judges giving subjective ratings in personality diagnosis situations, is taken to be a sign of the ratings' validity. Such an agreement is not a sufficient basis for concluding high validity. It can arise because the judges have the same bias in common, and the ratings perhaps express something entirely different from what was intended by the instructions.

When we estimate a test's validity we must know which trait we wish the test to measure. This trait is called the *criterion variable.* We are interested in knowing how well the individuals' positions on the *obtained distribution* of scores correspond to the individuals' positions on the *continuum which represents the criterion variable.* Validity is traditionally estimated by a correlation coefficient, called the *coefficient of validity*, which expresses the relationship between data obtained with the test and data which we use, with a known degree of certainty, as indices for the individuals' scores for the criterion variable. Thus, if we have constructed a test for predicting success as a salesman, we need an index of success in this field as a criterion with which a prediction can be compared. We can test a number of applicants and then take the sales figures for each individual after a certain period of employment as the criterion of success as a salesman. The correlation coefficient for the relationship between test results and sales figures is the coefficient of validity for the test with respect to its ability to predict success as a salesman of a given type.

If we now use the same test for predicting success in some other job, we will need a different criterion. Many tests are used in this way for more than one purpose. A test does not have a fixed coefficient of validity which holds for every purpose and for every group of individuals for which it might possibly be used. The test's validity varies according to the purpose for which it is used and the group within which it has to discriminate. A school readiness test has a certain validity when used to predict beginners' grades after the first school year, and a different validity when used for rating the beginner's social maturity. A validity coefficient expressing a test's ability to predict success as a supervisor cannot be used as an expression for its ability to predict success as an office worker. For every validation procedure the essential question is: For whom and for what is the test to be valid? We need, therefore, different criteria for different test purposes. As a criterion of the accuracy of a test measurement, we wish of course to have as exact an expression as possible for the individuals' positions on the true criterion distribution. This leads to a number of difficulties which will be discussed in the next section.

So far we have dealt with validity only as the correlation between measurements obtained from the test whose validity is to be estimated and another known measure for the criterion variable; in this case, validity is expressed as a coefficient of validity. Methods of testing validity in other ways will be dealt with later in this chapter.

10-2   CRITERION

Those criterion measurements which we use for testing the validity of a new instrument seldom give an exact measure of the individuals' positions on the continuum for the "true criterion." Some of the difficulties involved in obtaining good criterion measurements can be illustrated by an example.

Let us assume that we have constructed a test battery for the selection of nursing trainees. The purpose of the tests is clear. We wish to select those applicants who will become the best nurses. The criterion we attempt to predict is then the individuals' positions on a continuum representing "nursing success." Complications arise immediately. The nursing profession is not a single occupation, but a whole range of occupations, and different branches of nursing place different demands on individual capabilities. What constitutes a "good" nurse in one field does not necessarily hold in another. We thus have no concise definition of "nursing success" available when we choose criterion measures for success in this profession.

The criterion problem, however, is still complicated, even if we restrict ourselves to one limited branch of nursing. If we use ratings or grades based on observation of the nurses in training, these ratings will have been obtained from different judges. Judges who rate the same individuals can have seen the ratees in different situations, and different individuals can have been rated by different judges. Since judges do not always interpret the instructions in the same way or always rate the same behavior in the same way, the grades and ratings will not all be a measure of exactly the same kind of success.

It is difficult enough to obtain unambiguous criterion measurements which exactly represent the criterion variable we wish to measure, but we will also encounter purely administrative difficulties. After completing their training, the nurses will be assigned to various hospitals and will there be engaged in various branches of nursing. In order to determine the validity of the test instruments, we need criterion measurements for a relatively large number of trainees who all have the same type of work after the completion of their training. However, if this follow-up takes place one or more years after the completion of training, we find the former trainees working in different hospitals with different requirements for success in the profession, as well as in

different branches of nursing, which also have different requirements for
success. We can accept these differences and regard the ratings and grades we
obtain from different hospitals and different branches of nursing as expressions for the success which we wish to predict. Or we can wait until a sufficient
number of trainees have been tested and have done nursing work, so that
there is a relatively large number of individuals in each of a number of subgroups within which duties and aptitude required are so homogeneous that
we can compute the validity of the test's ability to predict success within each
of these groups. The first alternative is unsatisfactory and the results obtained
would certainly be discouraging and difficult to interpret. The second alternative is often impossible because of administrative difficulties.

In this situation, therefore, we choose a criterion which is both adminis-
tratively easier to obtain, and which gives a comparison between individuals
with respect to the same variable. The most common criterion is then a
measure of success in training (e.g., grades after completed training). It
should, nevertheless, be realized that this is in fact a rather poor measure of
the actual criterion variable. In the first place, we must expect the grades
to be unreliable, but even if we could expect them to be completely reliable,
their validity as an expression for the criterion variable would not be very
high. Grades have probably considerable shortcomings even as expressions
for success in training, and even though we can expect a relatively good
correlation between success in training and success in practice, grades will
be even more inadequate as an expression for success in practice than as an
expression for success in training.

When we estimate validity, we seldom have access to criteria which are
reliable and valid expressions for the criterion variable. We must therefore
distinguish between genuine, "true" criteria and the available intermediate
criteria. The true criterion in the example given would be a measure of
success in nursing, if it were possible to agree what is meant by this and to
measure it. The available criterion can be selected from a number of alternatives. It is an important fact that the size of the validity coefficient to a
certain extent depends upon the alternative which is chosen. But no matter
which alternative we use, we must expect deficiencies of reliability and validity
in the criterion data which we use for estimating the test's validity. When we
judge the value of some validity coefficient we must therefore take into
account both how closely the criterion used is related to the true criterion
and the reliability of the obtained criterion measure.

Even for a given purpose we cannot always expect a validity coefficient
giving an accurate expression for the test's validity. Every validity coefficient
must be judged in the light of the criterion which has been used.

The data we are dealing with are not always only predictor data or criterion
data. Data which in one situation are used as criterion data can in some other
situation be used as predictor data, and must then, of course, be tested for

validity in the usual way. The grades obtained upon completion of training, which we can use as an intermediate criterion for the accuracy of the selection of nursing trainees, can also (though they still have the inadequacies of an intermediate criterion) be used as a basis for a prediction of success in various special branches of nursing. We must then in the usual way test the validity of the prediction we make for each of these branches on the basis of the grades.

We have pointed out that criterion data also suffer from deficiencies of reliability and validity. Even if objective, standardized methods are used for obtaining criterion data, these will contain errors caused by unreliability. With reference to standardized methods, unreliability can, however, be kept within reasonable bounds and its size fairly accurately estimated. When the extent of the unreliability can be estimated it is possible to introduce a correction term and estimate the size of the validity coefficient for a completely reliable criterion measurement. We will deal more fully with this problem of unreliability in Chapter 11. Unreliability is a serious problem, particularly in the many situations where the only criterion data available are subjective judgments.

We are thus able to correct for unreliability in criterion data. Low validity in the criterion data, however, can never be corrected for. The only way to make the criterion data more valid is to refine the analysis of the variable we wish to measure and, as far as possible, relate the criterion measurement to what we consider to be the genuine criterion.

10-3 DIFFERENT TYPES OF VALIDITY

We distinguish here among four concepts of validity, each of which is related to a certain method of testing validity, in accordance with the recommendations on nomenclature presented in "Technical Recommendations for Psychological Tests and Diagnostic Techniques" (1954).

A. Predictive validity

When computing predictive validity, one wishes to use the test for predicting the individuals' positions on a distribution which becomes available only at a later date. The test predicts a certain outcome after a given time. The criterion data consist of some measure of the outcome (e.g., grades after completed studies or ratings after a certain period of employment). Predictive validity, computed as a validity coefficient, needs to be estimated for tests used in vocational guidance and in the selection and classification of individuals for training or work purposes.

B. Concurrent validity

In this case, measurement of the criterion variable is available at the same time as the test results are obtained. A clinical diagnosis of brain damage, on which a number of neurologists agree, can for instance be used as a criterion for the validity of a brain damage test. The reason for constructing tests to measure a variable for which one already has data is, in most cases, that the test saves time and expense, but gives the same result as the criterion measurement. Like predictive validity, concurrent validity is expressed as a validity coefficient.

Concurrent validity is used for tests in diagnostic situations. When assessing coefficients for concurrent validity, one should remember that the criteria which are used (e.g., in clinical situations) vary greatly in quality.

It is apparent that there are no differences in principle between the methods of computing predictive and concurrent validities. Most frequently, both are determined by computing the correlation between test scores and measures of a criterion variable, and the validity is expressed in both cases as a correlation coefficient. The coefficient of validity gives the test's validity with respect to the variable which is defined by the criterion measurement. For concurrent validity, the question is whether the test measures what it is intended to measure, and the validity coefficient indicates how adequate the test data are as a basis for diagnosis, in the widest sense of the word. For predictive validity, the question is the accuracy with which the test predicts what it is intended to predict—a question which is especially important for vocational guidance, selection, and classification. It should be noted here that good predictive ability presupposes good diagnostic ability. If something cannot be measured accurately, it cannot be used as a basis for valid prediction.

Validity has previously been defined as the accuracy with which an instrument measures what it is intended to measure, and we have said that validity is computed as a validity coefficient for the relationship between test data and criterion data. It should, however, be borne in mind that a high coefficient for the relationship between test and criterion does not necessarily mean that the test measures what we believe it to measure. Let us suppose that we have constructed a test in logical aptitude for predicting success in engineering studies, assuming that high logical aptitude is a necessary requirement for success in such studies. If we now obtain a high correlation coefficient for the relationship between test scores and grades in engineering studies, we cannot be certain that the test measures logical ability. It may perhaps in fact measure verbal ability, since comprehending each individual item places great demands on this ability. But, since verbal ability also is related to success in engineering studies, we still obtain a relatively good correlation. Many examples are available of cases where it was believed that a test measured a certain trait, and where this supposition was later shown to be false. (One example of this is a number of tests which were supposed to measure pure spatial aptitude. More careful control has shown that certain individuals solved the items using purely logical methods instead.)

When we are computing validity coefficients, it is necessary that test data and criterion data be determined independently. The following is an example of a common type of situation. A psychologist has a hypothesis concerning how two groups of individuals who differ in certain respects, also differ with respect to some other variable which is the object of his interest. Knowing the group membership, he rates the members of the two groups on the second variable and computes the correlation between ratings and the group membership, which constitutes the criterion. The psychologist has fallen prey to what is known as *criterion contamination*. He knew the criterion data (i.e., group membership) when he made the ratings which were to be tested for validity with group membership as criterion. Such a procedure is not permitted. No matter how the rater in this situation attempts to ignore his previous knowledge, he cannot avoid being influenced in some direction by his expectations.

In this example the psychologist had access to criterion data when he carried out the ratings which were to be validated. Obviously, we can expect the same result in the opposite situation, i.e., when the person who is to make the ratings to be used as criterion data has access to the test data which are to be validated. The validity coefficient will be different from that which would have been obtained if the estimates had taken place without the influence of this knowledge.

C. Content validity

This type of validity is applicable when we are estimating the extent to which a school test, for example, covers some field of study. The test items can be regarded as a sample from a population representing the content and the aims of the course. Content validity is then determined by the extent to which the sample of items in the test is representative of the total population. Before content validity can be estimated it is necessary to define explicitly the aims of the instruction given in the field to which the test refers, the material which the pupils should have grasped, the relative importance of different parts of the course, etc. Unlike predictive or concurrent validity, content validity cannot be expressed as a validity coefficient.

D. Construct validity

A new concept, construct validity, was launched in 1954 by a technical committee appointed by the American Psychological Association. The purpose of this committee was to define terminology and formulate rules for test standardization (cf. "Technical Recommendations," 1954, pp. 13–18). Construct validity, unlike predictive and concurrent validity, is not expressed as a single coefficient representing the correlation between test and criterion measurements.

The concept of construct validity is especially useful with reference to tests measuring traits for which external criteria are not available. The following example can illustrate such a situation. In personality psychology one often distinguishes between manifest aggressiveness (the aggressiveness shown by an individual's observable behavior) and latent aggressiveness (the more or less subconscious aggressive tendencies which an individual can have without ever showing them in observable behavior). After a period of observation of an individual in different situations, we can obtain ratings of manifest aggressiveness. It is difficult to obtain such ratings of an individual's latent aggressiveness, especially since one cannot expect the agreement between the individual's positions for the two variables (manifest and latent aggressiveness respectively) to be at all perfect. How can we now test the validity of estimates of an individual's latent aggressiveness—for example, with the aid of a projective test?

We begin from a logically defined variable, in this case latent aggressiveness. This variable is included as a logical construct in a system of concepts, in which all of the concepts logically belong, and where the relationships are explained by a theory. From this theory certain practical consequences can be derived about the outcome of the test under certain conditions. These consequences can be tested. If the result is what was expected in a series of such tests, the test is said to have construct validity for the variable tested.

Let us assume that we want to examine the construct validity of the projective test with respect to its ability to determine correctly the positions of a group of individuals for the variable "latent aggressiveness" as defined in psychoanalytic theory. Furthermore, let us assume that we can derive two hypotheses from this theory: first, that individuals who are subjected to frustration reply with aggression; second, that individuals with either a low or a high value for the latent aggressiveness variable will, when frustrated, respond with less manifest aggressiveness than those who have an intermediate value. When we evaluate the hypothesis empirically by presenting the test to a number of individuals, we estimate their values for the latent aggressiveness variable and establish which group each individual belongs in. These groups are subjected to the same form of frustration, and we investigate whether the different groups behave in the manner predicted. We can now continue the validation process, by reasoning out other consequences of the theory in which the concept is included, and testing to see whether these logical consequences occur in empirical testing. So long as the results agree with those predicted, we can state that our estimates of the individuals' values for the latent aggressiveness variable have construct validity.

Note that the accuracy refers to the variable "latent aggressiveness" as defined in the theory from which the tested predictions have been made. Note also that we do not measure exactly the variable defined, but the variable which is operationally defined by the test. The individuals' positions on the continuum for the conceptually defined variable can perhaps also be estimated by test methods other than those first applied. If hypotheses about the conceptually defined variable as measured by some other instrument are tested with these other methods, the measurement which is then carried out will be operationally defined by this new test instrument. If this measurement can be shown to have good construct validity, it can be used for estimating the positions of individuals on the continuum for the conceptually defined variable.

Let us now assume that the consequences which could be drawn from the theory of the concept were substantiated by empirical testing. If this were not the case the explanation could lie either in the theory, which could be reformulated after several such incorrect predictions, or in the instrument, which could be insensitive to latent aggressiveness.

Thus, construct validity cannot be summed up in a single measure as a correlation between test scores and criterion scores. Validity is determined by showing that the consequences which can be predicted on the basis of the theory with respect to data from the test can, in the main, be confirmed by a series of testings.

As can be seen from the above discussion, the procedure for testing construct validity is the same as the deductive method currently applied in all scientific research. The concept of construct validity is an application of this method to the problem of evaluating the accuracy of predictions based upon a test. This evaluation takes place in accordance with the classical procedure: theory—deduction—hypothesis—experimental testing—data which falsify or verify the hypothesis.

Construct validity can be tested in several different ways. (For a more complete account, cf. Cronbach and Meehl, 1955.) Only the most common methods will be given here:

1. The study of differences between groups which should differ according to the theory for the variable.

2. The study of how the test results are influenced by changes in individuals or environment which, according to the theory, should respectively influence or fail to influence the individuals' positions on the continuum.

3. The correlation between different tests which are assumed to measure the the same variable. Great care must be taken here that correlations between the measurements do not arise as a result of similarities in method. This could happen if (for example) the answers to the tests required some special aptitude other than that under consideration. A possible agree-

ment between the measurements could then arise purely as an effect of individual differences with respect to this special aptitude. This problem will be dealt with in greater detail in a later section of this chapter.

4. The correlation between single items or different parts of the test. The parts of the test must have a high intercorrelation if the test is to be regarded as measuring a unitary variable.

It should perhaps be mentioned that the introduction of the term "construct validity" has been widely accepted but has also given rise to debate, and a number of views have been presented concerning the advantages of introducing the new term. Some of these views have been rather critical (see, e.g., Bechtoldt, 1959).

10–4 AN EXAMPLE OF TESTING CONSTRUCT VALIDITY

The reasoning behind one of the methods of testing construct validity (by computing the correlation between ratings from different methods) can be illustrated by an example of ratings for one and the same variable, based on certain projective methods (cf. Magnusson, 1960). In this example, ratings of the variable "general adjustment" were obtained from the Rorschach test, from the CAT (Children Apperception Test) and from the Draw-a-man test. The ratings based on the different tests were obtained independently; each rater scored performance on only one of the tests. Every rating was carried out blind; i.e., the stories were not collected by the same psychologist who made the ratings, and the stories could be identified only through a code number. As well as from these ratings, data were also obtained from the Bender Visual Motor Gestalt Test, the raw scores from which were used as an expression for the degree of general adjustment. Thus there were four independent measurements of the variable "general adjustment," and each of the measurements was based on a test with specific characteristics. The coefficients shown in Table 10–1 were obtained when the intercorrelations between the measures from the different kinds of tests were computed.

When interpreting the coefficients in Table 10–1, we should bear the following factors in mind. There are no essential similarities between the stimuli

Table 10–1 Intercorrelation coefficients for ratings of the variable "general adjustment," based on different projective methods and scores for the Bender Visual Motor Gestalt Test

	CAT	Bender	Draw-a-man
Rorschach	0.35	0.40	0.46
CAT		0.38	0.03
Bender			0.67

used in the tests for which the scores were obtained: ink blots, animal pictures, instructions to draw a man, and geometrical patterns. Nor is there any similarity in the types of response: nouns, stories, a freehand drawing, and a drawing of geometrical patterns. No common factor can have affected the ratings and influenced the correlation computations through the judges, since they worked independently and never saw the individuals who gave the stories on which the ratings were based. Some common (and for our present purposes irrelevant) factor in the different methods can thus scarcely have given rise to the positive coefficients obtained throughout.

Bearing this in mind, we can interpret the coefficients in the correlation matrix in Table 10–1 as an expression for the construct validity in the ratings of general adjustment which are obtained from the different methods. To do this, we reason as follows: If these coefficients were not an expression for the validity of the ratings, then each of the three projective test raters must have rated something other than what they were instructed to rate. Nevertheless, independently they must have rated the same variable to some extent and also the variable expressed by the raw scores on the Bender test. The probability of this being the case must be regarded as very small.

10–5   COMPLETE VALIDITY TESTING WITH SEVERAL VARIABLES AND SEVERAL METHODS

From what has been said so far about validity, we can now state one of the basic differences in methodology between testing a method's reliability and its validity. Reliability is estimated by the agreement between two measurements of the same variable with methods as similar to one another as possible—parallel tests. Validity, on the other hand, is computed from measurements of the same variable carried out with methods which are as unlike one another as possible. This latter fact is particularly apparent in testing construct validity.

In the above discussion of a study of the construct validity of ratings based upon different projective methods, the importance of the methods' dissimilarity in various respects was stressed, in order that the obtained intercorrelations could be interpreted as expressing construct validity. In this section we shall deal more systematically with this problem.

Every method has its specific stimulus patterns and types of response. The variation between individuals as expressed by the distribution of scores obtained by a given method can be affected either by otherwise irrelevant differences in the individuals' reactions to the method's characteristic features, or by differences in positions on the continuum on which we intended the test to measure—or by both. The variation obtained in a distribution of ratings of a given personality trait, in which the estimates are based on TAT (Thematic Apperception Test) responses from a group of individuals, has been shown to be partly dependent upon the length of the stories which the individuals invented in response to the TAT pictures (cf. Magnusson, 1959). A certain portion of the variance of the distribution of ratings for this personality trait is therefore the result of the method's characteristic features. We would not obtain the same variance if we allowed the same judges to rate the same individuals with respect to the same personality trait on the basis of material from a method having properties completely different from those of the TAT method. Another part of the total variance of these TAT ratings arises from genuine differences between the individuals with respect to the trait being tested. It is this variance which expresses the genuine validity of the ratings and which we wish to estimate as accurately as possible when testing validity.

We can thus break down the systematic variance into (a) variance due to the properties of the method used and (b) variance due to relevant characteristics of the individuals tested.

The variance due to the properties of the method will give a sort of methodological "halo" effect.* Consequently, when ratings of a number of variables are based on the same method, the coefficients in the intercorrelation matrix will generally be larger than in situations in which the common-method factor has no effect. The ratings of different personality traits will be affected by the properties of the method, and a certain amount of common variance will result.

If two different methods having similar properties are used as a basis for ratings of a certain personality trait and are applied independently, a certain portion of the variance in the ratings based on one of the methods might reappear systematically in the ratings based on the other. For example, let us assume that the number of words spoken by individuals being interviewed has a systematic effect on the magnitude and direction of the ratings which the interviewer makes with respect to a certain personality trait. If this is so, we can expect a systematic relationship between the ratings of this personality trait which are based on an interview and the ratings of the same personality trait which are based on TAT stories, even if neither of the ratings is a valid expression for individual differences with respect to the personality trait in question. This common variance which is a result of similarities in method will thus lead to an overestimate of the construct validity, when this is tested by correlation computations between scores obtained from different methods.

---

* The halo effect is a systematic rater effect which must be taken into account in rating procedures. When human traits are rated, a positive or negative attitude on the part of the rater towards the ratee will generally affect the ratings for each trait in the direction of this attitude. The ratings for each individual trait will be colored by the overall impression of the ratee. The effect will be a decrease in intraindividual differences and an increase in the correlation between ratings of different traits.

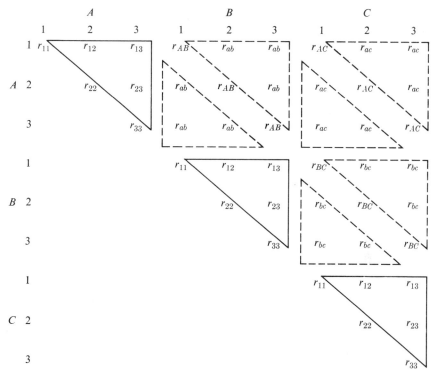

Fig. 10–1 A multivariable-multimethod matrix.

The preceding views can serve as a background to the requirements which Campbell and Fiske (1959) have formulated for a completely satisfactory validity test. These requirements are especially important in tests of construct validity, but they can also be applied to the testing of predictive and concurrent validity. The discussion will be based on references to the matrix shown in Fig. 10–1, which is what Campbell and Fiske call a *multivariable-multimethod matrix*. The correlation coefficients in the table are computed for data obtained for three different variables (1, 2, 3) using three different methods (*A*, *B*, *C*). The scores for each of the variables are correlated with the scores for each of the other variables, without regard to the method by which they were obtained. The diagonal values in the complete matrix, r_{11}, r_{22}, r_{33}, give the reliability of the measurements. These correlations are computed from scores obtained with the same method for the same variable.

The triangles (enclosed by solid lines) which lie along the diagonal of the complete matrix contain coefficients which give the relationship between measurements of different variables with the same method: r_{12}, r_{13}, r_{23}. Since the same method has been used as a basis for the measurement of different variables, the properties of the method will give rise to common variance for the different variables, to the extent that the properties of the method give rise to systematic variance when the individual variables are measured.

The triangles enclosed in dashed lines contain the coefficients of correlation between measurements of different variables obtained by different methods: r_{ab}, r_{ac}, r_{bc}. The diagonals between these triangles contain the coefficients of correlation between measurements of the same variable with different methods: r_{AB}, r_{AC}, r_{BC}. These last coefficients are the validity coefficients. Common variance which arises because of similarities in method will affect the size of all of these coefficients, to the extent that the methods have similar properties and are given the opportunity of affecting the measurements in a systematic way.

Campbell and Fiske now make the following requirements for a completely satisfactory validation process:

1. The coefficients of correlation between measurements of the same variable with different methods, r_{AB}, r_{AC}, r_{BC}, must be significantly greater than zero. This is the criterion which is normally considered sufficient.

2. The measurements of a variable must correlate more closely with measurements of the same type which are carried out with another method than with measurements of another type which are carried out with the same method. The validity coefficients, r_{AB}, r_{AC}, r_{BC}, for a certain variable should thus be greater than the coefficients for the same variable in the triangles enclosed by solid lines, r_{12}, r_{13}, r_{23}.

3. A validity coefficient for a given variable must be greater than the correlation between the measurements of this variable and the measurements of all other variables with any other method. A validity coefficient should thus be greater than the corresponding coefficients, r_{ab}, r_{ac}, r_{bc}, in the same row and column within the triangle enclosed by dashed lines.

The methods are said to have *convergent validity* if the first requirement—for significant agreement between measurements of the same type with different methods—is satisfied. For reasons given above we cannot, however (as has often been done), be satisfied with showing that this requirement is fulfilled. We must also show that the second and third are satisfied. If they are, the measurements are said to have *discriminant validity*.

It should be pointed out briefly that Campbell and Fiske's requirements cannot, of course, be considered without taking into account the methods' reliability. If unreliability affects the results, one must tolerate certain shortcomings in the exact fulfillment of the requirements for discriminant validity. A fourth requirement makes discriminant validity especially difficult to attain. Because of the difficulty of judging the effect of unreliability in a matrix of the size we must often deal with, this requirement appears unrealistic and impossible to maintain rigorously. It reads as follows:

4. Whether the same or different methods are used, the magnitude of the coefficients for the correlation between different variables should have the same pattern.

REFERENCES

AMERICAN PSYCHOLOGICAL ASSOCIATION (1954). Technical recommendations for psychological tests and diagnostic techniques. *Suppl. Psychol. Bull.*, **51.**

BECHTOLDT, P. (1959). Construct validity: a critique. *Am. Psychologist*, **14,** 619–629.

CAMPBELL, D. T., and D. W. FISKE (1959). Convergent and discriminant validation by the multitrait-multimethod matrix. *Psychol. Bull.*, **56,** 81–105.

CRONBACH, L. J., and P. E. MEEHL (1955). Construct validity in psychological tests. *Psychol. Bull.*, **52,** 281–302.

MAGNUSSON, D. (1959). *A study of ratings based on T.A.T.* Stockholm: Almqvist & Wiksell.

——— (1960). Some personality tests applied on identical twins. *Scand. J. Psychol.*, **1,** 55–61.

Suggested reading

ANASTASI, A. (1950). The concept of validity in the interpretation of test scores. *Educ. Psychol. Measmt.*, **10,** 67–78.

CURETON, E. E. (1951). Validity. In E. F. LINDQUIST (Ed.) *Educational measurement.* Washington, D.C.: Am. Council on Educ.

DUNNETTE, M. D. (1963). A note on the criterion. *J. Appl. Psychol.*, **47,** 251–254.

——— (1963). A modified model for test validation and selection research. *J. Appl. Psychol.*, **47,** 317–323.

EBEL, R. L. (1961). Must all tests be valid? *Am. Psychologist*, **16,** 640–647.

GELLERMAN, S. W. (1963). Personnel testing—what the critics overlook. *Personnel Psychol.*, **40,** 18–26.

GHISELLI, E. E. (1956). Dimensional problems of criteria. *J. Appl. Psychol.*, **40,** 1–4.

GHISELLI, E. E., and M. HAIRE (1960). The validation of selection tests in the light of the dynamic character of criteria. *Personnel Psychol.*, **13,** 225–231.

GHISELLI, E. E. (1964). *Theory of psychological measurement.* New York: McGraw-Hill.

LOEVINGER, J. (1957). Objective tests as instruments of psychological theory. *Psychol. Rep.*, **3,** 635–694.

MOSIER, C. J. (1951). Problems and designs in cross-validation. *Educ. Psychol. Measmt.*, **11,** 5–11.

NORMAN, W. T. (1965). Double-split cross-validation: an extension of Mosier's design, two undesirable alternatives, and some enigmatic results. *J. Appl. Psychol.*, **49,** 348–357.

SECHREST, L. (1963). Incremental validity: a recommendation. *Educ. Psychol. Measmt.*, **23,** 153–158.

THORNDIKE, R. L. (1949). *Personnel selection.* New York: Wiley.

CHAPTER 11

Prediction and its Dependability

11-1 THE STANDARD ERROR OF ESTIMATE

As was shown previously we can make a prediction from one of two variables to the other with the aid of the correlation coefficient. If we know the correlation between the scores for two variables x and y, we need only obtain an individual's score for x in order to be able to predict the same individual's probable score for y, using the equation $z'_y = r_{xy} z_x$ (Eq. 3–4). The accuracy of the prediction is directly dependent on r_{xy}, the size of the correlation. When $r = 1.0$ the prediction will be perfectly accurate—every individual will obtain the score on y predicted for him, if we later carry out a measurement for the y-variable. If $r = 0$ the prediction will be completely random—every individual will have the same predicted score, but only a limited number of the individuals involved will obtain this score when we measure the y-variable.

The uncertainty of prediction thus increases as the correlation between the variables decreases. When predicting from the x-variable to the y-variable we have a direct expression for this uncertainty in the distribution of y-scores around the predicted score (y') corresponding to each x-score (see Fig. 11–1). When we know the standard deviation of this distribution we have a numerical expression with which we can compute the interval within which an individual's y-score is to be found with a known degree of certainty, when his predicted score is of a given magnitude.

If linearity and homoscedasticity (see pp. 43–44) are present, it is also possible to derive a general equation for estimating from the validity coefficient the standard deviation of the errors we make in the prediction from x-scores to y-scores. This standard deviation for a given column (in future denoted by s_{yx}, the standard error of estimate from x to y) can be computed by means of the usual equation for the standard deviation. We let y denote the obtained individual score and y' the predicted score, both expressed as

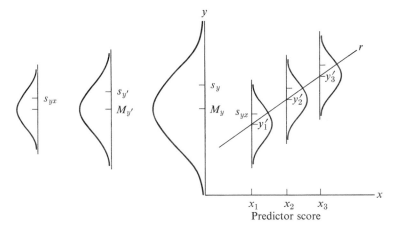

y

x₁   x₂   x₃
Predictor score

Fig. 11–1 Prediction of y-scores from known scores on the x-variable.

deviations from the mean of the y-distribution, and obtain

$$s_{yx} = \sqrt{\Sigma(y - y')^2/N_k},\tag{11–1}$$

where N_k is the number of individuals in the column.

The assumption of homoscedasticity for product moment correlation means that the variance of the distribution of y-scores around the predicted score is the same for every column, within the limits set by the size of the sample (see Fig. 11–1). Every deviation from predicted scores can then be used in the computation and we obtain the expression

$$s_{yx} = \sqrt{\Sigma(y - y')^2/N},\tag{11–2}$$

where y is the obtained score for the y-variable, y' is the predicted score for the y-variable, and N is the total number of individuals included in the correlation computation (y and y' are given as deviations from M_y).

Squaring both sides of the expression and expanding, and at the same time replacing y' by $r_{xy}(s_y/s_x)x$ (Eq. 3–9), we obtain

$$s_{yx}^2 = \frac{\Sigma[y - r_{xy}(s_y/s_x)x]^2}{N} = \frac{\Sigma y^2}{N} + r_{xy}^2 \frac{s_y^2}{s_x^2} \frac{\Sigma x^2}{N} - 2r_{xy} \frac{s_y}{s_x} \frac{\Sigma xy}{N}.$$

Since y and x are deviations from the distributions' means, $\Sigma y^2/N = s_y^2$, and $\Sigma x^2/N = s_x^2$. If we now multiply the numerator and denominator in the third term on the right-hand side by s_y, we obtain

$$s_{yx}^2 = s_y^2 + r_{xy}^2 s_y^2 - 2r_{xy}^2 s_y^2 = s_y^2 - r_{xy}^2 s_y^2 = s_y^2(1 - r_{xy}^2);$$

$$s_{yx} = s_y\sqrt{1 - r_{xy}^2}.\tag{11–3}$$

We have now derived the expression for the standard deviation of the probable distribution of y-scores around the predicted y-score corresponding to every single x-score. Equation (11–3) thus gives the *standard error of estimate*.

The magnitude of the standard error of estimate depends partly on the numerical value of the standard deviation of the distribution to which the prediction is made, and partly on the correlation between scores on this distribution and predictor scores. For a given correlation between the distributions the dispersion of y-scores corresponding to a given x-score will of course depend upon the scale on which the y-scores have been given. The standard error of prediction for a given correlation will not be the same if the total dispersion in y is 10 instead of 1. For a given standard deviation in y, the standard error is entirely dependent on the magnitude of the validity coefficient. When the correlation is 1.0 the standard error will be zero. In this case, there is also a perfect agreement between predicted and obtained y-scores, and there is no dispersion of obtained scores around the regression line. When the correlation is zero, the standard error of prediction will be equal to the standard deviation of the total distribution of y-scores. In this case we are unable to make any better prediction than a purely random one.

The derivation of Eq. (11–3) is based on the assumption that the variance of the distributions around predicted y-scores is the same for every x-score, i.e., that a homoscedastic relationship exists. This condition must be satisfied if the equation is to be applied.

It is easy to investigate empirically whether homoscedasticity is present. If the dispersion of obtained criterion scores is different for different predictor scores, the empirically obtained standard deviations should be given when one is reporting on the test standardization. They should also be used when one is applying the test results as a basis for counseling, diagnosis, or decision-making. Even if homoscedasticity is present, the practical use of the validity coefficient in evaluating the standard error of prediction is facilitated by recording in a scatter diagram the empirically obtained y-scores corresponding to various x-scores.

Equation (11–3) thus gives the probable deviation of obtained criterion scores around a predicted score. If we assume homoscedasticity, it can also be used for computing the interval on the y-axis within which we can expect the criterion score to lie with a known degree of certainty for individuals with a given predictor score. Let us examine a situation in which the standard error of prediction can be used in this way.

We choose the case in which a pupil's test score is known and we wish to predict his success as a student, expressed by the teacher's rating after the completion of his studies. A pupil's I.Q. is taken to be 120 on a scale where $M_x = 100$ and $s_x = 16$. The teacher's rating is on a 9-point scale where $M_y = 5$ and $s_y = 2$. We assume that the validity coefficient r_{xy} is 0.50, which is common for relationships of this type. What is now the best estimate of success, as expressed by the teacher's rating for the pupil with I.Q. 120? The deviation from the mean 100 is 20 units. If we insert the values given in Eq. (3–9) we obtain $y' = 0.50 \times 2/16 \times 20 = 1.25$. The best estimate of the teacher's rating of the pupil under the given conditions will then be 6.25, i.e., the mean 5 plus the computed deviation 1.25. We obtain the same result if we give the pupil's test score as a standard score and compute the estimated score using Eq. (3–4).

A further question remains. How great is the uncertainty involved in estimating the score 6.25? To calculate this, let us use the equation for the standard error of estimate and insert the known values, obtaining

$$s_{yx} = 2\sqrt{1 - 0.50^2} = 1.74.$$

This means that the score the pupil actually obtains on the rating lies with 68% certainty in the range 6.25 ± 1.74, i.e., in the range from 4.51 to 7.99, and with 95% certainty in the range from 2.84 to 9.66. The probability of obtaining a rating outside the area between 2.84 and 9.66 is approximately 5%.

The use of common validity coefficients for the interpretation of the standard error of estimate implies a linear and homoscedastic relationship between predictor scores and criterion scores. In other words, we assume that a trait has the same effect on an individual's performance, no matter what his position on the distribution of predictor scores and criterion scores.

In some cases it can be established that the relationship is not homoscedastic, i.e., that the variances in criterion scores differ for different predictor scores. The usual equation for the standard error of estimate is not then applicable and the variances of criterion scores for different predictor scores must be given. That the relationship is not homoscedastic may in some situations be due to the fact that the relation between predictor scores and criterion scores differs among different subgroups of the sample for which the validity coefficient has been computed. In such cases it has been possible to increase the magnitude of the validity coefficient considerably by splitting up an original sample into subsamples by means of suitable *moderator variables* (cf. Ghiselli, 1963, and Saunders, 1956).

11–2   THE COEFFICIENT OF ALIENATION

Equation (11–3) gives us the standard deviation of the distribution of errors involved in predicting from x to y. The error deviation in a given case depends partly on the total dispersion in the distribution to which the prediction takes place, and partly on the correlation coefficient which gives the magnitude of the relationship. We can now easily obtain a measure of the

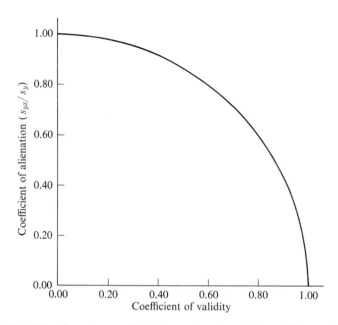

Fig. 11–2 The alienation coefficient as a function of the validity coefficient.

relative error deviation, i.e., the proportion of the total standard deviation which consists of the standard error, corresponding to a given correlation coefficient. This is done by dividing both sides by s_y. We then obtain

$$s_{yx}/s_y = \sqrt{1 - r_{xy}^2}. \tag{11–4}$$

Equation (11–4) gives the *coefficient of alienation.* Figure 11–2 illustrates the relationship between the alienation coefficient and the correlation coefficient. As can be seen already from Eq. (11–4), the curve in the figure is an arc.

The figure shows clearly the comparatively small decrease in relative error deviation that comes with increased validity coefficients, even those regarded as unusually high in practical situations. The relative standard error is still as high as 0.80 for validity coefficients of 0.60, a value above the average for our most common diagnosis and prediction instruments. Or, in other words, the error deviation we would have obtained for zero correlation has been reduced by only 20% by this relatively high validity coefficient. Even for a validity coefficient as high as 0.80, which scarcely ever arises in tests for practical use, the relative error deviation is 0.60. It is thus reduced by only 40%.

In the literature of psychology it is not uncommon to come across very low validity coefficients which, because they are significant, are used as a basis for drawing conclusions about the value of the test. It should be remembered, however, that a coefficient need not be particularly high in order to deviate significantly from zero, if the sample for which it is computed is large. The examples given should, however, be sufficient to show that validity coefficients for a test must in most situations attain a considerable magnitude before the test can be regarded as a source of dependable diagnoses or predictions. It should be stated here that the value of a validity coefficient cannot, however, be judged with respect *only* to its numerical magnitude. The value differs with the circumstances in which the coefficient is to be used. In some situations even small validity coefficients can be of considerable value.

11–3   THE VALIDITY COEFFICIENT AND VARIANCE OF PREDICTED SCORES

The score an individual j actually obtains for the y-variable (y_j) can now be divided into two components: a predicted score (y'_j) and an error score, the part of the obtained score which could not be predicted from another variable because of low correlation between the variables (y_{ej}).

$$y_j = y'_j + y_{ej}. \tag{11–5}$$

The error score is one of the components included in the distribution of obtained y-scores around a predicted y-score. We now obtain three distributions of y-scores: one for obtained scores, one for predicted scores, and one for error scores (see Fig. 11–1). Since the magnitude of the error scores, if we assume homoscedasticity, will be uncorrelated with that of the predicted scores, the variance of obtained y-scores can be written as the sum of the variance of predicted scores and the variance of errors around predicted scores:

$$s_y^2 = s_{y'}^2 + s_{yx}^2. \tag{11–6}$$

We obtain the following expression by expanding the equation for the standard error of estimate (Eq. 11–3):

$$r_{xy}^2 = (s_y^2 - s_{yx}^2)/s_y^2.$$

This gives

$$r_{xy}^2 = 1 - s_{yx}^2/s_y^2, \tag{11–7}$$

or

$$r_{xy}^2 = s_{y'}^2/s_y^2. \tag{11–8}$$

The square of the correlation coefficient thus expresses the proportion of the total variance on one of the distributions which can be predicted from the other. This fact will be used in Chapter 13 when we discuss factor theory. Since the square of the correlation coefficient gives the amount of a variance which is determined by the relationship with some other variable, it is also called the *coefficient of determination* and is denoted by d.

The part of the variance on the y-distribution which cannot be predicted from the x-variable, i.e., the variance denoted by s^2_{yx}, is usually called the *residual variance* or *partial variance*.

11–4 THE VALIDITY COEFFICIENT AND VARIATION IN TRUE PREDICTOR SCORES

We previously showed how the magnitude of the reliability coefficient is dependent on variation in true scores, (see p. 75). We shall now examine the effect of this variation on the validity coefficient.

As a rule, validity is tested by computing the agreement between scores obtained from the instrument whose validity is to be tested and criterion scores. In many situations, however, a systematic dropout of subjects occurs at one or other end of one of the two distributions. The size of the variance will be affected, and a measure of validity will be obtained, by computing the correlation of distributions with dispersions other than those which hold for the distribution in which the test's power to discriminate is to be tested. The effect of this on the validity coefficient is best illustrated by means of a practical example.

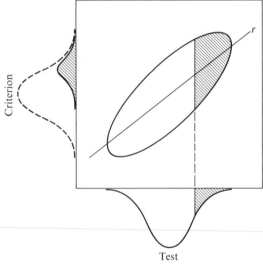

Fig. 11–3 The effect of restriction of range.

Consider Fig. 11–3. The example can be taken to illustrate what happens, for instance, in validity testing of a selection instrument for higher education. Every applicant to the course is tested and given a score on the distribution on the x-axis. A selection is made on the basis of the test scores; those who are above a certain level are selected for the course; those who have not reached this level are not allowed to continue (the unshaded part of the test distribution). The test is supposed to differentiate as accurately as possible among subjects with reference to success in higher studies. The best criterion is obviously then a measure of such success, e.g., grades after a certain period of study. A weeding out has already taken place, however, and we can obtain criterion scores only for those who have actually been allowed to begin studying. Instead of the total distribution on the y-axis, which we would have obtained if every applicant had been allowed to study, we will now obtain the smaller, shaded distribution which is a part of the larger one. This involves a considerable limitation of heterogeneity—a *restriction of range*—partly in the distribution of predictor scores, and partly in the criterion distribution, although to a smaller extent in the latter since the correlation between the distributions is not 1.0.

What effect does this systematic restriction have on the validity coefficient? The unshaded part of the correlation area in Fig. 11–3 represents the part which will be excluded because y-scores have not been obtained for individuals in the unshaded part of the distribution on the x-axis.

We begin from Eq. (11–7):

$$r_{xy}^2 = 1 - s_{yx}^2/s_y^2.$$

Under the assumption of homoscedasticity, s_y^2 will be reduced as a result of the systematic restriction which has taken place. However, s_{yx}^2, which is of course the variance of the probability distribution of y-scores around the predicted score corresponding to a particular x-score, will not be affected. The proportion of error variance will thus increase and the validity coefficient will be reduced.

The general effect of a restriction which leads to reduced variation in true scores is a reduction of the validity coefficient. In the extreme case the restriction will be so great that only individuals with one given x-score will be left on the y-variable after preliminary selection or weeding out. Every individual will then have the same predicted score; $s_{y'}^2$ will be zero and s_y^2 will equal s_{yx}^2, so that r_{xy} will also be zero. Nor will there be any differentiation based upon test results in such a situation.

The validity coefficient which can be computed for a sample where restriction has taken place will thus underestimate the instrument's validity, i.e., its ability to differentiate meaningfully on the total distribution for which it is actually supposed to discriminate. The extent of underestimation will of course be greater, the greater the number of dropouts.

Table 11–1 shows two series of validity coefficients for a number of tests administered to American pilot trainees during the Second World War (cf. Thorndike, 1949, pp. 170–171). Everyone tested was accepted for the preliminary training, and the validity coefficients for the various tests were computed with the training result as a criterion.

Table 11–1 Validity coefficients computed both for the total number of individuals and for a highly selected group

	Total number $N = 1036$	Selected group $N = 136$
Pilot stanine (composite score)	0.64	0.18
Mechanical principles test	0.44	0.03
General information test	0.46	0.20
Complex coordination test	0.40	−0.03
Instrument comprehension test	0.45	0.27
Arithmetic reasoning test	0.27	0.18
Finger dexterity test	0.18	0.00

The first column of the table gives the validity coefficients obtained when the computations were based on the results for everyone tested (1036 individuals). The second column shows the validity coefficients obtained when the computations were based on a highly selected group, namely, the 13% who had obtained the best results during the selection procedure.

What we wish the validity coefficient to express is, of course, the instrument's ability to discriminate between those who will do well and those who will do less well. The validity coefficients in the first column of Table 11–1 are expressions for the tests' ability to do this. If only the best 13% had been accepted—and in practical situations the test instruments are, of course, used for the very purpose of selecting among many applicants for a limited number of places—we would have obtained training results and criterion scores for this group only, and we would have obtained the validity coefficients shown in the second column of the table. These coefficients express the tests' ability to differentiate within the selected group (a differentiation which we are not really interested in) and considerably underestimate the power of the tests to differentiate among the total number of applicants.

A selection of persons from the total number of those originally tested can be based upon (a) the individuals' scores on the test whose validity is being computed, (b) the individuals' scores on the criterion variable, or (c) scores from some variable other than the predictor or criterion variable. In case (c), the selection is often made with a test battery in which the test whose validity is to be computed is included. This is a common situation. When the means and standard deviations of the distributions of obtained scores on which the selection is based are known, both for the total number of individuals and for the selected group, we can estimate, from the correlation coefficient for the selected group, the validity coefficient which would have been obtained for the total number (cf. Thorndike, 1949, pp. 172–176). In many situations the data necessary for a correction for a restriction of range are not available, since the actual selection is also based on subjective judgments which are not reported.

The relationship between validity and the dispersion of scores in the sample on which the validity is to be tested is important in situations where, for instance, the selection is to be made within a group which is the result of several successive selective procedures. The variables for which the individuals have been tested and found to form a homogeneous group through the previous selection procedures are clearly unsuitable as selection variables. For a group which is selected with respect to high intelligence, differences between individuals which are other than intellectual probably play a greater and more decisive role in determining success in, for instance, a given course of education.

11–5 CORRECTION FOR UNRELIABILITY

A validity coefficient expresses the extent of the agreement between test scores and a measurement of the criterion variable. Both these measurements will, however, contain errors which are results of the unreliability of the instruments with which the measurements have been carried out. It is possible to introduce a correction for these errors, and thus obtain an estimate of the relationship which would be obtained if the measurements were completely reliable.

What we are looking for is an equation for the correlation between true scores for two variables. We begin with the following expressions for an individual's true scores for two variables measured by tests t and g:

$$T_j = t_j - e_{jt}, \qquad G_j = g_j - e_{jg}.$$

(All scores are in deviation form.)

The desired correlation is obtained by summing the product for every individual and dividing by the number of products and the standard deviations of the two distributions:

$$r_{TG} = \frac{\sum(t - e_t)(g - e_g)}{N s_T s_G}; \qquad (11\text{–}9)$$

$$r_{TG} s_T s_G = \frac{\sum tg}{N} - \frac{\sum t e_g}{N} - \frac{\sum e_t g}{N} + \frac{\sum e_t e_g}{N}.$$

The direction of obtained scores (t and g) and error scores (e_t and e_g) can be assumed to be independent. Furthermore, error scores are assumed to be uncorrelated. Under these conditions, the last three terms will be zero. After multiplying both sides by $1/s_t s_g$ we obtain

$$r_{TG} = r_{tg} s_t s_g / s_T s_G.$$

From Eq. (5–7) we obtain $s_T = s_t\sqrt{r_{tt}}$ and $s_G = s_g\sqrt{r_{gg}}$. Inserting these expressions in the above equation we obtain

$$r_{TG} = r_{tg}/\sqrt{r_{tt}r_{gg}}, \qquad (11\text{–}10)$$

where r_{TG} is the estimated coefficient for the correlation between true scores for variables t and g (for instance, a test variable and a criterion variable), and r_{tg} is the obtained coefficient for the correlation between variables t and g. The equation is usually called the *correction for attenuation*.

We can thus obtain an estimate from Eq. (11–10) of the correlation between measurements of two variables, assuming that the measurements are free from error scores. The equation should, therefore, be used only in situations where we are interested in the correlation between true scores for the two variables. Let us, for example, suppose that we wish to investigate in which traits identical twins are most like each other. We cannot immediately compare coefficients for the correlation between their scores on a series of tests which, we assume, measure the variables we are interested in, and then use the magnitude of these obtained coefficients as an expression for the degree of similarity between the twins with respect to these traits. The reliability of a test sets an upper limit to the correlation we can obtain between true scores, and the magnitude of the coefficients we obtain will thus partly depend upon how unreliable the tests are. It is only when we have corrected for the unreliability of the measurements that the coefficients will be comparable as expressions for the degree of similarity between the identical twins with respect to the traits measured by the test. (In this case, the distributions from which the correlations are computed are made up of scores obtained from a single instrument. Since the measurements for both variables have to be corrected, the corrected intraclass coefficient $r_{i(c)}$ for the correlation between true scores for the variable measured by test t will be estimated from the equation $r_{i(c)} = r_i/r_{tt}$.)

It is primarily in the testing of construct validity that a correction of obtained coefficients by means of Eq. (11–10) is meaningful.

Equation (11–10), when used for correcting an obtained validity coefficient for predictive or concurrent validity, gives an estimate of the correlation between a completely reliable test and a completely reliable criterion. In many situations such a correlation is of little interest. The test measurement we shall use in the practical application of the test (for example, when making a prediction) is of course the contaminated measurement included in the obtained validity coefficient. A completely reliable criterion measure should, however, be used in order to obtain a correct assessment of the value of this contaminated measurement for prediction. In such cases the required correction is made by correcting for unreliability only in the criterion measurement. In this way, an estimate is obtained of the relationship between obtained test measurements and true criterion scores (r_{tG}). This correction is made with the equation

$$r_{tG} = r_{tg}/\sqrt{r_{gg}}. \tag{11–11}$$

It should be observed that corrected scores are estimates of the scores that would have been obtained if the factors for which one has corrected had not affected the results. The accuracy of these estimates depends on the accuracy of the scores on which the correction is based, and on the accuracy of the other scores which are used in the correction. When an obtained validity coefficient is corrected for unreliability, this is done by means of obtained reliability coefficients. It should be borne in mind that uncertainty in all correlation coefficients, including reliability coefficients, increases as the value of the coefficient decreases. If low reliability scores are used for correction, they will already contain a considerable error which will affect the correction. In the case of low reliability coefficients, correction can have a considerable effect which will arise partly from the errors to be found in the reliability scores. Corrected validity coefficients must under such conditions be interpreted with great caution. The above circumstances make the usual equation for testing the significance of correlation coefficients unsuitable for testing corrected correlation coefficients.

11–6 VALIDITY COEFFICIENTS FOR COMPLETELY RELIABLE CRITERIA AND TESTS

From Eq. (11–10) we can now find the theoretical upper limit for validity coefficients, assuming that we have completely reliable tests and completely reliable criteria.

The theoretical upper limit for the validity coefficient is 1.0 if both test and criterion in a given case are completely reliable and express exactly the same true scores. Both r_{tt} and r_{gg} are then 1.0, the denominator on the right-hand side of Eq. (11–10) will be 1.0, and the maximum value of the validity coefficient will also be 1.0.

If only the criterion measurement is completely reliable, all of the criterion variance can be predicted. The maximum value of the validity coefficient then depends upon the reliability of the test and can be written

$$r_{tg(\max)} = r_{tg}/\sqrt{r_{tt}}.$$

The maximum value of the obtained validity coefficient (r_{tg}) will then be $\sqrt{r_{tt}}$, or the reliability index for the test (see p. 68). This is the theoretical upper limit for the validity coefficient, and thus the maximum value we can obtain by improving the reliability of the criterion for a given test.

From Eq. (11–10) we can also estimate the maximum value of the validity coefficient which can be obtained for a completely reliable test with an unreliable criterion; r_{tt} will then be equal to 1.0 in Eq. (11–10). The maximum validity coefficient which can be obtained will theoretically be $\sqrt{r_{gg}}$. This value gives the theoretical limit we can attain for the validity coefficient by making a test more reliable.

11–7 VALIDITY AND TEST LENGTH

The reliability of a test is increased when we increase the length of the test by including additional items of the same type. The derivation of the Spearman-Brown formula, which gives the general relationship between the reliability after the test has been increased in length n times (r_{tt_n}) and the reliability of the original test (r_{tt}), was presented and discussed previously (pp. 68–74).

Since the test becomes more reliable when increased in length, it also becomes more valid. The greater the proportion of the test's variance which is made up of the true variance, the greater the amount of variance which the test will have in common with the criterion. This can also be seen from what was previously said about the maximum value of the validity coefficient. It is equal to the reliability index or the square root of the reliability coefficient. When the reliability increases the maximum validity coefficient also increases.

The maximum validity of a test with reliability r_{tt} is thus $\sqrt{r_{tt}}$. The maximum validity of the test after an increase in length is then the square root of the reliability coefficient after the increase, or $\sqrt{r_{tt_n}}$. The relationship between the maximum validity for the original test and the maximum validity of the test which has been lengthened n times is the same as that between the two reliability indices:

$$r_{t_n g(\max)}/r_{tg(\max)} = \sqrt{r_{tt_n}/r_{tt}}.$$

The maximum validity for the test after an increase in length can then be written in terms of the maximum validity before the increase and the two reliability indices:

$$r_{t_n g(\max)} = r_{tg(\max)}\sqrt{r_{tt_n}/r_{tt}}. \tag{11–12}$$

Equation (11–12) thus gives us the maximum validity coefficient for a test increased in length a given number of times.

The equation can, however, not only be used for computing, from the original maximum validity, the maximum validity after an increase in length. It can also be used for estimating the validity coefficient for a test increased in length n times, when the validity of the original test is known. The equation can then be written

$$r_{t_n g} = r_{tg}\sqrt{r_{tt_n}/r_{tt}}. \tag{11–13}$$

Table 11–2 Estimated reliability and validity coefficients for a test with r_{tt} equal to 0.80 and r_{tg} equal to 0.50, when increased in length

n	r_{tt}	r_{ty}
1	0.800	0.500
2	0.889	0.527
3	0.923	0.537
4	0.941	0.542
5	0.952	0.545
6	0.960	0.547

By simple expansion, Eq. (11–13) can be written so that r_{tt_n} need not be computed. We first obtain a simple expression for $\sqrt{r_{tt_n}/r_{tt}}$:

$$\frac{r_{tt_n}}{r_{tt}} = \frac{nr_{tt}}{r_{tt}[1 + (n - 1)r_{tt}]} = \frac{n}{1 + (n - 1)r_{tt}}.$$

Equation (11–13) can then be written

$$r_{t_n g} = r_{tg}\sqrt{n/[1 + (n - 1)r_{tt}]}. \tag{11–14}$$

Equations (11–13) and (11–14) thus give the estimated validity coefficient for a test increased in length n times. The assumptions are the same as for the Spearman-Brown formula. The items which are added to the original test should be parallel to the items in that test.

Let us see what happens when we increase the length of a test which has reliability 0.80 and validity 0.50. Table 11–2 shows the estimated reliability and validity coefficients for the test when increased in length a given number of times.

As can be seen from the values in Table 11–2, the validity coefficient does not increase as quickly as the reliability coefficient when the test is increased in length. This is generally the case. In the example given, the validity coefficient rose only from 0.500 to 0.547 when the test was increased in length six times, while the reliability coefficient rose from 0.800 to 0.960.

This example demonstrates a fact which should be borne in mind in test construction. Under normal circumstances it is correct strategy to increase a test's validity by increasing its length only in the case of very low validity scores on very short tests. In the example given, the small improvement gained by making the test six times as long could have been achieved much more easily by constructing another test to be included in the test battery together with the original. The relation between reliability and validity will be dealt with more fully in Chapter 13.

In this section we have assumed that the criterion remains unchanged when the test is increased in length. Thus Eq. (11–14) is properly described as the equation for the estimated validity of a test when increased in length n times, with an unchanged criterion.

REFERENCES

GHISELLI, E. E. (1963).   Moderating effects and differential reliability and validity. *J. Appl. Psychol.*, **47**, 81–85.

THORNDIKE, R. L. (1949).   *Personnel selection.*   New York: Wiley.

SAUNDERS, D. R. (1956).   Moderator variables in prediction.   *Educ. Psychol. Measmt.*, **16**, 209–222.

Suggested reading

GUILFORD, J. P. (1965).   *Fundamental statistics in psychology and education.*   New York: McGraw-Hill.

GULLIKSEN, H. (1950).   *Theory of mental tests.*   New York: Wiley.

NUNNALLY, J. (1960).   The place of statistics in psychology.   *Educ. Psychol. Measmt.*, **20**, 641–650.

RYDBERG, S. (1963).   *Bias in prediction: on correction methods.*   Stockholm: Almqvist & Wiksell.

CHAPTER 12

Individual Prediction, Classification, and Selection

12-1 COMBINATION OF SCORES

This chapter will deal with validity problems that arise when differential psychology data are used as a basis for counseling, decision-making, or diagnosis. A procedure common to all of these areas is that of combining results from more than one testing instrument. The final score for an individual is obtained by combining scores from several subtests, each of which has been scored independently. Using *test batteries* composed of unidimensional tests has a number of advantages. We have better control over what the total test measures, and by means of various weighting procedures, we can give different weights to certain factors for different purposes.

The individual subtest scores can be combined to give a total score in a number of different ways. The most common procedure, and the one which we shall devote most attention to, is to obtain the total score for each individual as a sum of unweighted or weighted subtest scores. If the distributions of raw scores for different subtests have different standard deviations, a summation of raw scores from the subtests to a total score for each individual will give the subtests varying degrees of importance for the total result. In other words, they will have different weights. The individual who has a very high score on a test with a large dispersion of raw scores is favored more, when we are summating to a total score, than an individual who has a very high score, with the same relative position as the former individual, on a distribution with little raw-score dispersion.

If we wish every subtest to have the same weight in the summation of scores, we can easily convert the scores on every subdistribution to standard scores before summating. This will give every subdistribution the same standard deviation.

When we have a number of subtests in a test battery, we can compute the validity for each of the tests and for the total test against a given criterion. We often find that the validity coefficient for the simple sum of unweighted subtest scores is higher than the validity coefficient for each of the subtests. We have in this case made every subtest, regardless of the relation of the subtests to the criterion, of equal importance when computing the validity coefficient for the total test. Since we know that the subtests contribute varying amounts to the total test's validity it seems reasonable to make use of this fact, so that the tests which predict the criterion distribution more accurately (i.e., have most common variance with it) are also given more importance when we determine the sums of scores which the individuals are to have in the total distribution. The weighting of the subtests is then determined, not by the size of the standard deviation in the raw-score distribution (which is, of course, not necessarily an expression for the test's validity), but by other factors.

The purpose of weighting the subtests is to ensure that the sum of the subtest scores gives the best possible agreement with a given criterion. The procedure for weighting the subtests so as to satisfy this requirement is *multiple-regression analysis*.

The determination of the weights is made by taking into account (a) the correlation between each of the subtests and a criterion measure and (b) the correlations among the subtests included in the battery. The best weighting is that which gives as little variance as possible in the distribution of differences between predicted and obtained scores in the criterion distribution, i.e., as little residual variance as possible.

It should be remembered that the best possible prediction of an individual's score on the y-variable is obtained from a predictor score on the x-variable by means of the equation $z'_y = r_{xy}z_x$, where r_{xy} is equal to b (the angle coefficient in the normal equation for a straight line) and gives the slope of the regression line (see Chapter 3). The equation can thus be used for predicting to a criterion distribution (y) from a single predictor score. When the prediction is based upon a complete test battery the best possible prediction for the single individual will be obtained from the multiple-regression equation:

$$z'_y = b_1z_1 + b_2z_2 + \cdots + b_nz_n. \tag{12–1}$$

In this equation, b_1, b_2, etc., are the regression weights which have to be computed in the multiple-regression analysis. They are constants with which every individual's subtest scores have to be multiplied before being included in the final test scores. Thus b_1 is the value with which Subtest 1 is to be weighted, i.e., every individual's standard score on Test 1 (z_1) has to be multiplied by b_1.

The best possible prediction of the criterion variable for a single individual thus consists of a weighted sum of subtest scores. The regression weights (b_1, b_2, etc.) for the subtests are computed so that the correlation between the weighted test battery and the criterion will be a maximum. This correlation coefficient is a *multiple-correlation coefficient*. The square of the multiple-correlation coefficient gives the proportion of the total variance in the criterion which can be predicted from the weighted test battery (see p. 143).

(The procedure for computing the regression weights is not dealt with here. Those interested are referred to a reference book on psychological statistics, e.g., McNemar, 1962, pp. 169–197.)

When subtest scores are weighted in order to give the highest possible correlation with a given distribution of criterion scores, full advantage is taken of all correlations obtained between the test and the criterion, as well as correlations which are the result of random effects in this particular sample and which do not recur in others. The multiple-correlation coefficient for the sample of individuals for which the regression weights are determined will therefore always be an overestimation of the weighted test's power of prediction with respect to this criterion. We must therefore test a new sample of individuals, i.e., make a *cross validation*. The best estimate of the validity of the weighted test battery will then be the correlation coefficient for the relation between the test data (obtained from subtests which have been given the weights we obtained for the first sample) and the criterion distribution.

The weighting of the subtests in the test battery may be done for the purpose of increasing the accuracy of prediction. We expect the total score obtained from weighted subtest scores to be more valid than the total score obtained from unweighted ones. This question of the effect of the weighting is important, since multiple-regression analysis involving the computation of regression weights is often a considerable undertaking. The cost of time and work must be outweighed by a sufficiently large increase in accuracy of prediction. The effect which weighting has on the relation between total score and criterion distribution is often overestimated. It depends on (a) the number of subtests to be weighted, (b) the correlation between the subtests, and (c) the variation in weights for different subtests. The effect of weighting increases (a) as the number of subtests decreases, (b) as the correlation between the subtests decreases, and (c) as the differences between the weights for the subtests increase. If the multiple-regression analysis is based upon weighted subtest distributions, the effect of weighting will also depend on the agreement between the original weights and the obtained weights. The lower this agreement is, the greater will be the effect of weighting.

12–2   INDIVIDUAL PREDICTION TO A CRITERION VARIABLE

The simplest situation is that of making a prediction from a predictor variable (i.e., from a distribution of test scores, for example) to a distribution of criterion scores for a single individual at a time. Here the predictor variable can be obtained from a single test or from several weighted tests. This sort of individual prediction occurs, for example, in certain counseling situations. We found previously that, even if the prediction we make for a given indi-

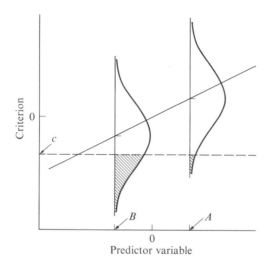

Fig. 12–1 Individual prediction.

vidual is based on a very high validity coefficient, we must be prepared for a rather high degree of uncertainty (see Fig. 11–2). We shall now study the situation more closely, taking a counseling situation as an example.

Let us suppose that we wish to use the score from a certain test or number of weighted tests as a basis for counseling about a certain college course. The tests have been constructed to measure the traits which, from previous empirical testing, we have found to be of importance for success in this course.

The certainty with which we can use the test score for a single individual as a basis for predicting his likelihood of satisfying the requirements made by the course depends on (a) the minimum level of the educational requirements, (b) the individual's capacity as measured by the test, and (c) the relation between test scores and criterion scores, i.e., the size of the validity coefficient.

The situation is illustrated in Fig. 12–1. Both of the marginal distributions of scores are given as standard scores with mean zero and standard deviation 1.0. The regression line for a validity coefficient of 0.70 is drawn. Suppose that individual A has a score corresponding to the standard score 1.0 and that individual B has a score corresponding to the standard score -1.0 on the test. What information can they obtain about their likelihood of passing the course, if the minimum level of the educational requirement is the score on the criterion distribution given by c in the figure?

Since the validity coefficient is 0.70, the best estimate of the standard score in the course will be 0.7 for A and -0.7 for B. In Fig. 12–1 the probable distribution of y-scores for the predictor score 1.0 and the predictor score -1.0 has been drawn around each of these predicted y-scores. If we assume homoscedasticity, the probability distributions will have the same magnitude for both the predictor scores. The horizontal line which is drawn through the critical score c in the criterion distribution cuts off the shaded parts of the error distributions around the predicted scores. This shaded part of an error distribution (e.g., for predictor score 1.0) represents the proportion of individuals with this predictor score who are likely to fall below the critical level on the criterion distribution, i.e., fail the course. It also gives the probability that an individual with this score will fail—in other words, the risk he is taking.

The critical level on the criterion distribution has the standard score -1.0. The distance from the predicted criterion score for A to the critical level c is clearly 1.7, expressed as a z-score. The standard deviation of the error distribution around the predicted score can be computed to be $\sqrt{1 - 0.70^2} = 0.714$. We can now transform the value 1.7 to a z-score on the error distribution for A by dividing 1.7 by the standard deviation (0.714) of the error distribution. We then obtain 2.380. From a normal distribution table we can read off how much of the error distribution lies below a z-score of -2.380. We find that it is 0.008 or 0.8%.

Thus, it is probable that 0.8% of the individuals who have obtained the same score as A will fail the course.

In the same way we can compute the risk for individuals with the same score as B. His predicted score -0.7 lies above the critical limit -1.0. More than half the individuals with this score can thus be expected to pass the course. The predicted score lies 0.3 standard-score units above the critical level. Expressed as a standard score on the error distribution, this is 0.420. The standard score -0.420 in the error distribution cuts off 0.334 or 33.4% of the distribution. This part of the distribution lies below the critical level c and is shaded in Fig. 12–1. We can now estimate that 33.4% of individuals with score -1.0 on the test will fail the course, if the critical level remains at c on the distribution of criterion scores.

The risk of failure for A is so small that he should certainly be advised to take the course, if no other difficulties or complications exist. However, B would need to have very pressing reasons for starting the course if he is to take such a large risk of failure as is indicated here.

The prediction of success will become more and more certain, the higher the predictor score obtained for a given critical requirement level in the training or occupation for which the prediction is made. The risks for individuals with different predictor scores can be estimated in advance. For a given risk level, the number for whom the risk of failure is great decreases with increased validity of the prediction instrument and with reduced requirements.

In the above example, we computed the risk for individuals with different predictor scores on the assumption that we had a normal bivariate distribution with homoscedasticity. When these conditions are not satisfied, as is frequently the case, the assessment of the risks for individuals in predictions of this type is based on empirically obtained values of dispersion of criterion scores corresponding to different predictor scores.

12–3   CLASSIFICATION

The previous section dealt with prediction to a single criterion variable. This is not, however, a particularly common situation in counseling, decision-making, or diagnosis. Instead, the problem usually consists of a choice among a number of different alternatives. It can be a question of different courses of education, different types of occupation, different types of treatment, or membership in different diagnostic groups. We wish to make as effective a placement as possible within one of these categories.

Each alternative has its own characteristic properties which can be expressed in a profile. For example, every college course has its own special requirements which we have to take into account when making a choice for each individual. We attempt to make as effective a choice of category as possible on the basis of a comparison between (a) individual profiles for those factors which we have judged to be relevant and measurable and (b) the trait profiles which are characteristic of the different categories in which the individuals can be placed. In other words, we make a *classification* of the individuals.

The classification situation is easiest to deal with when we can place the individuals one at a time, without taking into account the number of individuals for which the same alternative is best. In this situation, we have an unlimited number of places in each of the categories in which individuals can be placed. In other words, the number of individuals who can be placed in each of the alternative categories is not determined in advance. Instead, every individual can choose the alternative which is most suitable for him. This situation arises when we, for example, decide on a certain form of treatment for a patient on the basis of a clinical diagnosis, or when we give advice to someone seeking guidance in a choice among different courses of study. A favorable outcome of the decision on treatment would be an improvement in the patient's condition. A favorable outcome of the counsel about different courses of study would be that the person seeking advice succeeds in the course of study he has chosen as a result of guidance.

Classification is multidimensional. It is not safe to base the choice among alternative categories on a single test result, unless the requirements for the different categories differ only in level in one respect. Classification is therefore based on a test battery.

The classification situation is shown in Fig. 12–2. We have a number of alternatives to choose among for each individual, i.e., categories c_1–c_3, and five tests (t_1–t_5) whose results are to be the basis of the classification.

In the classification situation now being discussed, we have to make as certain a choice as possible for a single individual among the categories c_1–c_3 on the basis of the results from tests t_1–t_5. It seems reasonable to attempt this in the following way. Assuming that we have access to criterion measures for each of the categories, we compute for each the multiple coefficient for the correlation between the total test $(t_1 + t_2 + t_3 + t_4 + t_5)$ and the distribution of criterion scores. For each category we then weight the sub-tests in the prediction battery in such a way that the correlation between this battery and the criterion distribution is a maximum. This is done for each of the categories independently of the weighting of the subtests for the other categories. We have now made what Horst (1955) calls a *multiple-absolute prediction*.

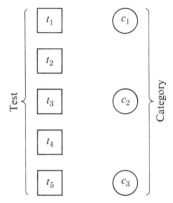

Fig. 12–2 The classification system.

With multiple-absolute prediction we make as certain a differentiation as possible among the individuals in the group with respect to each of the categories separately. This is not, however, what we really wish to achieve when classifying individuals. Rather, we want to make as precise a differentiation as possible among different categories for each individual. We wish to base the choice of category for an individual on as certain an estimate as possible of the differences in the requirements which the different categories make of the individual. We wish to make as certain a *multiple-differential prediction* as possible.

The object of multiple-differential prediction is therefore different from that of multiple-absolute prediction. This difference affects both the choice of tests in the test battery and the statistical treatment of the data.

In multiple-regression analysis we can determine regression equations for the total test battery with respect to each of the classification categories. A given subtest will then be assigned different weights in a test battery when we make placements in different categories. If the factor which the subtest measures is very important for success in a certain category, we should weight it heavily when computing the multiple-correlation coefficient for the battery with respect to this category. The same factor may be less important in other categories; the subtest will then have less weight when it is used for placement in these categories.

Let us suppose that we are to choose subtests for making a classification into a given number of categories with given distributions of criterion data. It may happen that the weights which we assign the subtests when making a multiple-absolute prediction will be highly correlated between different categories. This will mean that the relative position in a group for a single individual will be more or less the same for different categories. The results we then obtain as a basis for classification do not differentiate well among different categories, no matter how well they differentiate among the individuals with respect to each separate category. Certain tests must therefore be replaced by others if we wish to increase the accuracy of the differential prediction. The result may perhaps be a reduction in the accuracy of the multiple-absolute prediction. We choose tests which maximize the difference between the predictions to different categories for the individual, so that the differences between alternative courses of action are as clear as possible. This is done by choosing tests for the test battery which have as high a validity as possible with respect to as few categories as possible, i.e., tests with high *differential validity*. A test which has a high validity but is equally good for each of the categories is of little use as a basis for classification. It is apparent from what was said previously that, the more homogeneous the tests are, the easier it is to carry out differential prediction.

In the preceding section we touched briefly upon the situation where differential prediction can be made for each individual, independently of group membership, and where also the assessment of what is a favorable outcome of the prediction can be made for one individual at a time. The classification becomes considerably more complicated when the number of places in the different alternatives is limited. When assigning an individual to a category we are hampered by the fact that each category can contain only a more or less fixed number of individuals. The restriction can consist of an absolute or relative number of individuals in each category. We must in this case make an *optimal classification*.

This is the situation in military service when people are assigned to different branches of the armed forces, units, etc. We cannot consider the individuals separately and give to each the placement most suitable for him. If we did this, we would soon fill up certain categories, with the result that these alternatives could not be chosen for those remaining individuals for whom one of them would be best. We must thus take into account the solution for every individual at the same time. The solutions which different alternatives offer in a given situation vary in attractiveness. The purpose of the classification is to give a combination of solutions for every individual at the same time, so that the total outcome will be as favorable as possible.

In recent years much attention has been given to the complicated problems of classification in both its theoretical and practical aspects. A leading contributor to this development has been Horst (1954, 1955, 1960a, 1960b). Cronbach and Gleser (1964), with their application of a theoretical decision-making model to problems of differential psychology, have given a new approach to the problem of constructing the test battery for differential prediction and optimal classification so as to give as favorable an outcome as possible.

The purpose of classification is to give as correct an assignment of individuals to categories as possible. If the categories refer to occupations with different demands on the individuals' capabilities, the individuals should be placed or advised so that as many as possible will be rated as good workmen and experience job satisfaction when the assignment of categories has been functioning for a period of time. So far only regression-analysis solutions have been presented, and it is common for classification problems to be approached in this way. When this method is used, the composition of the test battery and the weighting of the results are based on the linear relationships, expressed as correlation coefficients, between each of the subtests, between each of the criterion measures, and between subtests and criterion measures.

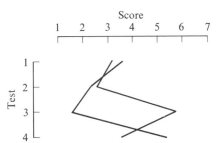

Fig. 12–3 Profiles of test scores for two professional groups.

Another method, one which is less common in practical situations, is classification by means of the *multiple-discriminant function* (cf. Johnson and Jackson, 1959). Here we make no assumptions about the form of the regression, nor do we use relationships between distributions in the form of coefficients for the correlation between predictors and criteria. Instead, we make use of the fact that groups of individuals belonging to the different categories to which the assignment is to be made differ with respect to average level on the selection variables. Let us suppose that the test profiles of two groups of workers, e.g., office workers and auto mechanics, differ with respect to means on four tests in the manner shown in Fig. 12–3. By simple significance testing of one mean difference at a time, we can obtain a measure of the accuracy with which each of the tests differentiates between the two occupational groups. If the reliability of the different tests is the same and the variances are the same for each of the groups on every test, we will then find that Tests 3 and 4 differentiate best, while Tests 1 and 2 differentiate poorly. The assignment of categories will, therefore, in the first instance be based upon Tests 3 and 4. In the multiple-discriminant function the use of every difference is formalized so that the classifications will be as certain as possible. The individual scores are weighted to make up a total sum such that the difference between the means of total scores for the groups of individuals in relation to the variance of total scores within the groups will be a maximum.

The multiple-discriminant function is thus based upon differences in level with respect to scores on the selection instrument. It was pointed out previously that one does not make any assumptions about the form of the regression for the correlation between test scores and success in each of the categories. It should, however, be observed that the presence of such differences between means of the groups' test scores, which are supposed to be valid with respect to category assignment, presupposes some systematic relationship between means of test scores and success in different categories.

When we use the multiple-discriminant function for classification, we place each new individual in the category whose profile of scores on the selection instruments most resembles his own. A consequence of this procedure is that the selection of individuals who are to represent a certain category, and on whose scores the profile for the category will be based, will determine the type of individual who will be recruited to that category. There are different ways of deciding which individuals should represent a certain category when we determine the multiple-discriminant function, in order to make as suitable a recruitment as possible. One well-known example of the application of the discriminant-function principle is the Strong Vocational Interest Blank (cf. Strong, 1955). The responses on this questionnaire for vocational interest are scored so that one can determine the extent to which each individual's interests are similar to those of each of a number of different occupational groups. In order to ensure that representatives of different vocational groups gave differentiating, characteristic responses to the questions, only those who had worked for a considerable time in the occupation with wages higher than the minimum were chosen. The assumption behind this choice is that individuals who remain in the occupation and are successful are suitable for the work and experience job satisfaction. Whether or not these assumptions are reasonable can of course be debated. What should be borne in mind, however, is the effect which a given method of choosing representatives has on the composition of an occupational category. This and other problems are discussed by French (1955), who also summarizes a comparison between multiple-differential prediction based on regression analysis and that based on the discriminant function (see also, e.g., Goldman, 1961, pp. 168–183).

12–4 SELECTION

A common employment situation is that we have a certain number of applicants for a smaller number of positions in a given occupation. We meet the same problem, for example, when we can accept only a fraction of the applicants to some non-compulsory course of education, e.g., a vocational training school. In both cases certain individuals will be accepted while the others must be rejected. We must make a *selection*.

We can distinguish between two selection situations which in part present different problems.

First, we have the situation where there is a given number of places available, which must be filled no matter what qualifications the applicants have. Assuming that we have a sufficient number of applicants, we accept those who have the highest scores on some selection test. The acceptance level on the distribution is determined such that a sufficient number of places are filled.

The acceptance level on the test distribution—often called the *cutoff limit* —will under these circumstances be determined by the qualifications of the applicants with respect to the factor measured by the selection instrument, and the number of applicants in relation to the number of places. Other factors being equal, the greater the number that must be rejected, the higher the cutoff level will be. The higher the members of the applicant group are on the distribution of total scores for the selection variable, the higher the cutoff limit will be. Whether or not a certain individual will be accepted is therefore, in this selection situation, determined by the relation between the characteristics of the individual and the characteristics of the group in which he is included at the time of selection.

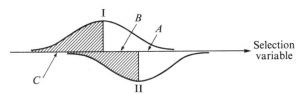

Fig. 12–4 Selection from two groups, I and II, without previously decided cutoff limit.

The situation is shown in Fig. 12–4. A cutoff limit for two groups of the same size but with different qualifications has been fixed so that 50% of the applicants will be accepted and 50% rejected. Individuals in the unshaded part of the distribution will be accepted; those in the shaded area will be rejected. Of the three individuals A, B, and C, A will be selected in both groups, B will be selected if he applies together with Group I but not if he applies in Group II, and C will not be accepted in either group.

A situation of this type where a previously determined number of the applicants is to be accepted is rather common, especially in selection among applicants for educational courses. The method does not present any great problems. We begin by selecting those who have the best qualifications and continue downwards in the distribution until the quota has been filled.

The effectiveness of a selection procedure can be expressed by the proportion of those accepted who succeed in the given course or occupation. This proportion is usually called the *success ratio*. Effectiveness expressed as a success ratio will of course be the greater, the smaller the proportion of the applicants who are to be accepted, i.e., the greater the number of applicants we have to choose among for a given number of places.

The proportion of the applicants who are to be accepted is usually called the *selection ratio*. The situation is shown in Fig. 12–5.

We have a group of applicants for which two cutoff limits X_1 and X_2 have been given. With the cutoff at X_1, we accept only a small number of the applicants; with the cutoff limit at X_2, considerably more. The error distribution around the regression line has been drawn for the cutoff limits X_1 and X_2. We let the score c on the y-axis represent the score on the criterion variable for which the result can be regarded as successful. We can immediately conclude that the risk of failure for those accepted with the

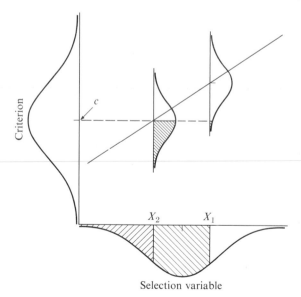

Fig. 12–5 The effect of the size of the selection ratio.

lowest acceptance score for the cutoff limit X_2 is approximately 50%. On the other hand, the risk of failure is very small for the last of those accepted with cutoff limit X_1.

Therefore, the smaller the selection ratio, the greater will be the effectiveness of the selection expressed as a success ratio. Also, as can be seen from Fig. 12–5, the higher the validity coefficient, the greater will be the effectiveness expressed as a success ratio. The higher the validity, the smaller the error deviation of criterion scores around the regression line will be. Thus, for a given critical level on the criterion distribution, the higher the validity, the smaller the risk of failure among those accepted at each level.

This treatment of the selection problem, whereby we consider each group by itself and accept a number determined in advance without considering their relative qualifications, has certain disadvantages. As has been shown, one consequence is that whether an individual is accepted or not depends upon the other applicants who happen to apply on that occasion. One way of minimizing this difficulty is to make selections as infrequently as possible with as many applicants as possible. Other factors being equal, the more often we make the selection, the smaller the groups will be who are tested on each selection occasion and the more the cutoff limit will fluctuate from occasion to occasion.

This difficulty can also be solved in another way if it is possible to estimate the number of individuals required and the number who will apply during a lengthy period of time. Since we then know the selection ratio for the total number of applicants during this period, we can fix a cutoff limit which will give us the number required. This cutoff limit will be the same for every group. A single individual will be judged in relation to the same norm regardless of the group of applicants in which he happens to be included. The fact that the selection ratio will vary from group to group is one of the difficulties which can sometimes restrict the application of this selection procedure.

In the second type of selection situation, certain degrees of given traits are required for the duties or training for which the selection is to be made. One attempts to measure these traits with the selection instrument. In order to be accepted, an individual must satisfy the minimum requirements. In this situation the decision whether or not a certain individual is to be accepted does not depend on characteristics of the other applicants or how many other applicants there are. Acceptance or rejection of the individual is determined by the relation between the individual's position on the selection distribution and the minimum requirements which have been determined for the training or job in question. Selection can be made for one individual at a time.

A question which must be answered in this selection situation is the following: Where is the cutoff limit to be located on the test distribution in order that the individuals who lie above this level and are accepted also lie above the critical level on the criterion distribution, i.e., in order that those accepted really fulfill the minimum requirements for the duties or training for which the selection is made? Knowing the error deviation for prediction from a distribution of test scores to a criterion for validity coefficients of normal size, we can see that the cutoff limit can scarcely be placed so high on the test distribution as to ensure with complete certainty that every individual selected really has the necessary qualifications. We must take a certain risk that individuals who are selected lack these qualifications, i.e., in fact lie below the critical level on the criterion. Furthermore, we are ignoring the personal sacrifices which must be made by those who will be rejected even though they are above the critical level on the criterion distribution.

Let us look at the simple case illustrated in Fig. 12–6. We know that to pass a certain college course requires the position z_c on the criterion. What will happen if we accept, for example, every individual for whom the best possible prediction—the predicted score—is at least this y-score?

The x-score which is to be determined in this case is that for which the critical y-score z_c can be predicted. This x-score is obtained from the equation $z_y' = r_{xy}z_x$ (Eq. 3–4):

$$z_x = z_y'/r_{xy}. \tag{12–2}$$

We can now see immediately that we will select a certain number of individuals who in fact lie below the critical level on the criterion distribution. These are represented by the shaded part of the probable distribution of y-scores around the predicted y-score in Fig. 12–6. For a randomly selected individual with a test score z_x, the probability is as great as 50% that he belongs among those who should be rejected. As a rule we do not wish to take such a risk for any single individual.

The higher the cutoff limit on the selection distribution, the less is the probability that an individual who is selected belongs among those who are below the critical level on the criterion distribution. In the example given, we should raise the cutoff limit if we wish to reduce the risk of an individual's being incorrectly selected. But how much do we have to raise it in order that the risk of selecting an individual who falls below the critical level on the criterion variable will be of a predetermined size?

We can, for example, decide that no individual will be accepted for whom the risk is greater than 10%. In this case the level on the selection distribution has to be determined so that the risk of incorrect placement for those individuals who have the lowest acceptance score is such that not more than one out of ten who were accepted should in fact have been rejected. A general equation can be derived for determining the required x-score in situations such as this. The situation is illustrated in Fig. 12–7.

We wish to find z_x, the prediction score for which 10% of the individuals will probably fail to fulfill the requirements made by level z_c on the criterion distribution. The probable distribution of criterion scores around the predicted score z_y' is drawn in Fig. 12–7. The shaded area makes up 10% of

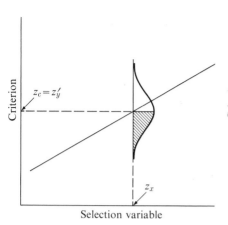

Fig. 12–6 The effect of the location of the cutoff limit so that the maximum chance of failure for a single individual is 0.50.

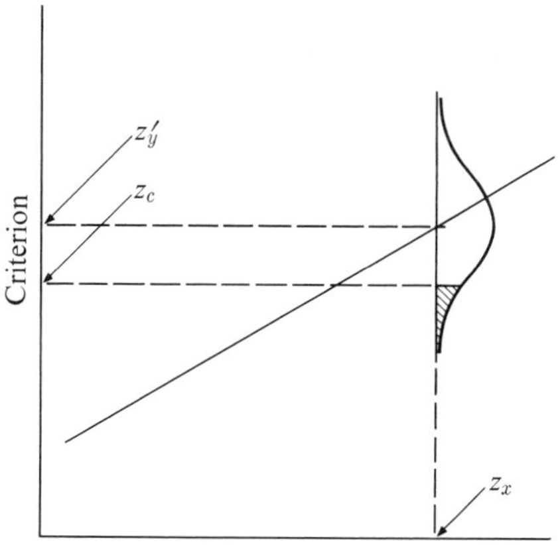

Fig. 12–7 The effect of the location of the cutoff limit for an estimated maximum chance of failure of a predetermined size.

the error distribution which represents the risk of incorrect placement we have decided to take.

The problem will be solved if we can determine the value of z_y', since we can then also obtain z_x from the equation $z_y' = r_{xy}z_x$. We assume that the validity coefficient r_{xy} is known.

Since we have decided upon the risk of failure we are prepared to accept, we can also give the standard score in a normal distribution with standard deviation 1.0 for the position which divides the probability distribution around the predicted y-score in the proportions determined by the risk we wish to take. This standard score is denoted by z_p. If the risk is 10%, z_p will thus be the standard score which divides a normal distribution in the proportion 10:90.

The critical level z_c on the criterion distribution can now be expressed as a standard score on the error distribution in question by means of the well-known equation $z_x = (X - M_x)/s_x$. This standard score is to be chosen so that it cuts off 10% of the error distribution; this means that it is to be the same as the standard score which cuts off 10% of a normal distribution, namely, z_p. Since the scores on the x- and y-distributions are expressed as z-scores, the standard deviation of the error distribution is $\sqrt{1 - r_{xy}^2}$. If we now express the critical level z_c as a standard score on the error distribution and equate this expression with z_p, we obtain the following:

$$z_p = (z_c - z_y')/\sqrt{1 - r_{xy}^2}.$$

Solving for z_y' we obtain

$$z_y' = z_c - z_p\sqrt{1 - r_{xy}^2}. \tag{12–3}$$

The numerator of the right-hand side of Eq. (12–2) can now be replaced by the right-hand side of Eq. (12–3):

$$z_x = \frac{z_c - z_p\sqrt{1 - r_{xy}^2}}{r_{xy}}, \tag{12–4}$$

where z_c is the critical score on the criterion variable, and z_p is the standard score which cuts off the part of a normal distribution which represents the given risk.

Equation (12–4) thus gives the formula for determining the cutoff limit (z_x) so that the risk for incorrect placement of an individual does not exceed a given value (p), when the qualifications required on the criterion distribution are of a given magnitude (z_c).

One should bear in mind when using Eq. (12–4) that the expression $z_p\sqrt{1 - r_{xy}^2}$ takes a negative sign as soon as p is less than 0.50, as is ordinarily the case in this type of situation. The critical level is then located in the part of the probability distribution which has negative z-scores. This means that, when p is less than 0.50 and the critical level lies *above* the mean of the y-distribution (and is therefore a positive standard score on the criterion distribution), we obtain the numerator as the *sum* of the critical limit score on y (i.e., z_c) and the distance $z_p\sqrt{1 - r_{xy}^2}$. Conversely, when p is less than 0.50 and the critical level lies *below* the mean of the criterion distribution (and is therefore a negative standard score on the criterion distribution), we obtain the numerator as the *difference* between z_c and $z_p\sqrt{1 - r_{xy}^2}$.

We can now compute from Eq. (12–4) the cutoff limits on the selection distribution which with varying degrees of risk correspond to various critical scores on the criterion distribution. These scores can be used to form an *expectancy table.*

We have dealt with two selection situations in this section: first, that in which we select a number of the applicants without determining any selection level in advance; second, that in which an individual in order to be selected must exceed a certain minimum level on the selection distribution. Many selection situations are in practice neither the one nor the other, but a combination of the two. For selection with a fixed cutoff limit, the number who are above this level may be greater than the number of available places. The same procedures which are used when there is no fixed cutoff limit are then applied to selection among those who satisfy the qualification requirements.

It should be pointed out that we have assumed a linear relationship between scores for the selection variable and measures of success. Sometimes, however, nonlinear relationships are obtained. In some situations where the regression line for the prediction of success in a certain occupation is curvilinear, we need to determine two cutoff limits. The situation is shown in Fig. 12–8.

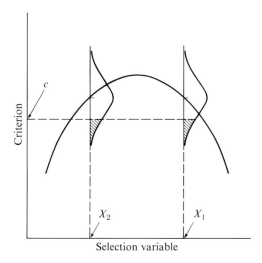

Fig. 12–8 Selection when regression is nonlinear.

The error distributions around the curvilinear regression line have been drawn for scores X_1 and X_2. If the shaded part of the distributions gives the risk of failure we are prepared to accept when selecting individuals, those individuals who have scores between X_1 and X_2 will be accepted, while those who have scores higher than X_1 or lower than X_2 will be rejected.

12–5   LINEAR COMBINATION OF SUBTEST SCORES; MULTIPLE-CUTOFF IN SELECTION

In most selection situations the final decision to accept or reject is based upon the results on several tests. The various subscores can be used as a basis for decision-making in several different ways. Here we shall deal with only the two most common ones.

For the sake of simplicity we shall choose an example consisting of two subtests which are to be used for selection with a fixed cutoff limit.

The most common method of using the two subtest scores has already been discussed in the first section of this chapter, where the principles of multiple-regression analysis were given. The critical level on the selection distribution lies on a total distribution where each individual has a total score made up of his weighted or unweighted subtest scores. The critical level can now be obtained in several different ways. The same total score can be obtained as the sum of a high score on Test 1 and a low score on Test 2, but also as a sum of a low score on Test 1 and a high score on Test 2. It is the sum of the subtest scores which decides whether an individual is accepted or not. It is of no importance on which of the subtests he has the better result.

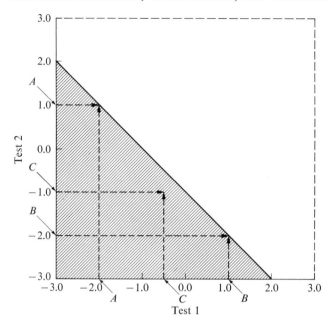

Fig. 12–9 Linear compensatory model for combination of data for selection and classification.

The principle is illustrated in Fig. 12–9. The two axes represent subtest distributions for Tests 1 and 2, which are to be combined. We assume that the cutoff level is the score −1.0 in the distribution of subtest scores. The subtest distributions have the same standard deviation, 1.0. The oblique straight line joins the points whose projection on the axis gives the same sum, namely, the critical level −1.0. The position of this straight line can be computed by means of Eq. (12–1). Every point on the line gives the same sum of subtest scores. Individuals *A* and *B* thus have the same total score and are situated on the cutoff limit. The sum of subtest scores for individual *C* is, however, lower than the cutoff level. All sums in the shaded area lie below the cutoff limit; individuals who obtain these total scores will therefore be rejected. Every sum in the unshaded area lies above the cutoff limit, and individuals obtaining these total scores will be accepted.

We have now made a *linear combination* of scores. This can be called a *compensatory model*. It is possible for someone who is weak in one area to compensate by being strong in another. Multiple-regression analysis and factor analysis are based on a linear combination of data from subdistributions. In both cases an individual's total score is obtained as a sum of scores. We give the various scores different weights—regression weights in multiple-correlation analysis, factor loadings in factor analysis (see p. 183).

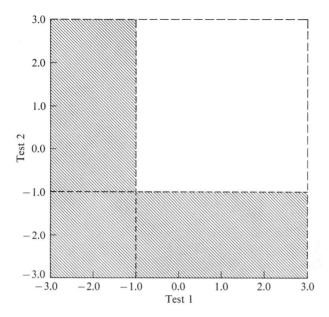

Fig. 12–10 Conjunctive model for selection and classification.

In some situations a linear combination of scores is not the best method. This is the case when a critical level must be exceeded on several subtest distributions. It is not possible to compensate for weakness in certain respects by strength in others. If the individual is to be accepted, he must exceed the cutoff limit on each of the subtests. We use a *multiple-cutoff method*. This can be called a *conjunctive model* (cf. Coombs, 1964). A pilot must have good eyesight *and* good theoretical training *and* good coordinating ability. He cannot compensate for poor eyesight no matter how good his theoretical training or coordinating ability might be.

The multiple-cutoff method is illustrated in Fig. 12–10.

The same test distributions as in Fig. 12–9 used here for selection by the multiple-cutoff method. We suppose that the cutoff level for both the subtests is located at the standard score −1.0. Those who will be selected by means of this model thus belong to the best 84% on each of the distributions. It is not sufficient to be located among the best 84% with respect to the sum of the results on Test 1 and Test 2, as is the case with linear combination of scores. The scores for all individuals in the shaded area are below the critical level on at least one of the subtests. These individuals will therefore be rejected.

Selection based on linear combination of scores leads to a somewhat different result from that obtained by selection with multiple-cutoff methods.

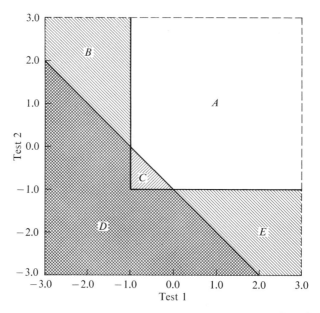

Fig. 12–11 Comparison between a compensatory and a conjunctive model.

Certain individuals will be selected with one method but rejected with the other. This effect is illustrated in Fig. 12–11 with the same cutoff levels as in Figs. 12–9 and 12–10. Individuals in the unshaded area *A* will be selected with both methods, and individuals in the shaded area *D* will be rejected with both methods. Individuals in the shaded areas *B* and *E* will be selected with a linear combination of scores, since the sum of the subtest scores lies above the critical level on the total variable. They will, however, be rejected with the multiple-cutoff method, since they fall below the cutoff level on one of the subtests. Individuals in the shaded area *C* will be accepted with the multiple-cutoff method but rejected if the decision is based on a linear combination of scores.

A third model should be mentioned, though it is one with very few practical applications. It is the *disjunctive model*, in which individuals to be selected must reach a certain level on *either* one of two distributions of scores on which the selection is based.

12–6   COST AND UTILITY IN SELECTION AND CLASSIFICATION

An important and recurrent question is this: What advantages do we gain by using a certain procedure for selection or classification in a given situation? The profit or utility must be judged in relation to the results obtained with some other method which requires less time and work. In most selection and classification situations, we obtain a better result even with traditional methods, without using (for instance) aptitude and intelligence tests, than with random procedures.

It should be realized that a certain success ratio will be obtained in selection and classification situations even by drawing lots, a completely random procedure. Even without a systematic selection procedure a certain proportion of those accepted will be successful. The size of this proportion depends on the quality of the applicants in relation to the requirements. The proportion of the accepted applicants who are successful will be equal to the proportion of the applicants who have sufficient qualifications for the given activity, job, or course. If 50% of the applicants can pass a given college course, we can expect to have a success ratio of 0.50 if the selection is made randomly, no matter what the proportion is between individuals accepted and applicants. In a similar manner, if 25% of the applicants fulfill the requirements, we can expect approximately 25% of those selected to be successful if the selection is made randomly.

We increase the effectiveness of the selection or classification procedure by basing it on scores from standardized test batteries. By making the test more and more valid with respect to relevant criteria we also increase the chance that those who are selected on the basis of the test data are in fact those who will be successful.

We saw previously that the effectiveness of selection as measured by the success ratio depends partly on the validity coefficient and partly on the selection ratio. We must also, however, take into account the proportion of the applicants who have sufficient qualifications to be successful in the given college course or job. The smaller this proportion, the greater is the advantage to be gained by putting the selection procedure on a more systematic basis. If every applicant satisfies the requirements, no improvement in the form of a smaller number of failures can be made by using a more comprehensive selection procedure. There can be no failures in this situation, no matter what selection procedure is used. In such situations one can often, however, find a better selection procedure by considering the differences between the study performance, production, or work quality that can be achieved on the average by workers chosen by means of random selection, and that achieved by workers selected by means of some more systematic procedure.

The possible improvement also depends on the dispersion of selection scores. The greater the dispersion, the greater is the improvement which can be made. If everyone who passes the qualification level has approximately the same qualifications, there is not much to be gained by a finer differentiation among the applicants. It is of little importance which we accept and which we reject. If the dispersion is great, i.e., if the applicants show considerable differences with respect to qualifications, we gain by determining more accurately the order in which the applicants should be selected.

The improvement made possible by more systematic selection also depends upon the selection ratio. The nearer the selection ratio is to 0.50, other things being equal, the greater is the gain obtained by a given selection procedure for a fixed cost, and the more work it is worthwhile to devote to the improvement of the selection instruments (cf. Cronbach and Gleser, 1964).

As was previously pointed out, the degree of improvement which can be made by a new selection procedure is obtained by comparing the outcome with what would have been obtained with a previously applied procedure or with a purely random one. We have also pointed out that we will obtain a certain number of successful outcomes even for purely random selection or classification. Assuming bivariate normal distributions, we can estimate in advance the probable number of successful outcomes for different validity coefficients. We can then estimate the improvement over a completely random selection or classification procedure. This computation is shown in Table 12–1, where the proportions of the individuals selected who can be expected to succeed in the training or occupation is given for different validity coefficients and for different selection ratios. It is assumed that 50% of the applicants would have succeeded if everyone had been allowed to make the attempt.

Table 12–1 Estimated success ratios for different validity coefficients and selection ratios, when 50% of the applicants satisfy the qualification requirements

r_{xy}	Selection ratios									
	0.05	0.10	0.20	0.30	0.40	0.50	0.60	0.70	0.80	0.90
0.00	0.50	0.50	0.50	0.50	0.50	0.50	0.50	0.50	0.50	0.50
0.20	0.67	0.64	0.59	0.59	0.58	0.56	0.55	0.54	0.53	0.52
0.40	0.82	0.78	0.73	0.69	0.66	0.63	0.61	0.58	0.56	0.53
0.50	0.88	0.84	0.78	0.74	0.70	0.67	0.63	0.60	0.57	0.54
0.60	0.94	0.90	0.84	0.79	0.75	0.70	0.66	0.62	0.59	0.54
0.70	0.98	0.95	0.90	0.85	0.80	0.75	0.70	0.65	0.60	0.55
0.80	1.00	0.99	0.95	0.90	0.85	0.80	0.73	0.67	0.61	0.55

We can confirm what was said earlier from the first row in Table 12–1. When the selection is made purely randomly, i.e., when the validity coefficient for the selection procedure is zero, the estimated proportion of individuals who are successful is equal to the proportion of the total number of applicants who satisfy the qualification requirements.

Taking any row whatsoever, for instance, the row for validity coefficient 0.50, we can establish that with an increasing selection ratio we have a decreasing estimated success ratio.

We can thus compute the probable improvement to be obtained by using a more comprehensive selection procedure than that used previously, assuming that we have normal bivariate distributions. Obtained improvements are often based in practice upon empirically obtained scores from similar selection and classification situations.

So far we have discussed possible improvements in the form of a reduction of the number of individuals who fail in the occupation or course of education. When we know the costs of employing individuals in an occupation in which they will be unsuccessful after a period of time, or of accepting individuals for a college course which they will fail, we can state the improvement which will be made in a certain selection or classification situation in terms of money.

We have said that a selection procedure can be improved by increasing the validity of the tests and by increasing the number of individuals tested in relation to the number selected. In many situations, considerable improvements can be made by these means, if we do not have to take a number of practical difficulties into account. Such steps cost money and require time and work. Every addition of a new test in order to increase the validity of the selection procedure, and every increase in the number of individuals tested, involves extra costs. We should also in certain cases include in the costs those individuals who are rejected although they would have been successful in the college course or occupation. Every improvement must thus be weighed against the costs involved. Somewhere on the way toward higher validity in the test battery and/or a lower selection ratio, we reach an optimum in the relation between improvements and costs. It should be observed, however, that the improvements made with even a relatively modest increase in the number of correct diagnoses or predictions are considerably greater than is usually thought.

The problem of improvements and costs has another aspect. If we have certain resources of time, labor, and money to spend on a series of improvements, these resources can be used in various ways in order to obtain information, and we can use a given amount of different types of information in a number of different ways. We can choose among a number of alternative actions, some of which give a better outcome than others. A contribution to the whole problem of the relationship between improvements and costs in classification and selection has been made in recent years on the basis of decision theory derived from mathematical statistics. The application of a decision-making model to differential psychology is presented by Cronbach and Gleser (1964). Decision theory gives a general model for collecting information and using it in a systematic test strategy, so that the total outcome of a series of decisions will be as favorable as possible.

PROBLEMS (Chapters 11 and 12)

1. Compute the criterion score which is the best possible prediction from the predictor scores (a) -1.0, (b) 0.0, (c) 0.75, and (d) 1.4, if the validity coefficient is 0.70. Predictor and criterion scores are given as standard scores. Assume linear regression.

2. In selection for a college course the applicants are rated after interviews on a nine-point scale, 1–9. The ratings were normally distributed with mean 5 and standard deviation 2. After completing the course the same individuals were rated on a scale from 1 to 19 with mean 10 and standard deviation 3. The correlation between the two ratings was found to be 0.35. A student obtained a score of 4 on the interview rating. What is the best estimate of his final rating? Within which rating scores will his obtained score lie with (a) 68%, (b) 95% certainty?

3. The correlation between entrance examination scores and final grades is 0.60. Scores on the entrance examination are transformed to T-scores ($M = 50$, $s = 10$). The grades have $M = 4.0$ and $s = 1.2$. Individual A has a score of 55 on the entrance examination. (a) Predict his final grade. (b) What is the risk that he will drop below the pass level 3.0? Draw the figure.

4. A predictor is measured on the scale 1–21 ($M = 11$, $s = 3$). The criterion variable is measured on the scale 1–11 ($M = 6$, $s = 2$). The coefficient of validity is 0.66. Above which criterion score will approximately 2.5% of those tested with predictor score 7 be located? Draw the complete figure.

5. The correlation between scores for Tests 1 and 2 in a vocational guidance test battery is 0.50. Scores are on a T-scale ($M = 50$, $s = 10$). An individual has obtained the score 60 for Test 1. Compute (a) the risk that he will fall on or below the mean 50 for Test 2 and (b) the probability that he will obtain 70 or more on Test 2. Draw the figure.

6. How much will the relative standard error of estimate be reduced when the validity coefficient is (a) 0.30, (b) 0.60, (c) 0.90, and (d) 0.95?

7. Draw the curve for the relation between r_{xy} and the proportion of the variance which is predicted.

8. Insert the values $s_{yx}^2 = 0.1$ and $s_y^2 = 1.0$ in Eq. (11–6). Compute r when the value of s_y^2 is reduced. Draw the curve of the relation between them. Compare the curve with that obtained in Problem 7.

9. The correlation between test scores (t) and criterion scores (g) has been found to be 0.60. The reliabilities are $r_{tt} = 0.85$ and $r_{gg} = 0.78$ respectively. Compute (a) the theoretical correlation between the variables measured, and (b) the correlation between obtained test scores and the true scores for the criterion variable.

10. A newly constructed test has split-half reliability 0.86. The correlation between test scores and criterion scores is 0.54. The reliability of the criterion is 0.62. Estimate the correlation, correcting for the unreliability of the criterion measurement.

11. What will be the reliability and validity of a test which is increased in length 4 times when the original validity is 0.65 and reliability 0.88?

12. A school entrance examination gives scores with $M = 70$ and $s = 10$. School grades are added to give a total score for each individual, where $M = 18$ and $s = 4$ and where the pass level is 12. The correlation between the entrance examination and the grades is 0.65. Determine a cutoff limit such that no one who is accepted has a risk of failure greater than 10%. Draw the complete figure.

13. Test the result in Problem 12 by predicting grades from the score obtained as the suitable cutoff limit (Eq. 3–13), and compute the risk of obtaining grades lower than 12 with this score.

14. The critical level which must be exceeded on a given criterion variable is a standard score of $+0.6$. The validity of the prediction instrument is 0.60. (a) Where should the cutoff limit be placed so that the poorest of the individuals accepted will have less than a 10% risk of failure? (b) Where should the cutoff limit be placed if the critical level is -1.2 and the risk of failure must not be greater than 5% for any single individual? Draw the complete figure.

REFERENCES

COOMBS, C. H. (1964). *A theory of data.* New York: Wiley.

CRONBACH, L. J., and G. C. GLESER (1964). *Psychological tests and personnel decisions.* Urbana: University of Illinois Press.

FRENCH, J. W. (1955). The logic of and assumptions underlying differential testing. In *Invitational conference on testing problems.* Princeton, N.J.: Educational Testing Service.

GOLDMAN, L. (1961). *Using tests in counseling.* New York: Appleton-Century-Crofts.

HORST, P. (1954). A technique for the development of a differential prediction battery. *Psychol. Monogr.,* **68,** No. 9.

——— (1955). A technique for the development of a multiple absolute prediction battery. *Psychol. Monogr.,* **69,** No. 5.

——— (1960a). Predictor elimination techniques for determining multiple prediction batteries. *Psychol. Rep.,* Monogr. Suppl., 1.

——— (1960b). Optimal estimates of multiple criteria with restrictions on the covariance matrix of estimated criteria. *Psychol. Rep.,* Monogr. Suppl., 6.

JOHNSON, P. O., and R. W. B. JACKSON (1959). *Modern statistical methods: descriptive and inductive.* Chicago: Rand McNally.

McNEMAR, Q. (1962). *Psychological statistics.* New York: Wiley.

STRONG, E. K. (1955). *Vocational interests 18 years after college.* Minneapolis: University of Minneapolis Press.

Suggested reading

ANASTASI, A. (1961). *Psychological testing* (2nd ed.). New York: Macmillan.

FRENCH, J. W. (1964). Comparative predictions of high-school grades by pure-factor aptitude, information and personality measures. *Educ. Psychol. Measmt.,* **24,** 321–329.

GHISELLI, E. E. (1964). *Theory of psychological measurement.* New York: McGraw-Hill.

JONES, L. V., and R. D. BOOK (1960). Multiple discriminant analysis to "ways to live" ratings from six cultural groups. *Sociometry*, **23,** 162–176.

LORD, F. M. (1952). Notes on a problem of multiple classification. *Psychometrika*, **17,** 297–304.

——— (1962). Cutting scores and errors of measurement. *Psychometrika*, **22,** 19–30.

——— (1963). Cutting scores and errors of measurement—a second case. *Educ. Psychol. Measmt.*, **23,** 63–68.

MADDEN, J. M., and R. A. BOTTENBERGER (1963). Use of an all possible combination solution of certain multiple regression problems. *J. Appl. Psychol.*, **47,** 365–366.

McQUITTY, L. L. (1961). A method for selecting patterns to differentiate categories of people. *Educ. Psychol. Measmt.*, **21,** 85–94.

——— (1963). Best classifying every individual at every level. *Educ. Psychol. Measmt.*, **23,** 337–345.

MOLLENKOPF, W. G. (1952). Some aspects of the problem of differential prediction. *Educ. Psychol. Measmt.*, **12,** 39–44.

NUNNALLY, J. (1964). *Educational measurement and evaluation.* New York: McGraw-Hill.

RAO, C. R. (1952). *Advanced statistical methods in biometric research.* New York: Wiley.

SOLOMON, H. (1961). *Studies in item analysis and prediction.* Standford: Stanford University Press.

THORNDIKE, R. L. (1949). *Personnel selection.* New York: Wiley.

CHAPTER 13

Factor Theory, Reliability, and Validity

13–1 SUBTERMS OF TRUE VARIANCE

Every obtained score is considered to be composed of two components, a true score T and an error score e; thus $t = T + e$. The total variance is composed of the variance of true scores and the variance of error scores ($s_t^2 = s_T^2 + s_e^2$). The error variance is in turn considered to be composed of a number of uncorrelated variance terms, as has been discussed in Chapter 8.

The variance of true scores can be broken down into subvariance terms in the same way as the error variance. The different parts of the true variance are then taken to be determined by factors which are independent of each other. This assumes that each individual true score T_j can be broken down into components ($T_{ja} + T_{jb} + T_{jc} + \cdots$), where the magnitude of each component for an individual j is determined by a single factor (A, B, C, etc.) which is uncorrelated with every other. The various true components which are included in each obtained score will therefore be uncorrelated with each other, and the true variance will be made up of the sum of the variances determined by the m different factors:

$$s_T^2 = s_a^2 + s_b^2 + s_c^2 + \cdots + s_m^2, \qquad (13\text{–}1)$$

where s_a^2 is the variance determined by factor A, s_b^2 is the variance determined by factor B, and s_m^2 is the variance determined by factor M. The total variance (s_t^2) can now be written

$$s_t^2 = s_a^2 + s_b^2 + s_c^2 + \cdots + s_m^2 + s_e^2. \qquad (13\text{–}2)$$

Dividing both sides by s_t^2, the contribution of each factor to the total variance can be expressed as a proportion of the total variance:

$$\frac{s_t^2}{s_t^2} = \frac{s_a^2}{s_t^2} + \frac{s_b^2}{s_t^2} + \frac{s_c^2}{s_t^2} + \cdots + \frac{s_m^2}{s_t^2} + \frac{s_e^2}{s_t^2} ;$$

$$1.00 = a_t^2 + b_t^2 + c_t^2 + \cdots + m_t^2 + e_t^2, \tag{13–3}$$

where a_t^2 is the proportion of the total test variance which consists of true variance and is determined by factor A, b_t^2 is the proportion of the total test variance which consists of true variance and is determined by factor B, m_t^2 is the proportion of the total test variance which consists of true variance and is determined by factor M, and e_t^2 is the proportion of the total test variance which consists of error variance.

13–2   COMMUNALITY, SPECIFIC VARIANCE, AND ERROR VARIANCE

The terms communality and specific variance should be introduced here.

Communality is the proportion of the total variance which a test has in common with other tests in a given correlation matrix, a variance which thus gives rise to correlation between the given test and the others. It is determined by factors which are common to the given test and the others. This variance is based entirely upon true components. Communality is written h^2.

The *specific variance* of a test is that part of the true variance which does not appear systematically in other tests in a given correlation matrix, and does not therefore contribute to the correlation between the given test and other tests or criteria included in the matrix. The proportion of the total test variance which consists of specific variance is written v^2. The proportion of the total variance which consists of true variance can therefore be expressed as the sum of the communality and specific variance:

$$s_T^2/s_t^2 = h_t^2 + v_t^2. \tag{13–4}$$

It should now be apparent that the relative magnitudes of the communality and the specific variance for a given test are not determined once and for all, but depend instead on the properties of the other tests which are included in the correlation matrix on a given occasion. However, they always constitute all of the variance of true components.

Reliability was previously defined as the proportion of the total variance which is made up of the variance of true components. Reliability can now be written in the following way by splitting up the true variance into communality and specific variance (see the discussion on true variance of parallel tests, pp. 102–104):

$$r_{tt} = h_t^2 + v_t^2. \tag{13–5}$$

Since the main object of the following discussion is to illustrate the dependence of validity on the test's factor structure, we will distinguish between, on the one hand, communality (h^2) and, on the other hand, *unique variance* (denoted here by u^2), i.e., the variance which is unique to the test and is composed of the specific variance and error variance. It follows from this that

$$h^2 + u^2 = 1.00. \qquad (13\text{--}6)$$

It should be observed that the communality (h^2) is the only part of the total test variance which can be used for meaningful predictions or diagnoses. It sets a limit to the maximum validity we can hope to achieve for the test. Specific variance with respect to a given criterion, though it is true variance and contributes to the reliability, does not contribute to the validity of the test with that criterion.

Table 13–1

Test	Common factor variance, Factor A B C D $\cdots$ M	Communality h^2	Unique variance u^2
1	$a_1^2\ b_1^2\ c_1^2\ d_1^2 \cdots m_1^2$	$a_1^2 + b_1^2 + c_1^2 + d_1^2 + \cdots + m_1^2$	u_1^2
2	$a_2^2\ b_2^2\ c_2^2\ d_2^2 \cdots m_2^2$	$a_2^2 + b_2^2 + c_2^2 + d_2^2 + \cdots + m_2^2$	u_2^2
3	$a_3^2\ b_3^2\ c_3^2\ d_3^2 \cdots m_3^2$	$a_3^2 + b_3^2 + c_3^2 + d_3^2 + \cdots + m_3^2$	u_3^2
$\vdots$			$\vdots$
g	$a_g^2\ b_g^2\ c_g^2\ d_g^2 \cdots m_g^2$	$a_g^2 + b_g^2 + c_g^2 + d_g^2 + \cdots + m_g^2$	u_g^2
$\vdots$			$\vdots$

a_g^2: the proportion of the total test variance in test g which is made up of true variance and is determined by factor A

m_g^2: the proportion of the total test variance in test g which is made up of true variance and is determined by factor M

Table 13–1 shows in matrix form the terms now being discussed. A numerical example is given in Table 13–2. The total variance in four tests included in a correlation matrix can be explained in terms of five independent factors. Thus 36% of the variance in Test 1 is determined by factor A, 4% by factor B, 36% by factor C, and 9% by factor D, while factor F has no effect on the variation in the test. All in all, the common factor variance thus makes up 85% of the total variance in Test 1, which is denoted by the communality score 0.85. The unique variance of the test thus makes up 15% of the total variance.

Table 13–2

Test	Factor					h^2	u^2
	A	B	C	D	F		
1	0.36	0.04	0.36	0.09	0.00	0.85	0.15
2	0.16	0.00	0.12	0.00	0.64	0.92	0.08
3	0.00	0.49	0.00	0.25	0.16	0.90	0.10
⋮							⋮
g	0.25	0.25	0.16	0.09	0.04	0.79	0.21
⋮							⋮

13–3 FACTOR LOADING

We can now continue the discussion begun in Chapter 11, where the following expression was derived:

$$r_{xy}^2 = s_{y'}^2 / s_y^2.$$

According to this expression the squared correlation coefficient, the coefficient of determination, gives the proportion of the total variance of the one distribution which can be predicted from the other. If there is a causal relationship such that the individuals' scores on y are dependent on their scores on x, the squared correlation coefficient gives the proportion of the total variance in y which is determined by the variation in x.

If the positions on the continuum for factor A are known for individuals whose scores have been obtained on test t, the squared correlation coefficient for the relation between scores on the continuum for factor A and test scores (r_{At}^2) will give the proportion of the total variance of obtained scores which consists of variance determined by the individuals' positions on the continuum for factor A. But this is the variance previously denoted in this chapter by a_t^2. We thus obtain the following:

$$r_{At}^2 = a_t^2; \tag{13–7}$$

$$r_{At} = a_t. \tag{13–8}$$

If the total test variance is 1.0, the correlation coefficient for the relationship between factor and test (r_{At}) is thus equal to the standard deviation of the distribution of test scores which can be predicted from the individuals' positions on the factor continuum.

The variance terms can now be replaced by the squared correlation coefficients for the relationship between test and factor in question, as shown in Table 13–3. Only the common variance terms have been included.

Numerical values for the squared correlation coefficients in Table 13–3 can be found in Table 13–2. We need only take the square root of these values in

Table 13–3

Test	Factor				
	A	B	C	D	F
1	r_{1A}^2	r_{1B}^2	r_{1C}^2	r_{1D}^2	r_{1F}^2
2	r_{2A}^2	r_{2B}^2	r_{2C}^2	r_{2D}^2	r_{2F}^2
3	r_{3A}^2	r_{3B}^2	r_{3C}^2	r_{3D}^2	r_{3F}^2
⋮					⋮
g	r_{gA}^2	r_{gB}^2	r_{gC}^2	r_{gD}^2	r_{gF}^2
⋮					

order to obtain the numerical values of the correlation coefficients. These coefficients are shown in Table 13–4, which thus expresses the degree of relationship between the individuals' positions on each of the five factor continua and on each of the test distributions.

The coefficients shown in Table 13–4 give the correlation between test scores and factor scores. The correlation between Test 1 and factor A is 0.60, the correlation between Test 1 and factor B is 0.20, etc. A matrix with coefficients of this type is called a *factor matrix*, and the coefficients *factor loadings*.

The size of the factor loadings in a factor matrix is determined by means of *factor analysis*. One starts from a correlation matrix which contains every intercorrelation for the tests on which the factor analysis is based. By factor analysis we determine (a) the smallest number of factors needed to explain all of the tests' common variance, and (b) the correlation between each of these factors and each of the tests, and consequently the proportion of the total test variance which is determined for each of the tests by each of the factors. (A classic in the literature about factor analysis is Thurstone, 1947. A standard modern work is Harman, 1960.)

Table 13–4

Test	Factor				
	A	B	C	D	F
1	0.60	0.20	0.60	0.30	0.00
2	0.40	0.00	0.35	0.00	0.80
3	0.00	0.70	0.00	0.50	0.40
⋮					⋮
g	0.50	0.50	0.40	0.30	0.20
⋮					⋮

The true component of the score which an individual obtains on a multi-factor test (i.e., a test in which the obtained variance is determined by more than one factor, a heterogeneous test) can be divided into subcomponents, each of which can be predicted from one of the factors which determine the total variance. The subcomponents will therefore be uncorrelated. When we know the correlation between the individuals' positions on two distributions, we can, starting from an individual's position on the one distribution, predict the same individual's score on the other distribution (Eq. 3–4). We can now express the position of an individual j on the continuum for factor A as a standard score, z_{aj}. From this score, the individual's standard score can be predicted on each of the test distributions where factor A determines a part of the variance and with which factor A thus has a positive correlation. The standard score for variable x predicted from factor A can then be written

$$z'_{xj(A)} = r_{xA}z_{aj}. \tag{13–9}$$

But the factor loadings are numerical expressions for the correlation between scores on each of the tests included in the factor matrix and on each of the factor continua. The correlation coefficient (r_{xA}) for the relation between test scores for x and factor scores for A can thus be replaced by the factor loading (a_x) for x with respect to A:

$$z'_{xj(A)} = a_x z_{aj}. \tag{13–10}$$

In the same way, the component in individual j's standard score on x which is determined by his position on factor B can be predicted from his standard score for that factor:

$$z'_{xj(B)} = b_x z_{bj}.$$

Every component in the individual's total true standard score can be predicted in this way from the factors which determine the total variance of the variable in question. The individual's total predicted score is made up of the sum of the predicted subcomponents. The total *predicted* score on x (z'_{xj}) can then be written

$$z'_{xj} = a_x z_{aj} + b_x z_{bj} + \cdots + m_x z_{mj}. \tag{13–11}$$

An individual's total *obtained* score will then consist of this total predicted score and an error score whose magnitude depends on the test's unreliability:

$$z_{xj} = a_x z_{aj} + b_x z_{bj} + \cdots + m_x z_{mj} + z_{ej}, \tag{13–12}$$

where z_{xj} is the score obtained for individual j on variable x, a_x is the factor loading in variable x with respect to factor A, z_{aj} is individual j's standard score on factor A, $a_x z_{aj}$ is the component in the obtained score predicted from individual j's standard score on factor A, and z_{ej} is the error component for individual j on variable x.

Similarly, the obtained result for variable y can be written as a standard score as the sum of components predicted from different factors plus an error score:

$$z_{yj} = a_y z_{aj} + b_y z_{bj} + \cdots + m_y z_{mj} + z_{ej}. \qquad (13\text{--}13)$$

Since we have obtained, in Eqs. (13–12) and (13–13), individual standard scores for x and y, the correlation between the two variables can now be written as the mean of all the products (Eq. 3–6):

$$r_{xy} =$$

$$\frac{\sum(a_x z_{aj} + b_x z_{bj} + \cdots + m_x z_{mj} + z_{ej})(a_y z_{aj} + b_y z_{bj} + \cdots + m_y z_{mj} + z_{ej})}{N}$$

$$(13\text{--}14)$$

On expanding the equation, two types of terms are obtained.

(a) We obtain $m + 1$ terms of the type

$$\frac{\sum a_x z_{aj} a_y z_{aj}}{N}, \quad \frac{\sum b_x z_{bj} b_y z_{bj}}{N}, \text{ etc.}$$

Each of these terms can be expanded in the following way. We take the first term as an example. Since a_x and a_y are constants they can be removed from the summation and we obtain

$$a_x a_y \frac{\sum z_{aj} z_{aj}}{N}.$$

But the mean of the squares of standard scores gives the correlation coefficient 1.0, so that the whole expression can be reduced to $a_x a_y$. The m first terms of this type can be simplified in the same way. The correlation coefficient for the last term will be zero, since this is a correlation between random errors. The other m terms thus give the following contribution to the correlation between the distributions for x and y:

$$a_x a_y + b_x b_y + \cdots + m_x m_y. \qquad (13\text{--}15)$$

(b) In addition we obtain $(m + 1)m$ terms of the type

$$\frac{\sum a_x z_{aj} b_y z_{bj}}{N}.$$

The constants can also be removed here and we obtain

$$a_x b_y \frac{\sum z_{aj} z_{bj}}{N}. \qquad (13\text{--}16)$$

The mean of the products of the standard scores expresses here the correlation between scores for factors A and B. Since they are assumed to be uncorrelated, the correlation coefficient and the whole term will be zero. This will be the case for every term of this type.

It should perhaps be stressed once again that this discussion ignores the specific variance, i.e., the specific variance for each test which is made up of true components not measured by other tests in the matrix. We have treated the problem as if all true variance were common variance. Under such conditions, all true variance will also be predictable from the common factors. If we had also taken the specific variance into account, a further term would have been added to Eqs. (13–12) and (13–13). This would have given additional terms in the expansion of Eq. (13–14). All of these terms would, however, have been zero. The exclusion of the specific variance terms does not, therefore, limit the validity and application of the derivation.

We have thus arrived at a theorem which is important when we are dealing with validity in factor theory: The correlation between two variables (e.g., between two test distributions or between a test distribution and a criterion distribution) is equal to the sum of the products of the factor loadings. The theorem has the following form when expressed in the symbols used previously:

$$r_{xy} = a_x a_y + b_x b_y + c_x c_y + \cdots + m_x m_y, \qquad (13\text{–}17)$$

where r_{xy} is the correlation between variables x and y, a_x is the correlation between variable x and factor A, i.e., the factor loading for variable x with respect to factor A, and a_y is the correlation between variable y and factor A, i.e., the factor loading for variable y with respect to factor A.

The correlation between Tests 1 and 2 in Table 13–4 can now be computed from the factor loadings shown there:

$$
\begin{aligned}
r_{12} &= 0.60 \times 0.40 + 0.20 \times 0.00 + 0.60 \times 0.35 + 0.30 \times 0.00 \\
&\quad + 0.00 \times 0.80 \\
&= 0.24 + 0.00 + 0.21 + 0.00 + 0.00 \\
&= 0.45.
\end{aligned}
$$

If test g in Table 13–4 is a criterion for Tests 1, 2, and 3, the validity coefficients for these tests can be computed from Eq. (13–17) to be 0.73, 0.50, and 0.58. From the factor loadings in a factor matrix we can in this way reproduce every correlation coefficient in the correlation matrix on which the factor analysis is based. Table 13–5 shows that part of the correlation matrix which can be reproduced from the factor matrix in Table 13–4.

We can now state a fact which is important when we are discussing validity: The magnitude of the correlation between two tests or between a test and a criterion depends on (a) whether the variances of the two distribu-

Table 13–5 Correlation matrix

Test

Test	1	2	3	...	g
1	...	0.45	0.29	...	0.73
2	0.45	...	0.32	...	0.50
3	0.29	0.32	...	...	0.58
⋮					⋮
g	0.73	0.50	0.58	...	...
⋮					⋮

tions are determined by the same factor or factors, and (b) the extent to which each common factor determines equal proportions of the variance in the two distributions.

The validity, expressed as a correlation coefficient, will be zero if the variation in test scores is determined completely by factors other than those which determine variation in criterion scores. The validity coefficient will be a maximum when each factor involved determines exactly the same proportion of the variance in the distribution of criterion scores as in the distribution of test scores. Under such conditions, the factor loadings corresponding to each other in the test and criterion will be equal in magnitude, and the validity coefficient of the test will be equal to the communality of the test and the communality of the criterion. The two communalities will, of course, be the same.

It should be particularly stressed that the previous discussion is based on the assumption that the factors (A, B, C, etc.) are uncorrelated. The factor matrix should therefore be the result of an orthogonal rotation of axes in the procedure for finding the best solution. The situation will be more complicated if the factor matrix has been obtained by oblique rotation, which means that the obtained factors are intercorrelated. Differences in rotation procedure have no effect on the interpretation of a row or column in the factor matrix (Table 13–4). The correlation between different variables cannot, however, be computed in the way described from a factor matrix in which the factor loadings give the correlation between tests and positively correlated factors. Consequently, in this case, the complete correlation matrix on which the factor analysis is based cannot be computed in this way either.

13–4   FACTOR STRUCTURE AND RELIABILITY

It was shown in Chapter 5 that reliability increases with the length of the test. This is true, however, only if the items with which a test of a given length is expanded can be considered parallel to the original items. The items which are added should measure the same factor as those which made up the original test.

We shall study the problem of reliability in relation to factor structure more closely by means of variance terms. We begin by assuming a one-factor test (t_1) of a given length and with a given reliability ($r_{t_1 t_1}$). What will be the effect on the reliability (a) if we expand the test with an equal number of items of the same type (i.e., retain the test's one-factor structure), and (b) if we expand the test with an equal number of items of a different type (i.e., items which measure a variable other than that measured by the original items and make the test a two-factor one)? Every item, both original and added, is assumed to have the same reliability. The total test in both cases will be made up of $t_1 + t_2$, if the additional part of the test in both cases is denoted by t_2.

The reliability can easily be computed for case a. The reliability increases in accordance with the Spearman-Brown formula, since t_2 can be considered as parallel to t_1. The reliability of the total test will be

$$\frac{2r_{t_1 t_1}}{1 + r_{t_1 t_1}}.$$

Case b presents a different picture. Reliability was previously defined by the expression $1 - s_e^2/s_t^2$ (Eq. 5–8). The total variance of the two-factor test can be computed from the variance of the test halves:

$$s_{(t_1 + t_2)}^2 = s_{t_1}^2 + s_{t_2}^2 + 2r_{t_1 t_2} s_{t_1} s_{t_2}.$$

The two test halves will be uncorrelated, since t_1 and t_2 measure different, uncorrelated factors. Thus $r_{t_1 t_2}$ will be zero, as will the third term on the right-hand side. In the same way, the error variance of the two-factor test can be computed from the error variances for the two test halves:

$$s_{e(t_1 + t_2)}^2 = s_{e_1}^2 + s_{e_2}^2 + 2r_{e_1 e_2} s_{e_1} s_{e_2}.$$

The third term on the right-hand side will also be zero, since the error terms are uncorrelated. We have assumed that every item is equally reliable. The second test half in the two-factor test will then be as reliable as the first and the proportion of true variance and error variance equal in each of the test halves. If we allow the variance terms to represent the proportions of the total variance in a test half, we find that $s_{t_1}^2 = s_{t_2}^2$ and $s_{e_1}^2 = s_{e_2}^2$. The reliability of the two-factor test can now be written

$$1 - 2s_{e_1}^2/2s_{t_1}^2 = 1 - s_{e_1}^2/s_{t_1}^2.$$

But this last expression is the same as for the reliability of the original test half ($r_{t_1 t_1}$). We have thus established that the reliability of the two-factor test, of which each of the halves is assumed to measure a different factor, will be the same as the reliability of the test which was half as long and measured one of these factors.

The reliability of a single-factor test is greater than that of a multifactor one, other things being equal. For two tests which have an equal number of items all having the same reliability but differing with respect to the number of factors determining the variance of test scores, the test with the smaller number of factors will be the more reliable.

13–5   FACTOR STRUCTURE AND VALIDITY

Bearing the above discussion in mind, let us study reliability and validity in a situation of practical importance in conjunction with our discussion of factor theory.

We begin by assuming that we have a one-factor test with moderate reliability (e.g., 0.81) among the tests which have supplied the factor matrix in Table 13–4. Furthermore, we assume that the whole of the test's true variance consists of common variance and that the test measures only factor B. We can now easily establish that the test's validity with test g as the criterion will be estimated to be $0.90 \times 0.50 = 0.45$. All other products will of course be zero, since the test's factor loadings are zero for every factor other than B.

If we now consider the validity we have obtained to be too low, how can we increase it?

First of all, we can increase the reliability of the test. By doing so, the communality is increased in this case—since we assumed that all of the true variance was common variance—and the factor loading with which we have to multiply the corresponding factor loading in the criterion will be greater. In order to increase the reliability by means of the Spearman-Brown formula, we must expand the test with items which measure the same factor. The validity can also be increased by this method, and its maximum value will be equal to the factor loading for the criterion with respect to the factor measured by the test. The maximum reliability which we can obtain is of course 1.00. The square root of this value will be included in the factor matrix as the factor loading for the test with respect to factor B, and the test's validity coefficient will be $1.00 \times 0.50 = 0.50$. Under the given conditions, we have increased the validity from 0.45 to 0.50 by increasing the reliability of the test from 0.81 to 1.00. For a validity of 0.45, 20.25% of the variance is predicted; for a validity of 0.50, 25%. We have thus, by means of the obtained increase in reliability, increased by a mere 5% that part of the total variance of the criterion which can be predicted. This relatively modest improvement in validity must be seen in relation to the costs in time and money which a reliability increase of the magnitude assumed would involve. A reliability of 1.00 presupposes an infinite number of items and is thus only a theoretical case. If we in practice choose to increase the test's reliability to 0.90, this will mean that the validity is increased to 0.949 $\times$ 0.50 = 0.474. As can easily be verified by the Spearman-Brown formula, an increase of reliability from 0.81 to 0.90 requires the test to be more than doubled. For this considerable increase in administrative and scoring work, we would thus gain only a small increase in validity by this method. When the criterion is a multifactor one, the advantages of increases in reliability for one-factor tests are as a rule small, and are often so small that the improvement in validity bears no relation to the extra work which the increase in reliability requires (see also the discussion on p. 151).

It is easy to see why the improvement in validity is so small even if the reliability is increased. The new items which are added in order to increase reliability measure the same factor as the original ones. The increase in validity is obtained, not because the new items measure something in the criterion other than what is measured by the original items, but because the new items make a more certain measurement of what has already been measured.

We found in the previous example that, by doubling the length of the test, we increased the reliability of a one-factor test from 0.81 to 0.90, and raised the validity from 0.45 to 0.474. Let us now try another approach, attempting instead to increase the test's validity by adding items of a different type which measure some other factor. For the sake of comparison, let us also assume in this case that we double the length of the test, i.e., add as many new items as were originally included in the test. Furthermore, let us assume that the new items measure factor C and that they are each as reliable as the previous ones.

Under the given conditions, the reliability of the two-factor test with twice as many items as the original one-factor test will be the same as in the original test, namely, 0.81 (see the discussion of factor structure and reliability, pp. 187–189).

The effect on validity of the addition of new items which measure factor C can be computed in the following way. In accordance with the previous discussion the two-factor test's communality will be the same (0.81) as that of the initial one-factor test. We must now divide 81% common variance for the total test equally between the two factors B and C. This means that 40.5% of the total test variance is measured by that half of the test whose common variance is determined by factor B, and 40.5% of the total test variance is measured by the other half, whose common variance is determined by factor C. If we replace percentages (40.5) with proportions (0.405), we now obtain the factor loadings for the test with respect to the factors B and C by taking the square root of the proportion. This gives the value 0.636. The factor loadings for the criterion with respect to factors B and C were 0.50

and 0.40 respectively, so that the validity for the two-factor test with respect to the criterion g in the factor matrix in Table 13–4 can be estimated to be $0.636 \times 0.50 + 0.636 \times 0.40 = 0.572$. By doubling the test length, we have achieved an increase of validity from 0.450 to 0.572 by adding items which measure a completely new factor which is also included in the criterion. The increase in validity is best expressed by the percentage increase in the variance which can be predicted. In this case the part of the variance which can be predicted rises from 20.25% to 32.72%. Thus approximately 12.5% more of the variance can be predicted with the two-factor test than with the original one-factor test, which was half as long. This improvement should be compared with the improvement in prediction which was obtained by adding an equally large number of items with the same factor structure as the original items in the test. In that case the predicted part of the total test variance rose from 20.25% to 22.47%, an increase of approximately 2.2%. Thus, for a situation such as this, we can state that the improvement in validity will be considerably greater if one makes the test more heterogeneous when increasing the test length than if one makes it more reliable. This is the case if new factors in the criterion are measured by the new items added to the test.

Let us return once more to Table 13–4. The increase in validity we obtained by adding new items to the test depended on our choosing items which represented factor C. If instead we had chosen factor A, the obtained validity coefficient for the two-factor test could have been estimated to be $0.636 \times 0.50 + 0.636 \times 0.50 = 0.636$, and if we had chosen factor D the validity would have been $0.636 \times 0.50 + 0.636 \times 0.30 = 0.509$. The validity improvement in such cases will thus depend upon the proportion of the criterion variance determined by the factor for which we choose new items to be included in the test for predicting the criterion variable.

Under the given conditions we also find that we increase the validity more rapidly by allowing the new items to measure new factors in the criterion than by adding similar items to the test in order to make it more reliable. If we were to increase the test $t_1 + t_2$ with a further part t_3 and make this part as long and as reliable as each of the two previous parts, we should clearly attempt to measure a further new factor in the criterion, e.g., factor A. Knowing the factor structure of the criterion, we could continue in this way and add to the test an equally long and equally reliable part for each of the other factors which determine variation in the criterion. We would then obtain a multi-factor test $(t_1 + t_2 + t_3 + t_4 + t_5)$ in the example given in the factor matrix in Table 13–4. It could also be called a multifactor test battery with the homogeneous subtests t_1, t_2, t_3, t_4, and t_5. The reliability of the total multifactor test would then be the same (0.81) as the reliability of each of the subtests (see the discussion on p. 188). The communality has been taken to be the same size as the reliability. The proportion of common variance for the total test will then also be 0.81. In this case the common variance has to be divided equally among the five tests in order for us to be able to compute, from the proportion of the variance which is measured by each of the tests and is determined by each of the factors, the factor loading for the total test with respect to each of the factors. These factor loadings can now be computed to be 0.403, and the validity of the total heterogeneous test will be $0.403 \times 0.50 + 0.403 \times 0.50 + 0.403 \times 0.40 + 0.403 \times 0.30 + 0.403 \times 0.20 = 0.765$. In this way we have further increased the validity from 0.572 to 0.765 by adding the test parts t_3, t_4, and t_5. By doing so we have increased the part of the variance in the criterion which can be predicted from 32.72% to 58.52%.

The purpose of this example was to illustrate the fact that increased heterogeneity leads to increased opportunities for raising the validity. This statement must, however, be qualified. After increasing the heterogeneity of the test to a certain limit, we do not gain more in predictive information by adding items which measure new factors. This can best be shown by a further example from the multifactor test we have just discussed. We can easily establish—as long as we are interested only in predicting the total criterion g in the factor matrix in Table 13–4—that the validity is not increased by adding subtest t_5 to the four others. The total common variance in the test would have been divided by four instead of by five if we had kept the four original subtests, and the factor loadings with respect to the different factors would thus have been 0.451 instead of 0.403. The test's validity with respect to the criterion g would then have been $0.451 \times 0.50 + 0.451 \times 0.50 + 0.451 \times 0.40 + 0.451 \times 0.30 = 0.767$. A test consisting of the first four subtests would thus have more or less the same validity as a test in which subtest t_5 is also included. Whether this effect arises, and if so how great the effect will be, depends of course on the factor structures of test and criterion.

In general we can make an equally certain and equally good prediction in both of the given cases, but it should be observed that the factors which are measured by the test, and on which the prediction is based, are somewhat different. This means in practice (e.g., in a selection situation) that certain individuals who would be accepted with tests t_1–t_5 would be rejected with tests t_1–t_4, while other individuals who would be accepted with the latter test battery would be rejected with the former, since the individuals have different factor scores.

In the above example we have given the parts of the test which measure different factors the same weight in the total test; i.e., the different subtests determine equal amounts of the total test variance. We could have further increased the test's predictive power, with other conditions unchanged, by fixing the lengths of the different subtests so that each determines a proportion of the total test variance such that the sum of the products of the test's and the criterion's factor loadings is a maximum. A consequence of this, in the case in question, would be that the subtests whose variation is determined by factors *A* and *B* would have the same weight, which would however be greater than the weights of the other subtests. By this procedure we should achieve the same results as from multiple-correlation computations. The weights to be assigned to each of a series of subtests in a test battery are determined by computing multiple correlations such that the battery will give maximal validity (see p. 154). In practice one never has the ideal situation, zero correlations between the subtests. Computation of the weights with which each of the subtest scores has to be multiplied before being included in the total sum must, therefore, take into account the magnitude of both (a) the correlation between each of the subtests and the criterion and (b) the correlation between subtests. It should be pointed out that one often over-estimates the increase in validity achieved by means of the weighting made when computing multiple correlation. In the present example, the work involved in determining the regression coefficients by means of multiple correlation would theoretically lead to an increase in the validity to $\sqrt{0.81} \times \sqrt{0.79} = 0.80$.

13–6   MULTIFACTOR TESTS; TEST BATTERY WITH ONE-FACTOR TESTS

When the variance of the criterion is determined by more than one factor, as is usually the case in practical situations, there are two methods, different in principle, of constructing an instrument which is as accurate as possible. Each of the methods has certain advantages and the method used will depend partly on the situation and the purpose for which the instrument is constructed (see Chapter 12). Let us assume that a fixed time is available for testing, thus determining the number of items which can be included in the test. The total test length for both solutions is therefore the same.

First: the problem can be solved by constructing a test with items chosen so that they cover the same area as the criterion. Different factors can thus be assigned different numbers of items, or items can be weighted so that the relationship between different factors will be the same for the test and the criterion. A multifactor test is thus constructed in order to predict the multifactor criterion. The result for an individual on this test will consist of only a single score which gives the position of the individual on the distribution of obtained test scores. A test constructed in this way can be used, for example, in simple selection procedures.

A second way of solving the problem involves dividing the total number of items into several subtests which together make up a test battery. Each subtest should contain a fixed type of item, i.e., measure one of the factors included in the criterion. When choosing items, we will thus try to obtain (a) high correlations between the items in each subtest, in order to make it as accurate a measurement as possible of the factor which the subtest measures and is intended to measure, and (b) low correlations—preferably zero correlations—between different subtests, so that each subtest as far as possible measures something different from other subtests. For a given individual a score is obtained both for each of the subtests and as a total score. The latter can be an unweighted sum of scores from subtests with the same mean and standard deviation, or a weighted sum of subtest results where the weighting is achieved either by giving the different subtests different means and variances during test construction or by computing regression coefficients by means of multiple correlation.

A multifactor test which is not divisible into homogeneous subtests gives for each individual only one total score which is often difficult to interpret because of the composite nature of the test. An individual's total score of a certain magnitude can have arisen in many different ways. The group of items solved with special ease in a particular case cannot be determined from the total result. A test battery with one-factor subtests gives subscores as well as a total score. This makes a discriminatory description of the individuals' scores for different factors possible. We can make both interindividual comparisons with respect to total scores and subtest scores and intraindividual comparisons for different factors.

The composite nature of a multifactor test implies in certain cases that it gives a satisfactory correlation not only with a fixed criterion variable but also in a number of other situations in which the factors measured by the test can have some significance. The multifactor test is consequently unsatisfactory as a basis for a differentiated prognosis or diagnosis. The various uncorrelated one-factor subtests in a test battery can for a given situation be given optimal weights such that the total score gives the best possible prediction without at the same time giving a high correlation with other criteria. We can thus meet the requirement of a many-sided and varied prediction with one and the same battery by giving the total test a relevant factor structure for every situation. Test batteries of this type provide the best basis for satisfactory classification (see pp. 158–163).

PROBLEMS

1. The following values are taken from the first row of a factor matrix.

		Factor	
Test	A	B	C
1	0.40	0.60	0.10

The specific variance is 0.25.

(a) What is the communality of the test?

(b) What is the reliability of the test?

(c) What is the unique variance?

2. Factor matrix

Factor

Test	A	B	C	D
1	0.30	0.00	0.50	0.20
2	0.00	0.60	0.40	0.00
3	0.50	0.00	0.00	0.60
4	0.30	0.70	0.00	0.40

Reconstruct the correlation matrix.

3. Obtain the correlation matrix for the tests included in the following factor matrix.

Factor

Test	A	B	C	D
1	0.10	0.70	0.40	0.50
2	0.60	0.40	0.10	0.45
3	0.45	0.00	0.55	0.52
4	0.00	0.00	0.80	0.32
5	0.30	0.50	0.62	0.14

4. What is the validity of each of the tests in Problem 3 if the criterion has given the following factor loadings?

Factor	A	B	C	D
Criterion	0.15	0.60	0.60	0.00

5. Factor matrix

Factor	A	B	C	D	E	F	
Test 1	0.00	0.00	0.00	0.93	0.00	0.00	$(v^2 = 0.00)$
Criterion	0.20	0.60	0.30	0.50	0.40	0.00	$(v^2 = 0.03)$

The matrix has been obtained by means of orthogonal rotation.

(a) Compute the reliability of Test 1 and the criterion.

(b) Compute the validity.

(c) Correct for unreliability in the criterion.

(d) Estimate the validity which will be attained if the test's reliability is raised by doubling its length with items which measure factor D.

(e) Compute the validity that will be attained if the test is doubled in length, but with items which measure factor B.

(f) Compute the validity that will be attained if the test is doubled in length with items which measure factor C. Compare the results in (d), (e), and (f).

(g) Compute the validity that will be obtained when the test is lengthened with items which measure factor B and items which measure factor E, in each case with as many items as the original test contained.

(h) Do the same for factors A, B, C, and E.

(i) Do the same for factors A, B, C, E, and F. Compare the results for (g), (h), and (i) and for (d), (e), and (f).

(j) Estimate the maximum validity which can be attained by using all possible means, with unchanged reliability.

REFERENCES

HARMAN, H. H. (1960). *Modern factor analysis*. Chicago: University of Chicago Press.

THURSTONE, L. L. (1947). *Multiple factor analysis*. Chicago: University of Chicago Press.

Suggested reading

ANASTASI, A. (1948). The nature of psychological "traits." *Psychol. Rev.*, **55**, 127–138.

CATTELL, R. B. (1962). The basis of recognition and interpretation of factors. *Educ. Psychol. Measmt.*, **22**, 667–698.

CATTELL, R. B., and J. A. RADCLIFFE (1962). Reliabilities and validities of simple and extended weighted and buffered unifactor scales. *Brit. J. Stat. Psychol.*, **15**, 113–128.

GUILFORD, J. P. (1954). *Psychometric methods* (2nd ed.). New York: McGraw-Hill.

——— (1965). *Fundamental statistics in psychology and education* (3rd ed.). New York: McGraw-Hill.

HENRYSSON, S. (1957). *Applicability of factor analysis in the behavioral sciences*. Stockholm: Almqvist & Wiksell.

HUMPHREYS, L. G. (1962). The organization of human abilities. *Am. Psychologist*, **17**, 475–483.

ROYCE, J. R. (1963). Factors as theoretical constructs. *Am. Psychologist*, **18**, 522–528.

CHAPTER 14

Item Analysis

An individual's obtained score on a test as a rule consists of the number of correctly solved items. It is the dependability of this obtained score for an individual, both as an estimate of his true score (i.e., the reliability of data) and as a basis for a diagnosis or prediction (i.e., the validity of data), which determines the value of the test. The reliability and validity of the data depend on the properties of the individual items which make up the test. The total test has no properties which cannot be derived from those of the single items or the relationships between them. In Chapter 4 we studied how the variance of the total test distribution is dependent on the frequency of correct response for the individual items and on the intercorrelations of the items. This chapter deals with methods for estimating the contribution of each item to reliability and validity.

This is a practical problem in all test-construction work. We do not have unlimited time for testing and scoring; we wish to use the testing time effectively by making as reliable and as valid a measurement as possible with as small a number of items as possible. This is achieved by choosing items which contribute maximally to reliability and validity. The choice must be based on an analysis of the likelihood of each item's increasing the reliability and validity. This item analysis can be carried out by a number of different methods, the most common of which will be presented in this chapter.

In test construction, situations can arise in which the requirements of high reliability and high validity respectively vary somewhat in importance. Such a situation arises when, for example, we wish to construct a test to measure a factor found by factor analysis and to be used in a number of situations where the factor measured can be relevant. In this situation the only purpose of item analysis is to satisfy the demand for as high a reliability as possible in the test, and this is done by testing the contribution of every item to the reliability.

We have already shown that the validity of a test can be increased by making the test more heterogeneous. If this is done by replacing certain items which correlate highly with other items in the test, with items which measure some factor other than that measured by those originally included (the original length of the test being thus retained), the increased validity will be gained at the expense of reliability. This is defensible in certain situations, but not in all: for instance, when we wish to make a differential prediction, we cannot permit the reliability to fall below a certain level. Thus, when analyzing an individual item, we must take into account its contributions to reliability and validity at the same time.

An item contributes to a test's reliability by measuring the same sort of true score as the other items in the test; i.e., it contributes to reliability if the true component in the item is determined by the same factor which determines the magnitude of the true components measured by other items. Likewise, an item contributes to the test's validity if it measures the same sort of true score as the criterion measurement. If the item contributes to the test's reliability, this should be shown by a positive correlation with other items in the test; if it contributes to the test's validity, there should be a positive correlation with the criterion measurement. In item analysis we attempt to establish the extent of these relationships. The methods used can be divided into two main groups: (a) short-cut methods which investigate differences between extreme groups on the test and criterion distributions respectively, with reference to ability to solve a certain item, and (b) methods which determine the extent of the relationship as a correlation coefficient. The immediately following section is devoted to some correlation methods which were not discussed previously but are used in item analysis.

14–1 CORRELATION METHODS

A. Point-biserial correlation

We previously derived the equations for computing the correlation between two continuous distributions (Eq. 3–6) and for computing the correlation between distributions in which the scores on each of the variables consist of only two categories (Eq. 3–14). Let us now examine the following practical situation. We have administered a test to 50 men and 50 women and wish to investigate whether there is a relationship between sex and test results. We have the situation illustrated in Fig. 14–1. On the x-axis we have two categories, for men (1) and women (0). The y-scores make up a normal distribution. The test distribution can now be divided into two halves, one containing test scores for men (i.e., individuals who are included in category 1 on the x-axis), the other containing test scores for women (i.e., individuals who are included in category 0 on the x-axis). If there is no relation between test results and sex category, the means of the test distributions for men and women should clearly be the same, and thus also the same as the mean of the

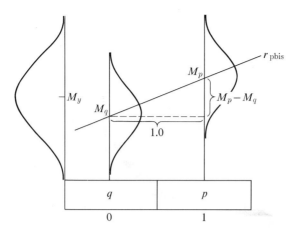

Fig. 14–1 Point-biserial correlation.

test distribution (M_y). The regression line for prediction c f y-scores from x will then be horizontal. The example given in Fig. 14–1 h is been chosen to illustrate a positive correlation between male sex and high scores on this test. This correlation is, of course, shown by the fact that the mean of the scores for men (M_p) is higher than the mean for women (M_q).

We can now derive an equation to express the relation between the two variables as a correlation coefficient.

We previously derived the expression for the regression coefficient for prediction from x to y:

$$b_{yx} = r_{xy} \frac{s_y}{s_x}.$$

This can be written

$$r_{xy} = b_{yx} \frac{s_x}{s_y}. \tag{14–1}$$

In this equation, b_{yx} is the angle coefficient which gives the slope of the regression line, and is equal to the tangent of the angle between the x-axis and the regression line. Since the difference in means between the two categories on the x-axis is 1.0 (the mean of category 0 will of course be zero and the mean of category 1 will be 1.0), b_{yx} will be equal to the difference $M_p - M_q$. Equation (14–1) can now be written

$$r_{xy} = \frac{(M_p - M_q)s_x}{s_y}.$$

Since the scores on the x-axis consist of only ones and zeros, s_x is equal to $\sqrt{pq}$. On inserting $\sqrt{pq}$ we obtain the equation for computing a *point-biserial* correlation coefficient (r_{pbis}), which is a special case of the more general product moment coefficient:

$$r_{\text{pbis}} = \frac{M_p - M_q}{s_y} \sqrt{pq}, \tag{14–2}$$

where M_p is the mean of y-scores for individuals in category 1 on the dichotomous distribution (the x-axis), M_q is the mean of y-scores for individuals in category 0 on the dichotomous distribution, p is the proportion of individuals in category 1 on the dichotomous distribution, and q is the proportion of individuals in category 0 on the dichotomous distribution.

When the values for M_p and M_q are determined, the value of M_y (i.e., the mean of the continuous distribution) will also be known. Both the differences $M_p - M_y$ and $M_p - M_q$ are expressions for the same slope of the regression line. The extent of the relation can then be expressed equally well by the relation between M_p and M_y. This way, the computations are simplified, since M_q must be computed for every individual item, while M_y is a constant whose value need be computed only once. The equation for computing the point-biserial correlation coefficient by using the difference $M_p - M_y$ can be derived from Eq. (14–2):

$$r_{\text{pbis}} = \frac{M_p - M_y}{s_y} \sqrt{\frac{p}{q}}. \tag{14–3}$$

Let us suppose that we have obtained the distribution of scores shown in Table 14–1 for 50 boys and 50 girls on a questionnaire referring to mechanical interests.

With the values for M_p (12.78), M_q (8.26), and s_y (3.49) which are given in the table, we can now compute the point-biserial coefficient for the relation between sex and interest as expressed by the responses to the questionnaire. Since p and q are 0.50, r_{pbis} obtained from Eq. (14–2) will be $(12.78 - 8.26)/3.49 \times \sqrt{0.50 \times 0.50} = 0.648$. The reader can see that Eq. (14–3) gives the same numerical value for the coefficient.

The point-biserial correlation coefficient is computed for the relation between a variable for which there are only two categories of scores and a variable for which the scores exist on a continuous distribution. The maximum value of the coefficient depends on the relation between the proportions p and q in the dichotomous distribution. Even for equal proportions of p and q the maximum coefficient is less than 1.0, and it is further reduced as the difference between these proportions increases. This can be shown in the following way. It is apparent from Eq. (14–2) that the point-biserial coefficient will be greatest when p and q have the same value, other things being equal. When this is the case it follows from Eq. (14–3) that $r_{\text{pbis}} = (M_p - M_y)/s_y$. When we have the most favorable relation for the coefficient $(p = q)$, the size of $(M_p - M_y)/s_y$ thus determines the size of the coefficient. We let M_y equal zero and s_y equal 1.0. The difference $M_p - $

Table 14–1

Score	Girls	Boys	Total
20		1	1
19			
18		1	1
17		3	3
16		4	4
15		6	6
14		6	6
13		7	7
12	4	4	8
11	4	6	10
10	8	5	13
9	10	3	13
8	9	2	11
7	3	2	5
6	4		4
5	5		5
4			
3	3		3
2			
1			
N	50	50	100
Σ	413	639	
M	8.26	12.78	
	$s_y = 3.49$		

$M_y = M_p$ must then be 1.0 if r_{pbis} is also to be 1.0. For a perfect correlation between the scores on the dichotomous distribution and scores on the other distribution, there must be no overlapping between the two groups of scores on the latter distribution corresponding to the two categories in the former. All scores on the y-distribution for individuals in category p on the x-distribution—and only these scores—lie above the mean M_y. Thus M_p is the mean of all y-scores which lie above the mean. We have set the mean of y at zero and the standard deviation at 1.0. This means that all scores on y are expressed as z-scores. The mean of all positive z-scores (M_p) is 0.7978. It follows that when $p = q$, the maximum value of r_{pbis} is 0.7978.

In testing the significance of the difference from zero for the point-biserial correlation coefficient, the standard error for large samples is computed from the equation $s_{r_{\mathrm{pbis}}} = 1/\sqrt{N}$. Its magnitude thus depends only on the number of individuals on whose scores the computation of the coefficient is based. For small samples of individuals, the significance of the coefficient's deviation from zero is tested by evaluating the difference $M_p - M_q$ with the t-test. (This t, usually called Student's t, should not be confused with the t generally used in this text as a notation for an obtained score. The t-statistic is treated in the standard books in elementary statistics. See, e.g., Ferguson, 1959.)

B. Biserial correlation

The equation for the point-biserial correlation coefficient has been derived from the regression coefficient on the assumption that the distribution of scores on one of the variables consists of only two categories. No special assumptions were introduced in the derivation. It is reasonable, however, to assume in certain situations that the individuals' true scores are normally distributed on the continuum on which the dichotomous distribution is placed. One fundamental assumption often used in test theory is that individuals' true scores for psychological variables have a normal distribution. We will, however, obtain a dichotomous distribution if we allow the test to consist of a single item and rate the responses 1 for a correct response and 0 for an incorrect response (see p. 14). This distribution with two categories will then be the result of splitting a normal distribution into two parts: individuals who are above the pass level on the performance continuum are put in one category, and those below this level are put in the other.

An equation can now be derived for the correlation between (a) a dichotomous distribution which can be regarded as the result of a differentiation with *one* item on a hypothetical normal distribution on at least an interval scale, and (b) a distribution of scores on some other continuous variable (linearity between the two distributions is assumed). The derivation follows the same steps as that of the point-biserial correlation equation. However, when we compute the angle coefficient, the denominator—the difference between the means of scores on the assumed normal distribution for the two categories—will not be 1.0 as in the derivation of the point-biserial correlation. For a normal distribution which has been split into two parts with the proportions p and q, the difference between the mean of the scores in the part consisting of proportion p and the mean of the total distribution is equal to y/p, and the difference between the mean of the scores in the part of the distribution consisting of proportion q and the total mean is equal to y/q (y is the ordinate at the dividing point between the two parts of a normal distribution with area 1.0 and standard deviation 1.0). The difference we will have in the denominator when computing the angle coefficient will thus be

$y/p + y/q$. This expression can be expanded in the following way:

$$\frac{y}{p} + \frac{y}{q} = \frac{yq + yp}{pq} = \frac{y(p + q)}{pq}.$$

But $p + q$ is equal to the total area (1.0) in the distribution of which p and q are the two parts. The expression for the correlation coefficient (Eq. 14–1) under the given conditions can thus be written

$$r_{xy} = b_{yx}\frac{s_x}{s_y} = \frac{(M_p - M_q)pqs_x}{ys_y}.$$ (14–4)

The standard deviation for the presumed normal distribution on the x-axis (s_x) will be 1.0, so that the equation for the correlation coefficient—the *biserial* correlation coefficient—will be

$$r_{\text{bis}} = \frac{M_p - M_q}{s_y}\frac{pq}{y},$$ (14–5)

where M_p is the mean of y-scores for individuals in category 1 on the dichotomized distribution (the x-axis), M_q is the mean of y-scores for individuals in category 0 on the dichotomized distribution, p is the proportion of individuals in category 1 on the dichotomized distribution, q is the proportion of individuals in category 0 on the dichotomized distribution, and y is the ordinate of the dividing line between the proportions p and q in a unit normal distribution.

It was pointed out in the discussion of the point-biserial correlation coefficient that the computation of the coefficient can be based equally well on the difference $M_p - M_y$ as on the difference $M_p - M_q$. An equation can also be derived for obtaining the biserial correlation coefficient from the difference $M_p - M_y$:

$$r_{\text{bis}} = \frac{M_p - M_y}{s_y}\frac{p}{y}.$$ (14–6)

Let us suppose that the two frequency columns of scores on the interest questionnaire shown in Table 14–1 have been obtained for two groups of students in a vocational training course. The right-hand column represents students who have completed the training; the left-hand one, students who have failed to complete the training and have left during its course. If we assume that the ability to succeed in this type of training will be normally distributed for the given total number of students, the relation between success in training and scores on the interest questionnaire can be computed as a biserial correlation coefficient with Eq. (14–5) or Eq. (14–6). M_p and M_q have the same values as they did when we computed the point-biserial correlation. The same is true of s_y. The size of pq/y is obtained from available tables (cf., for example, Guilford, 1954, pp. 568–569). The biserial correlation coefficient can now be computed from Eq. (14–5) to be $(12.78 - 8.26)/3.49 \times 0.6267 = 0.812$.

When deriving the equation for the biserial correlation coefficient, we use the assumption that the dichotomized variable has in fact a normal distribution. The biserial correlation should be computed only when there is reason to believe that this assumption holds. This may be the case in situations such as the one described above, where we measure the variable with an instrument which divides the assumed distribution into only two parts, as of course a single test item does. The biserial correlation coefficient is therefore a suitable measure if we wish to compute the correlation between the single item and a test. In other situations we may, as a result of shortcomings in the instrument used, have obtained scores on a strongly skewed distribution on the one variable, while having good reason to believe that the distribution would have been normal if we had had access to an instrument which gave scores on an interval scale. The degree of relationship between this variable and some other where the scores are on a continuous distribution is also expressed by a biserial correlation coefficient. The proportions p and q in the dichotomized variable are thus obtained by splitting the skewed distribution at a suitable point.

The biserial correlation coefficient is a special case of the product-moment coefficient, and its magnitude is independent of the size of p and q. The standard error for the biserial correlation coefficient is, however, greater than for the usual coefficient for product-moment correlation. To test the significance of a deviation from zero for a biserial coefficient, the equation $s_{r_{bis}} = 1/y\sqrt{pq/N}$ can be used as a rough estimate of the standard error (Ferguson, 1959, p. 204; see also McNemar, 1962, pp. 191–192). As can be seen, the standard error depends on the relation between p and q as well as on the number of individuals. It will be smallest when $p = q$, that is, when both p and q are 0.50. The estimate of the slope of the regression line will thus be most certain when the dichotomy is such that the proportions are the same— whether this has been obtained directly from the measuring instrument or afterwards, by dichotomization of a skewed distribution. Thus, if there is no specific reason for dichotomizing at another point on the distribution, the ordinate dividing a skewed distribution should be placed at the median.

Let us suppose that we obtain correlation coefficients for the same set of data from a number of samples of individuals drawn from the same population (a) with the usual equation for product-moment correlation, (b) with the equation for biserial correlation, and (c) with the equation for point-biserial correlation. We will obtain three distributions of correlation coefficients, one for each of the three methods. It is important to study the relation between the means of the three distributions. The distributions of ordinary product-moment coefficients and biserial coefficients will have the

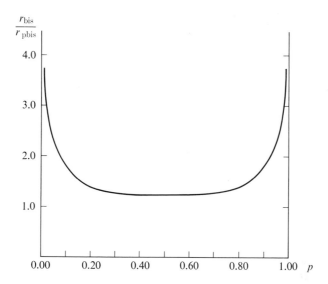

Fig. 14–2 The relationship between biserial and point-biserial correlation coefficients for different p-values.

same mean, but the distribution of biserial coefficients will have a greater standard deviation. The standard error for r_{bis} is greater than for the product-moment coefficient. The distribution of point-biserial coefficients will, however, differ from the two others with respect to both mean and standard deviation. The mean of this distribution will be numerically smaller than that of the two other distributions. Point-biserial coefficients thus give systematically lower values for the same set of data than do ordinary product-moment coefficients and biserial coefficients. The size of the point-biserial coefficient is systematically dependent on the relation p/q in the dichotomous distribution of scores (as shown on pp. 200–201). This means that biserial and point-biserial coefficients will give different values for the correlation between distributions where the scores are in two categories on the one distribution and on a continuous distribution on the other. The relation between the values obtained by the two correlation methods can be derived from Eqs. (14–2) and (14–5):

$$\frac{r_{bis}}{r_{pbis}} = \frac{\sqrt{pq}}{y}.\tag{14–7}$$

Figure 14–2 shows, for different values of p and q, the relation between the numerical expressions for the correlation we obtain with the two methods.

As can be seen from the figure, it is likely that, if the two methods are applied to the same set of data, the biserial coefficient will give a value which exceeds the point-biserial coefficient by 25%, even when p and q are 0.50.

We can also establish this empirically by comparing the results ($r_{\text{pbis}} = 0.648$ and $r_{\text{bis}} = 0.812$) obtained from the data in Table 14–1.

In certain situations data can be obtained in three categories on the one distribution, although there is reason to assume that this distribution is the result of the splitting of a latent normal distribution into three parts. This may be the case when successive selection procedures are administered during a course of training. The first category consists of individuals who were rejected at the first selection; the second, individuals who were rejected at the second selection; and the third, the remaining individuals. The relation between category membership and test results can then be expressed in a *triserial correlation coefficient* (cf. Jenkins, 1956). Like the biserial correlation coefficient, the triserial correlation coefficient can theoretically take values between -1.0 and 1.0. But since the estimate of the slope of the regression line is based on the means of three columns instead of two, it has a smaller standard error.

C. Tetrachoric correlation

The two correlation methods discussed above, biserial and point-biserial, are used for estimating the extent to which an item measures the same variable as the other items in the test. We compute the correlation between the distribution of scores for the item—a distribution with only two score categories, ones and zeros—and the distribution of scores for all other items. In certain circumstances we may wish to estimate the extent to which different items measure the same variable. The relation can be shown for two items at a time in a fourfold table, which is also the basis for computing a measure of the agreement between the two items in question. We have already described a method for computing the relation between two distributions each of which has only two categories (pp. 45–47). The correlation can be computed as a ϕ-coefficient. This measure has, however, the drawback that the size of the coefficient obtained is systematically affected by factors other than those we wish to measure. Differences in the frequency of correct response between the two items influence the size of the ϕ-coefficient. It is possible, however, to estimate the correlation between two items with a coefficient which does not have this characteristic. We assume that each of the items has discriminated within a normal continuous distribution, and that linearity exists between the two hypothetical normal distributions. On these assumptions, the equation for computing the *tetrachoric* correlation coefficient has been derived. This equation is, however, complicated and tedious to apply directly. Simplified methods have been presented for estimating such coefficients (cf., for example, Ferguson, 1959, pp. 204–206). It is customary to use a graphic method which simplifies the computation of the coefficient considerably (cf. Chesire et al., 1933).

Tetrachoric coefficients give an estimate of the product-moment correlation between the hypothetical normal distributions of scores, within which the items are assumed to have differentiated in the manner expressed empirically by the dichotomous distributions on which the estimate is based. This form of correlation computation can also be used for distributions with more than two categories (e.g., for the correlation between obtained distributions for whole tests), when one wishes to obtain a measure quickly for the relationship estimated by the product-moment coefficient. Hence the obtained distributions are dichotomized, preferably by division as near the median as possible.

14–2   ITEM ANALYSIS; DIFFERENCES BETWEEN EXTREME GROUPS

When performing an item analysis, let us assume that we wish to test the contribution of an item to the reliability of a test. The greater the correlation between the test measurement and the measurement made with the item, the greater is this contribution. Figure 14–3 illustrates two conceivable extreme cases. The score distribution for the test has been placed on the x-axis and the score distribution for the item on the y-axis. We assume that the item's frequency of solution is 0.50 ($p = q$). Half of those tested have thus been able to solve it. If the item and test were able to differentiate completely reliably on the same continuum (a purely theoretical case), only those who lie above the mean of the test-score distribution would be able to solve the item. This case is illustrated in Fig. 14–3(a). The case where there is no systematic relation between test scores and item scores is shown in Fig. 14–3(b). The item has been solved just as frequently by individuals with scores below the mean of the test-score distribution as by those with scores above this mean.

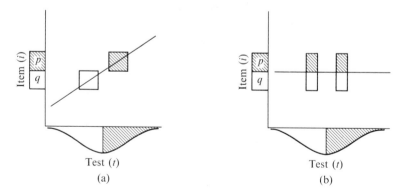

Fig. 14–3 The correlation between item and test for (a) perfect positive correlation and (b) zero correlation.

We can thus obtain an expression for the item's correlation with the test by comparing the proportions of individuals with scores in the upper and lower halves respectively of the test-score distribution who have been able to solve the item. It is this method which is in fact often used in practice. The difference $p_u - p_l$, where p_u is the proportion of the upper half of the distribution of test scores who have passed the item and p_l is the proportion of the lower half of the distribution who have passed it, is a measure of the degree of relationship between the item and the test. Thus it is a measure of the contribution of the item to reliability (or validity, if the test measures the criterion variable).

In the example given, the two halves of the test distribution were compared with respect to performance on the single item. This means that, when studying the extent to which the item discriminates, we consider every individual in the test distribution. However, if we assume that there is a positive correlation between measurements on the item and the test, it is clear that the item discriminates more accurately between individuals in the two parts of the test distribution the further they lie from the mean. The probability that they should in fact be in the other part of the test distribution is greatest for individuals who are located near the mean. The probable difference $p_u - p_l$ will thus be greater if we ignore the scores near the mean of the test distribution and base the computation only on the extreme scores. In doing so we reduce the number of individuals whose scores we use for the computation of the difference. This means that the standard error of the difference increases at the same time as the probable difference increases. The relation between the magnitude of the difference and the magnitude of the standard error will be most favorable if the computation of p_u is based on the 27% of the test distribution who have the highest scores, and p_l on the 27% who have the lowest scores (cf. Kelley, 1939). This method saves time, since only 54% of the individual scores need to be considered.

A choice between different items with respect to their ability to discriminate between extreme groups on the distribution of test scores and on the distribution of criterion scores cannot be based directly on the size of the difference $p_u - p_l$. The standard error for such a difference depends on the values of p_u and p_l (see, e.g., Ferguson, 1959, pp. 146–148, 169–170). Since p_u and p_l vary from item to item, the difference should be evaluated in relation to the standard error when the order in which different items are selected for a test is determined.

This relation between the difference and the standard error cannot, however, be used to determine whether or not a single item should be included. Critical ratios can be used when we have to test a hypothesis, in this case a null-hypothesis: namely, that there is no actual difference concerning ability on the item between the population of individuals who belong in the upper part of the test distribution and the population of individuals who belong in the lower half. By testing this hypothesis we can establish whether the difference in a certain direction is so large that the probability of its arising by chance, when there is no systematic correlation between item scores and test scores, is so small that it can be ignored. This result supports the belief that the item in fact discriminates between individuals in the same way as the test. However, we cannot verify the null-hypothesis. For many items the obtained difference will be less than that required for a given significance level, simply because the standard error for these items reduces the difference.

14–3   ITEM ANALYSIS; CORRELATION BETWEEN ITEM AND TEST

The relation between the item and the test can, of course, be expressed as a correlation coefficient. Measurement of one of the variables then gives a dichotomous distribution (the item distribution) and measurement of the other usually gives a continuous distribution. The correlation methods which are then most suitable are biserial and point-biserial correlations.

The choice of biserial or point-biserial correlation depends partly upon the item-analysis situation. On the one hand, the fact that the item distribution consists of two categories (the individuals having obtained either one or zero on the item) ought to justify the choice of point-biserial correlation. On the other hand, the item distribution is scarcely indicative of a genuine dichotomy. Assuming that the variables which we measure with test items are normally distributed, we would more naturally use the biserial correlation coefficient to express the relation between item and test.

We have previously mentioned that r_{pbis} depends on the relation between p and q, other things being equal. One should bear this fact in mind when choosing between biserial and point-biserial correlation. The greater the difference between p and q (i.e., the farther away from the median the dichotomization has taken place), the smaller will be the maximum point-biserial correlation. This means that, with point-biserial correlation, very easy or very difficult test items will have systematically lower coefficients for the correlation with the test than items of medium difficulty. Thus, if the coefficients are to be used as a basis for deciding which items in a preliminary version are to be retained and which are to be rejected, items which differentiate in the extreme areas of the test distribution will be rejected to a greater extent than items which differentiate in the middle.

This possible objection to the point-biserial correlation coefficient does not affect the biserial coefficient, which is independent of fluctuations in the relation p/q.

The fact that the point-biserial correlation coefficient depends on the relation between p and q makes it less applicable as an expression for the correlation between item scores and test scores than the biserial coefficient. A method based on the contribution of every individual item to the total variance will be discussed in a later section of this chapter. In the situations discussed there, the point-biserial correlation method is the correct one.

We saw previously that the difference between the proportions of individuals in the upper and lower parts of a test distribution who pass an item depends on the proportion of the test distribution which is used for the computation. As a result, the most certain measure of the item's ability to discriminate is obtained when the difference computation $p_u - p_l$ is based upon the extreme 27% in each half of the test distribution. When p_u and p_l are computed in this way, the discriminating ability of the item can still be expressed by a correlation coefficient for the relation between item and test. It is possible to estimate the correlation coefficients for different combinations of values for p_u and p_l, and with these estimations construct tables or graphs. Flanagan (1939) has published one of the most well-known and most frequently used of these tables (it can be found in Thorndike, 1949, pp. 345–351). There are also tables and graphic solutions for estimating other types of correlation coefficient—point-biserial, tetrachoric, and ϕ-coefficient (cf. Guilford, 1954, pp. 427–453). In many cases a considerable amount of time is saved by using them.

Figure 14–4 shows a graphic solution for estimating the product-moment correlation between item scores and test scores. The estimate is based on the computed proportions p_u and p_l, where p_u as before gives the proportion of the 27% having the highest scores on the test distribution who have also solved the item, while p_l gives the proportion of the lowest 27% on the test distribution who have solved the item. After computing numerical values for p_u and p_l, we find the point on the two lines corresponding to these values. The point where the straight line between these points cuts the middle line in the figure gives the estimated value of the product-moment correlation. If the proportion 0.60 of the 27% with the highest scores on the test distribution, and the proportion 0.25 of the 27% with the lowest scores, have solved item i, the correlation between item scores and test scores can be estimated from Fig. 14–4 to be 0.36.

It should perhaps be pointed out at this stage that the proportion of individuals who manage to solve a test item depends partly on the opportunities for guessing correctly. If guessing may have affected the frequency of correct response, we can make a correction for this effect before using the proportions to estimate the correlation between item and test. Methods of making such corrections are dealt with in Chapter 15.

When testing the contribution of an item to reliability, we want to know whether the reliability of the test is greater when the item is included than when it is not. This is done by testing whether the item measures the same factor as other items: a positive correlation between the item and other items

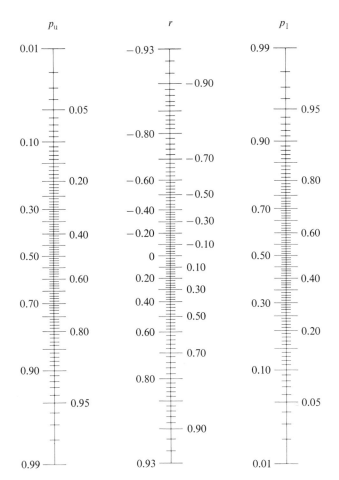

Fig. 14-4 Nomograph for estimating the correlation between an item and the total test. (Modified from Colver, 1959.)

will indicate that it does. In order to obtain a correct result, the item should be excluded from the total test when we compute the correlation coefficient for the relation between it and other items. If we allow the item to be included in the total test, we will obtain a positive correlation between item scores and test scores, even if the correlation between the given item and the other items in the test is zero. If there is a large number of items in the test, it can be a tedious procedure to exclude each new item from the computation of the required values from the score matrix.

The positive correlation we obtain between item scores and test scores because of the item's inclusion in the test is the result of the reappearance in the total test score of the two components which together constitute the score on the single item. Both the true component and the error component included in each individual's score for the item will be included with the same sign in the total test score for the individual.

It is possible, however, to derive an equation for computing the correlation between the given item and the other items in the test, which necessitates computing only the correlation between the item scores and the test scores and the standard deviation for the item and test.

We thus require the correlation between (a) item scores (i) and (b) test scores minus item scores [$r_{i(t-i)}$]. We begin with the correlation between the item scores and the total test scores, which can be written in the following way:

$$r_{it} = \frac{\sum i(a + b + \cdots + i + \cdots + n)}{N s_i s_t}, \tag{14–8}$$

where a, b, c, etc., are obtained individual scores on single items, expressed as differences from respective means.

The sum of the scores in parentheses in the numerator can be written as the sum of scores for the item and the scores for other items [$i + (t - i)$]. Expanding Eq. (14–8) we thus obtain the following:

$$r_{it} = \frac{\sum i^2}{N s_i s_t} + \frac{\sum i(t - i)}{N s_i s_t} = \frac{s_i^2}{s_i s_t} + \frac{r_{i(t-i)} s_{(t-i)}}{s_t} = \frac{s_i + r_{i(t-i)} s_{(t-i)}}{s_t}.$$

Multiplying both sides by s_t we obtain

$$r_{it} s_t = s_i + r_{i(t-i)} s_{(t-i)}; \qquad r_{i(t-i)} = \frac{r_{it} s_t - s_i}{s_{(t-i)}}.$$

The variance in the distribution of differences between item scores and test scores can be computed from Eq. (7–1):

$$s_{(t-i)}^2 = s_t^2 + s_i^2 - 2 r_{it} s_i s_t.$$

The required correlation between scores for item i and scores for the other items in a test (t) in which the item is included will thus be obtained from the equation

$$r_{i(t-i)} = \frac{r_{it} s_t - s_i}{\sqrt{s_t^2 + s_i^2 - 2 r_{it} s_i s_t}}. \tag{14–9}$$

14–4 RELIABILITY INDEX

For equal item variances the total test variance is dependent on the magnitude of the correlation between the items. Under these conditions the contribution of an item to the reliability can be computed in a variance-covariance matrix by examining its contribution to the test variance. Since the number of covariance terms to be computed increases very rapidly with the number of items [according to the formula $n(n - 1)/2$], this procedure is usually applicable only if data machines are available. However, a simpler procedure can also be used.

The correlation between an item i and the test t can be written

$$ r_{ti} = \frac{\sum_{j=1}^{N} x_{tj} x_{ij}}{N s_t s_i}, \tag{14-10} $$

where x_{tj} is individual j's score on test t, expressed as a deviation from M_t, and x_{ij} is individual j's score on item i, expressed as a deviation from M_i. This gives

$$ N r_{ti} s_t s_i = \sum_{j=1}^{N} x_{tj} x_{ij}. \tag{14-11} $$

But the obtained score x_t for individual j is equal to the sum of obtained scores on the individual items:

$$ x_{tj} = x_{1j} + x_{2j} + \cdots + x_{kj} + \cdots + x_{nj}, \tag{14-12} $$

where k is any item and n is the total number of items. We thus have

$$ x_{tj} = \sum_{k=1}^{n} x_{kj}. \tag{14-13} $$

Equation (14-11) can now be written

$$ N r_{ti} s_t s_i = \sum_{k=1}^{n} \sum_{j=1}^{N} x_{ij} x_{kj}. \tag{14-14} $$

But

$$ \frac{\sum_{j=1}^{N} x_{ij} x_{kj}}{N s_i s_k} = r_{ik}. $$

Equation (14-14) can now be written

$$ N r_{ti} s_t s_i = N \sum_{k=1}^{n} r_{ik} s_i s_k. $$

Dividing both sides by N we obtain

$$ r_{ti} s_t s_i = \sum_{k=1}^{n} r_{ik} s_i s_k. \tag{14-15} $$

In Eq. (14-15), n terms are included in the summation on the right-hand side, and i and k denote the same item for one of these terms. Thus the single item in question is to be correlated not only with $n - 1$ other items but also with itself. When i and k are the same item, the correlation will of course be 1.0 and the standard deviations s_i and s_k will be equal, so that $s_i s_k$ can be written s_i^2. The right-hand side of Eq. (14–15) will then consist of *one* variance term (s_i^2) and $n - 1$ covariance terms $(r_{ik}s_i s_k)$, and the equation will have the following appearance:

$$r_{ti}s_t s_i = s_i^2 + \sum_{k=1}^{n} r_{ik}s_i s_k. \qquad (i \neq k) \qquad (14\text{–}16)$$

The right-hand side of Eq. (14–16), however, consists of the sum of the scores in a row of the variance matrix in Table 4–2. The contribution of the item to the total variance is obtained by summing over every score in a row. The total variance consists of the sum of every item variance and every co-variance term, i.e., every score in the total matrix. The equation for the variance of a composite test (Eq. 4–4) also shows that the right-hand side of Eq. (14–16) constitutes the contribution of an item to the total test variance. The total test variance s_t^2 is then the sum of n terms of the same type as the right-hand side of Eq. (14–16). The total test variance can also be written as the sum of n terms of the same type as the left-hand side:

$$s_t^2 = \sum_{i=1}^{n} r_{ti}s_t s_i. \qquad (14\text{–}17)$$

The standard deviation of the test (s_t) is constant, and is included in all of the terms in the summation. We can remove it from the summation by dividing both sides of the equation by s_t:

$$s_t = \sum_{i=1}^{n} r_{ti}s_i. \qquad (14\text{–}18)$$

The standard deviation of a test distribution can thus be expressed in terms of the correlation between the test and the individual items and the standard deviation of the individual items. The term $r_{ti}s_i$, the *reliability index* for item i, is a measure of the item's contribution to the total test variance and hence to the reliability (see p. 212). The standard deviation of the distribution of obtained scores is made up of the sum of every item's reliability index.

For a fixed number of items and unchanged variances in the single items, the reliability is directly related to the magnitude of the total variance, according to the Kuder-Richardson formula (Eq. 9–12). The effect on the test's reliability of adding a single item can now be computed by inserting obtained scores in this formula.

We first compute s_t^2 (which is equal to the squared sum of the reliability indices) and $\sum s_i^2$ with the item excluded from the test, and then with it included. The reliability coefficients obtained by inserting the two sets of variance scores in the Kuder-Richardson formula are then compared.

It should be pointed out that no special assumptions or approximations have been introduced in the derivation of Eq. (14–16). The numerical value of s_t^2, computed as the squared sum of the reliability indices for the items, will thus be identical with that obtained by computing the variance with the usual equation. The correlation coefficient included in the reliability index is then a point-biserial coefficient.

The fact that the correlation is to be computed as a point-biserial coefficient makes a simple expression for the reliability index available for computational purposes. Inserting Eqs. (14–3) (for the correlation between item and test, r_{ti}) and (2–10) (for the standard deviation of a single item) in the equation for the reliability index, we obtain

$$r_{ti}s_i = [(M_p - M_t)/s_t]\sqrt{p/q}\sqrt{pq} = p[(M_p - M_t)/s_t]. \quad (14\text{–}19)$$

When we make an analysis of a set of items in, say, a preliminary version of a test, the mean and the standard deviation (M_t and s_t) of the test distribution will be the same for every item. The only score which needs to be computed for each individual item is M_p, the mean of the test distribution for those who have solved item i.

Equation (14–18) was derived on the assumption that item i, whose correlation with the test is computed in every particular case, is included in the test. A correction similar to that described in the previous section is thus unnecessary.

The most important application of the reliability index occurs in item analysis which must take into account the requirement that the test have, in addition to high reliability, as high a validity as possible.

14–5   VALIDITY INDEX

The following expression for the correlation between test scores (t) and criterion scores (g) (i.e., for the validity coefficient r_{tg}) can be derived by using the complete variance-covariance matrix for the relation between test and criterion:

$$r_{tg} = \frac{\sum_{i=1}^{n} r_{gi}s_i s_g}{s_t s_g}. \quad (14\text{–}20)$$

In this equation s_t is equal to the sum of the reliability indices of the items (Eq. 14–18). The standard deviation of the criterion (s_g) is a constant included in every term in the summation in the numerator and can, therefore, be removed from the summation. Cancelling s_g, we obtain the following expression for the validity coefficient:

$$r_{tg} = \frac{\sum_{i=1}^{n} r_{gi}s_i}{\sum_{i=1}^{n} r_{ti}s_i}. \quad (14\text{–}21)$$

The expression $r_{gi}s_i$ is the *validity index* for item i. The magnitude of an item's validity index thus depends on the magnitude of the correlation between item scores and criterion scores, and on the magnitude of the item's standard deviation. The correlation between an item and the criterion should also in this case be computed with point-biserial correlation. Therefore an equation analogous to Eq. (14-19) can be used for computing the validity index of an item.

A direct numerical expression for the validity coefficient is thus the ratio between the sum of the validity indices of the items and the sum of their reliability indices. In order to obtain, for a given criterion, as high a validity as possible in a test, we should obviously choose items which have as high a ratio as possible between the validity and reliability indices. We want high correlation between item and criterion scores (r_{gi}), and low correlation between item and test scores (r_{ti}). An item whose validity index is equal to its reliability index measures the criterion variable to the same extent as it measures the test variable, and thus contributes the same amount to the test's validity as to its reliability.

The easiest way of choosing items is to plot the reliability and validity indices against each other in a coordinate system with the reliability indices along one axis and the validity indices along the other. A coordinate system with the points plotted for a number of test items is shown in Fig. 14-5. The test items most suitable for inclusion in the final version of the test will in the first instance be those in the top right-hand quadrant. The items there

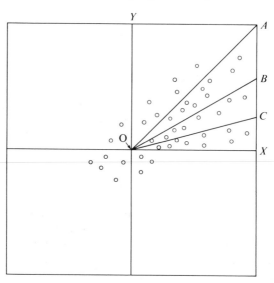

Fig. 14-5 Coordinate system with reliability index (X) plotted against the validity index (Y).

have positive values for both the reliability index and the validity index. Whether we should also include items in the top left-hand quadrant, which have a higher validity index than reliability index, depends on how the test is to be used (see the discussion on differential prediction and classification in Chapter 12).

The items found in sector AOY have a higher validity index than reliability index. This can, of course, be the case only for a limited number of items. Since the ratio between reliability and validity indices is greater than 1.0, such items will make a considerable contribution to the validity of the test. Validity is, of course, increased by the addition of test items which measure some variable other than that measured by previous items. It was demonstrated in Chapter 13 that making a test more heterogeneous can lead to a reduction in reliability. Considerations of reliability should therefore determine whether or not these items should be included.

As has already been said, if we are interested only in validity, we should choose items with reliability and validity indices as nearly equal as possible. This means that we should first include the items in sector AOB in the test, then items in sector BOC, and so on. However, for the sake of accuracy in individual prediction from one variable to the other and in the differences between measurements of other variables, it is also necessary to satisfy the requirement that the reliability be as high as possible. Items close to the origin in sector AOB will, to be sure, make a somewhat greater contribution to validity than items farther from the origin in sector BOC. However, the latter items will often be preferred to the former, since, at the same time as they increase the test's validity, they contribute to its reliability to a greater extent.

14–6   THE CONTRIBUTION OF ITEMS TO RELIABILITY AND VALIDITY

There are two factors to be taken into account in item analysis. The first concerns the accuracy of the values computed for the contribution of each item to reliability and validity respectively, whether this be expressed as a difference measure, a correlation coefficient, a reliability index, or a validity index. These values are naturally subject to the usual random variation, and their accuracy as estimates of the correlation between item scores and test scores or criterion scores depends on the size of the sample on which the computations are based. The smaller the sample of individuals, the more uncertain is the order in which we select items for the test. We will then include items in the test which are poor from the point of view of reliability and validity, at the expense of others which are better in these respects. One consequence of this situation is that the random variation is used systematically for computing different discrimination indices. This will lead to an overestimate of the reliability and validity of the test composed of the items chosen. The genuine reliability and validity of the final test must, therefore, be estimated by cross validation for a sample of individuals other than that on which the choice of items was based. If the size of the sample permits, the cross validation can be made by randomly dividing the sample into two equal parts and computing the relevant measures for each of these parts.

The second factor affects every method for computing the contribution of the single item to reliability, but does not affect the testing of the item's contribution to validity. When the effect of an item on reliability is tested for a preliminary version of a test, the correlation between the item and the total number of items is computed. It contains, however, a number of items which will not be included in the final version. The correlation between the single item and the preliminary version is thus an inaccurate measure of the relation between the item and the final version of the test. The extent of the deviation between (a) the correlation of item and preliminary version and (b) the correlation of item and test will of course depend partly on the relative difference in the number of items in the test and preliminary version, and partly on the extent to which the exclusion of items in the preliminary version changes the factor structure of the test.

The only completely satisfactory procedure for avoiding this latter difficulty is based on the use of a complete variance-covariance matrix (see p. 57). From this matrix we can determine both the sum of the variances of the single items from the diagonal scores and the sum of the covariance terms for different constellations of items. The reliability of the different groupings of items is then tested by inserting the values for the sum of the variances of the individual items and the total variance in the Kuder-Richardson formula. With the introduction of electronic computers, it is now possible to apply this procedure, which was formerly too laborious and tedious.

Limitations of this type in the methods applicable in practice to reliability analysis of individual items do not affect validity analysis. In the latter, the criterion measure used will of course be of constant length and independent of the number of items included in the preliminary and final versions of the test respectively.

14–7 FREQUENCY OF CORRECT RESPONSE AND CORRELATION BETWEEN SINGLE ITEMS

It was shown in Chapter 4 that the magnitude of the variance in the distribution of obtained scores depends partly on the frequency of correct response for the items, and partly on the magnitude of the correlation between the single items. The items' frequencies of correct response also affect the appearance of the distribution of scores. The frequency of correct response is then an important factor in item analysis, since, when we construct a new test, we often attempt to obtain a specific type of distribution of scores. But this cannot be done without also taking into account the correlations of the items. Consideration of the frequencies of correct response and intercorrelations at the same time leads, however, to certain complications.

The frequency of correct response for an item is usually expressed as a p-score, which gives the proportion of the total number of individuals tested who manage to solve the item. A high p-score means that the item has been easy and has been solved by most individuals. This high p-score will correspond to a low standard score: the item has discriminated at a very low level on the hypothetical distribution (see p. 14). A preliminary version of a test with many easy items will give a negatively skewed distribution of scores. An item with low frequency of correct response has a high standard score, and a surplus of these items gives a positively skewed distribution of test scores.

Each individual item discriminates maximally at the p-score 0.50. The average number of individuals from which each individual is discriminated will then be a maximum. However, every item will discriminate in the middle of the hypothetical distribution. If we choose items with as high intercorrelations as possible in order to secure high reliability, the result is then a tendency toward a bimodal distribution (see p. 55). In the extreme case of a correlation of 1.0 between the items, the result will be a distribution of individuals in two categories, the first category having a score of zero and the second having a score equal to the number of items (see Fig. 4–1b). In this case every single item will discriminate between exactly the same individuals as every other item. Thus we cannot obtain a normal distribution of test scores by choosing items which have at the same time maximum discriminating power and maximum intercorrelations.

What will happen if we maintain maximal discriminating power for the individual items (i.e., p-scores of 0.50) but ignore the requirement of high intercorrelations? If we choose the other extreme value for the intercorrelations, namely zero, we will clearly obtain the same distribution as if we had obtained the individual's score on each item by tossing a coin. It is probable that we would obtain a binomial distribution (see p. 55). A test constructed according to these principles would be of little use in practical situations. An intercorrelation of zero between items means that every item measures something different from every other item. The variable defined by items which are so heterogeneous would be difficult to interpret. Reliability would of necessity be low; if we assume that the reliability of each of the items is the same, the reliability of the test would not be higher than that of a single item.

The problem must be solved by a compromise between maximum discriminating power for the individual items and maximum correlation between items. Consider Fig. 1–10. A hypothetical distribution is split up by items 1–6 in a completely homogeneous test in which the difficulty of the items is chosen so that their positions on the continuum give equal scale units. The test's perfect homogeneity would be shown by biserial correlation coefficients of 1.0 between each item and the test. The ϕ-coefficient for the correlation between the items would not, however, be 1.0, even if the test's homogeneity were perfect. The maximum value of the phi-coefficient which expresses the relation between single test items is dependent on the relation between p-scores for the items, and can be 1.0 only when these are the same. This would not be the case for any pair of items in the test which has given the score distribution t in Fig. 1–10.

The problems we have dealt with concerning the relation between frequencies of correct response and (a) the items' intercorrelations and (b) the appearance of the score distribution become apparent when we wish to construct an instrument which gives a normal distribution of scores. It was pointed out in Chapter 1 that situations arise where we do, in fact, wish to obtain a bimodal distribution of scores, and these are perhaps as common as those cases where we require an interval scale. We want a bimodal distribution whenever we wish the instrument to distinguish between those who are above a certain level on the given variable and those who are below this level. One application of the most common individual intelligence tests for children is to determine whether a certain child has the intellectual capacity to take part in normal classwork, i.e., whether the pupil has an I.Q. which lies above or below a critical level in the area 85–90. We wish to make as reliable and valid a differentiation as possible at this specific critical level, and we are relatively uninterested in the exact position of the pupil within either part of the distribution. The practical consequence for test construction will be that the items' p-scores are so chosen that every single item differentiates within this area. Clearly, items with p-scores between 0.75 and 0.84 should be chosen, since the level in the example given lies between $-0.67s$ and $-1.00s$. Furthermore, the items should show a high intercorrelation, so as to ensure high reliability in the discrimination within the critical area. So long as the object was to construct an interval scale, a test consisting of items with the same p-scores and high intercorrelations was considered inadequate, since it gave a bimodal distribution. In the present situation, however, this is the very distribution we require.

In item analysis for testing the contribution of the single item to reliability and validity in this last-mentioned situation, we make use of ϕ-coefficients. The magnitude of the ϕ-coefficient depends systematically on the relation between the p-scores on the two distributions which are correlated with each other, and maximum ϕ-coefficients of 1.0 can only be obtained when these p-scores are the same. This is normally considered a disadvantage when ϕ-coefficients are used. Identical p-scores should, however, be an advantage in the present situation, since all of the items we wish to include are those with p-scores corresponding to the standard score at which we wish the total test to discriminate. The above method of selecting items is suitable in a number of practical situations, especially in selection and placement situations where a specific critical level is fixed.

PROBLEMS

1. See Table 2–2 in the text.

   (a) Compute r_{pbis} for each item (i.e., the correlation of each item with the total score). Use Eq. (14–2) or (14–3).

   (b) Compute r_{bis} for the same items. Use Eq. (14–5) or (14–6).

2. Compute the correlation between items and total score in the same matrix, expressed as a ϕ-coefficient [dichotomization of the score distribution at, for example, 4.5 (i.e., the poorer part is made up of those with $X_j = 1$–4)].

3. Some boys and girls took part in a test procedure and the following scores were obtained.

Raw score	Boys	Girls
	Frequency	Frequency
3	0	1
4	0	0
5	1	1
6	0	3
7	2	1
8	3	2
9	3	1
10	1	1

   (a) Compute the correlation between sex and raw score in the form of an r_{pbis}. Interpret the result.

   (b) Can the correlation be computed in the form of an r_{bis}?

4. Some pupils passed and others failed in an examination. In a second examination in the same subject the results were as follows for the two categories.

Raw score	Passed in Examination 1	Failed in Examination 1
	Frequency	Frequency
1	0	1
2	1	3
3	1	1
4	0	2
5	2	1
6	1	2
7	3	0
8	2	0

   (a) Compute the correlation between the two examinations in the form of an r_{pbis}.

(b) Compute the correlation in the form of an r_{bis}. Compare the results in (a) and (b).

5. Compute r_{bis}/r_{pbis} for the data in Problem 4. Compare the result with the relation in Eq. (14–7).

6. See Table 2–2 in the text. Compute r_{bis} using Flanagan's method. Use Fig. 14–4 to read off values for each item.

7. Compute the reliability index for each item in Table 2–2, both by multiplying r_{ti} by s_i, and by Eq. (14–19), which is used in practice.

8. Sum the reliability indices for every item and check Eq. (14–18).

9. For the score matrix below, compute the standard deviation of the distribution
   (a) as the sum of the reliability indices,
   (b) using the usual equation for computing the standard deviation.

Item

Subject	1	2	3	4	5	6
1	1					
2	1	1				
3	1	1	1			
4	1	1		1		
5	1	1	1	1		
6	1	1	1	1		
7	1	1	1		1	
8	1	1		1	1	
9	1	1	1	1	1	
10	1	1	1	1	1	1

10. The following criterion scores are available for the ten individuals whose scores are given in the score matrix in Problem 9.

Subject	1	2	3	4	5	6	7	8	9	10
Criterion	5	2	5	4	8	5	4	7	5	6

(a) Compute the validity index for each of the items in Problem 9.

(b) Compute the validity of the test consisting of the items in the score matrix in Problem 9 both as the correlation between obtained scores on the test and the criterion, and as the ratio of the sums of the validity and reliability indices.

11. Plot the items for selection purposes in the same way as in Fig. 14–5.

12. The following values were obtained from an item analysis of a test with 60 items: $pq = 13.25$, $s_t = 10.5$. This gives $r_{KR} = 0.895$. One item has $p = 0.6$ and $r_{ti} = 0.10$. Compute the internal consistency of the test if this item is removed.

13. The matrix below shows the results of a test procedure. Rank the items according to their ability to discriminate between the better and poorer halves of the test scores for the individuals tested.

Subject

Item	A	B	C	D	E	F
1	+	+		+	+	+
2		+	+	+		+
3		+		+	+	
4		+	+		+	

14. For a test with 10 items, the following results were obtained from an item analysis with criterion (g) data available.

Item	p	r_{ti}	r_{gi}
1	0.10	0.30	0.20
2	0.20	0.50	0.40
3	0.30	0.40	0.10
4	0.50	0.60	0.30
5	0.50	0.70	0.50
6	0.60	0.50	0.30
7	0.60	0.20	0.20
8	0.70	0.40	0.10
9	0.80	0.30	0.20
10	0.90	0.40	0.10

Compute the internal consistency (Kuder-Richardson) and the validity. Determine which item should be removed first if

(a) the test is to be made as homogeneous as possible,

(b) only the validity is to be taken into account.

Determine the internal consistency and the validity of the remaining items in these two cases.

REFERENCES

CHESIRE, L., M. SAFFIR, and L. L. THURSTONE (1933). *Computing diagrams for the tetrachoric correlation coefficient.* Chicago: University of Chicago Press.

COLVER, R. M. (1959). Estimating item indices by nomographs. *Psychometrika*, **24**, 179–185.

FERGUSON, G. A. (1959). *Statistical analysis in psychology and education.* New York: McGraw-Hill.

FLANAGAN, J. C. (1939). General considerations in the selection of test items and a short method of estimating the product moment coefficient from data at the tails of the distribution. *J. Educ. Psychol.*, **30**, 674–680.

GUILFORD, J. P. (1954). *Psychometric methods* (2nd ed.). New York: McGraw-Hill.

JENKINS, W. L. (1956). Triserial *r*—a neglected statistic. *J. Appl. Psychol.*, **40**, 63–64.

KELLY, T. L. (1939). The selection of upper and lower groups for the validation of test items. *J. Educ. Psychol.*, **30**, 17–24.

McNEMAR, Q. (1962). *Psychological statistics.* New York: Wiley.

THORNDIKE, R. L. (1949). *Personnel selection.* New York: Wiley.

Suggested reading

GHISELLI, E. E. (1964). *Theory of psychological measurement.* New York: McGraw-Hill.

GUILFORD, J. P. (1954). *Psychometric methods* (2nd ed.) New York: McGraw-Hill.

GULLIKSEN, H. (1950). *Theory of mental tests.* New York: Wiley.

HENRYSSON, S. (1962). The relation between factor loadings and biserial correlation in item analysis. *Psychometrika*, **27**, 419–424.

HENRYSSON, S. (1963). Correction of item-total correlations in item analysis. *Psychometrika*, **28**, 211–218.

MYERS, C. T. (1962). The relationship between item difficulty and test validity and reliability. *Educ. Psychol. Measmt.*, **22**, 565–572.

SOLOMON, H. (1961). *Studies in item analysis and prediction.* Stanford: Stanford University Press.

CHAPTER 15

Guessing

In many so-called multiple-choice tests, alternative responses are given, which the subject has to choose between. This type of test makes objective scoring easier, but on the other hand the individual has a greater chance of responding correctly by guessing to items which he would otherwise have been unable to solve. Because of guessing, the number of ones in the score matrix will be changed. Consequently, the items' frequencies of correct response and the individual test scores, and hence the total test variance, will also be affected. Some common methods of correcting for the effect of guessing will be presented, since both the items' frequencies of correct response and the total test variance affect the reliability of a test and the choice of items in test construction.

The effect of guessing on p-values for individual items is obvious. For each item we will obtain a number of ones in the score matrix, although not all those individuals who obtain the ones will in fact know the correct solutions. Through guessing, the frequencies of correct response will be greater than they would have been otherwise.

When assessing the effect of guessing on reliability, we must distinguish between two different factors. Guessing can add both a systematic variance and a pure error variance to the total test variance.

The strength of the tendency to guess when one cannot solve an item varies from individual to individual. If a multiple-choice test is administered to a number of individuals who are unable to solve every item, some will guess more than others. This guessing will add to the total test variance a systematic variance which will also be obtained if we test the same individuals with a parallel test. This variance will thus be a true variance which will contribute to the test's reliability. It will also be an expression for genuine interindividual differences with respect to risk-taking. A correction can be introduced if this variance is considered to be irrelevant in a given situation.

If individual differences in guessing tendency are kept under control by, for instance, instructing the individuals to guess on every item which they are unable to solve, a pure error variance will be added to the total variance. The score matrix will randomly contain ones which are the result of guessing. Since the error variance is increased without a corresponding increase in true variance, this error variance will have the effect of lowering reliability. No correction can be introduced for this error variance.

When we assess the effect of guessing on the validity of the test, it is also necessary to distinguish between systematic and random influences. The variance which is systematic, and is to be found in (for instance) parallel tests, expresses interindividual differences in a personality trait and therefore can be used as a basis for prediction and diagnosis. It is a variance which can also be found in a distribution of criterion scores and will thus contribute to increased validity. If this is not the case, it will lower the validity coefficient. The unsystematic error variance which is a result of guessing cannot, of course, contribute to the validity of the test and is merely a handicap in this respect.

15–1 INDIVIDUAL CORRECTION

When we are testing with multiple-choice methods, we can take a test score t_j to be the sum of two subscores: R, the number of items to which the individual has responded correctly because he has genuinely been able to determine which responses are correct, and R_g, the number of items which the individual has responded to correctly through guessing:

$$t_j = R + R_g. \tag{15–1}$$

The magnitude of R_g cannot be computed empirically. We are unable to determine definitely on which items, if any, an individual has guessed correctly. A value for R_g can, however, be estimated in the following way. If every alternative is considered an equally probable choice for an individual who does not know the correct response, the probability that he will answer correctly by guessing on a given item will be $1/m$, where m is the number of alternative responses. For five alternatives the probability of guessing correctly on an item is $1/5$. The probable number of correct responses on two guessed items is clearly double ($2/5$), and the probable number of correct responses on three guessed items is three times as great. If the number of items on which the individual guessed were known, we could then estimate R_g as G/m, where G is the number of items on which the individual guessed. We do not know this number, but we do know the number of incorrect responses he has recorded. We assume (a) that every incorrect response is the result of guessing, and (b) that every alternative response for items which the individual is unable to solve is equally attractive. The number of incorrect responses (F) should then be distributed equally over the $m - 1$ incorrect alternatives. For each of these, the number of incorrect guesses can then be estimated to be $F/(m - 1)$. But on the assumption that every alternative is an equally probable choice for an individual who guesses, an equal number of guesses should have arrived at the correct alternative. Thus

$$R_g = \frac{F}{m - 1}. \tag{15–2}$$

It follows from Eq. (15–1) that

$$t_j = R + \frac{F}{m - 1} \tag{15–3}$$

and

$$R = t_j - \frac{F}{m - 1}, \tag{15–4}$$

where t_j is the number of items marked correctly for individual j, R is the number of items which j has been able to solve without guessing, F is the number of incorrectly marked items for individual j, and m is the number of alternative responses.

The correction of individual scores with the help of Eq. (15–4) has the effect of equalizing the differences between individuals in the tendency to guess. Individuals A and B have solved 25 and 22 items respectively on a test with 40 items and four alternative responses. A has 15 incorrect responses and B has 6; this indicates that A has guessed on every item which he has been unable to solve, while B has guessed to a considerably lesser extent. Using Eq. (15–4) we can now estimate the number of items which A has really been able to solve to be $25 - 15/3 = 20$ items, and the number of items which B has been able to solve to be $22 - 6/3 = 20$ items. If we assume that the correction functions properly, A and B were in reality able to solve an equal number of items, but the number of correct responses was different because of different tendencies to guess. It is such differences which are cancelled by using Eq. (15–4). The effect of guessing on the number of correct items, and hence also the effect of the correction, are obviously dependent on the number of alternative responses. The greater the number of alternative responses, the smaller will be the probability of giving correct responses through guessing and, consequently, the smaller will be the correction term.

Equation (15–4) gives an estimate of the number of answers which the individual really knows. The result is in fact an estimate whose validity depends on the extent to which the assumptions are satisfied, i.e., that the individual has guessed on the items which he has responded to without being able to solve, and that every alternative, correct as well as incorrect, is equally attractive.

The differing guessing tendencies of individuals can also be controlled without correcting for guessing with the above equation. This is done in the instructions by asking those tested to respond to every item and to guess in those cases where they do not know the correct solution. Individual differences in guessing tendencies will not have any effect in this case. The method has, however, the disadvantage that reliability is reduced through increased guessing. This form of control over individual guessing tendencies is seldom used in practice. Another method which is often recommended is to inform the subjects about the correction made for guessing. Such information normally has the effect of reducing the guessing tendency.

It should be noted that the reliability of scores which have been corrected for guessing is not the same as the reliability of uncorrected scores. The reliability of the corrected scores must therefore be estimated independently. Of even greater interest, however, is the effect of the correction on the validity of the test. We stated previously that guessing normally reduces the test's validity by providing the test distribution with a variance which is unlikely to have a corresponding variance in the distribution of criterion data. The purpose of the correction is to eliminate this part of the variance of the test data, and if it is successful, it leads to increased validity. Lord (1963) has derived an equation for computing the validity of data corrected for guessing. He states, however, like the majority of other experts, that the effect of correction on the validity coefficient is so small that only in special circumstances is it worth the time and expense involved. According to Lord, it is of most value when (a) the tendency to guess varies considerably from individual to individual, (b) the number of alternative responses is fewer than five, and (c) the test is very difficult. Assumptions (a) and (c) are related: the harder the test items, the fewer the number of items the individual will in fact be able to solve, and the greater the opportunities for differences in guessing tendency to come into play.

One reason for correcting for guessing, which in most situations is considered more important than the possible positive effect on the test's validity, is the psychological effect on the individuals tested of knowing that they will be punished for guessing. This assumes, of course, that they are told in the instructions that the correction will be made. Even if this knowledge does not have the same restraining effect on everyone, it probably leads to a reduction in the dispersion of the irrelevant variance obtained through guessing.

15–2 CORRECTION OF FREQUENCIES OF CORRECT SOLUTION

The derivation of an equation for correction for the effect of guessing on frequencies of correct solution is based on the same assumptions as Eq. (15–4) for the correction of individual scores.

The frequency of correct solution for item i (f_i) can be written as the sum of the number of individuals who know the correct solution (R) and the number of individuals who answer correctly by means of guessing (R_g):

$$f_i = R + R_g. \tag{15-5}$$

It can easily be shown that Eq. (15-2), which is used for individual correction, also holds in this case. Equation (15-5) can thus be written

$$f_i = R + \frac{F}{m-1}; \tag{15-6}$$

$$R = f_i - \frac{F}{m-1}, \tag{15-7}$$

where f_i is the frequency of correct solution for item i, R is the number of individuals who know the solution to item i, F is the number of individuals who record an incorrect solution, and m is the number of alternative responses.

Since the items will be subject to varying amounts of guessing, the correction by Eq. (15-7) will, of course, affect the relation between p-values for different items.

Equation (15-7) is based on the assumption that every alternative is equally attractive when the individual tested does not know the correct response but is obliged to guess if he is to answer the question at all. For tests with a certain type of item it can be relatively easy to find alternative answers such that this condition is fairly well satisfied, but for other tests it may be more difficult.

Horst (1933) has derived a correction equation for a test with five alternative responses which are considered to vary in attractiveness. We take $5a$ to be the number of individuals tested for whom all five alternatives are equally attractive, $4b$ the number for whom four alternatives are equally attractive, $3c$ the number for whom three alternatives are equally attractive, and $2d$ the number for whom two alternatives are equally attractive. Furthermore, we assume that the correct response is included among the equally attractive alternatives for each group. The number who can really solve the item is m, and the distribution of the number of items for each alternative can now be written as shown in the matrix in Table 15-1. The total number of individuals (N) is equal to $5a + 4b + 3c + 2d + m$.

What we wish to find, of course, is the numerical value of m, the number who gave the correct response without guessing. The value of m can now be estimated from columns 1 and 2—i.e., the column which contains m and thus gives the obtained frequency of response for the correct response, and the column which gives the response frequency for the most attractive of the incorrect alternatives. The two columns give identical estimates of the probable number of guesses on the alternatives and the difference between

Table 15–1

Response alternative	Correct	Incorrect				
	1	2	3	4	5	
	a	*a*	*a*	*a*	*a*	5*a*
	b	*b*	*b*	*b*		4*b*
	c	*c*	*c*			3*c*
	d	*d*				2*d*
	m					*m*

the two columns represents the estimated number of individuals who are able to solve the item without guessing. The estimate of m is thus the difference between the number of correct responses and the number of times the most attractive of the incorrect alternatives is chosen.

When we discussed the correction of individual scores, we mentioned that the correction in this case can only be used to cancel interindividual differences in guessing tendencies, and that the correction can thus be used only in a situation where every individual does not attempt to solve every item. This limitation of the application of the correction equation holds only for correction of individual scores, and does not affect the application of the equations to correction for the effect of guessing on frequencies of correct solution.

PROBLEMS

1. In a multiple-choice test with 100 items, a pupil had 40 correct and 36 wrong. The number of alternative responses was 7. Estimate the number of correct solutions (correct for guessing).

2. A multiple-choice test with three distractors (wrong alternatives) was used in an experiment. The sample consisted of 200 boys aged 10–11. On item 57, 130 of them gave the correct answer while 63 answered incorrectly. Calculate the number of boys who could really solve the item.

3. In another multiple-choice test, also with three distractors, 80 of the 200 boys answered item 29 incorrectly. The three distractors had 20, 25, and 35 answers respectively. Calculate the number of individuals who really knew the correct answer.

4. For item 30 on the same test, the answers were distributed as follows among the four alternative responses: 27, 83, 40, 50. The second alternative was the correct answer. (a) Correct the frequency of correct solution for guessing. (b) How many individuals had no idea of the correct answer to the item?

REFERENCES

HORST, A. P. (1933). The difficulty of a multiple choice test item. *J. Educ. Psychol.*, **24,** 229–232.

LORD, F. M. (1963). Formula scoring and validity. *Educ. Psychol. Measmt.*, **23,** 663–672.

Suggested reading

GULLIKSEN, H. (1950). *Theory of mental tests.* New York: Wiley.

LORD, F. M. (1964). The effect of random guessing on test validity. *Educ. Psychol. Measmt.*, **24,** 745–747.

MATTSON, D. (1965). The effects of guessing on the standard error of measurement and the reliability of test scores. *Educ. Psychol. Measmt.*, **25,** 727–730.

TRAXLER, A. E. (1951). Administering and scoring the objective test. In E. F. Lindquist (Ed.) *Educational measurement.* Washington, D.C.: Am. Council on Educ.

CHAPTER 16

Scales, Transformations, and Norms

16–1 INTRODUCTION

In many situations where measurements obtained by the methods of differential psychology are applied, we need to compare results obtained by different methods. This is true, for example, in every situation where a score profile is the best basis for decision, diagnosis, or counseling. We have previously assumed that an individual's test score is obtained by simply adding up the number of correctly solved items. However, the raw score obtained for an individual by such a procedure is dependent not only on his own performance but also on the properties of the test (e.g., number of items in the test, difficulty of the items, etc.). A comparison between the raw scores 75 and 15 which individual A has obtained on Tests I and II gives no information unless we know something about the tests. If we are told that Test I contains 100 items and Test II contains 25 items, we know something about the subject's relative performance in the two tests. But it is only when we have received the information that the distributions of obtained raw scores in the population to which the subject belongs are (say) normal with means 50 and 10 respectively and standard deviations 10 and 3 respectively, that we can make a meaningful comparison of the individual's two scores. In the distribution for Test I he has the standard score $(75 - 50)/10 = 2.50$, and in the distribution for Test II the standard score $(15 - 10)/3 = 1.67$. We can now state that, relatively speaking, the individual has performed better on Test I than on Test II.

The example shows that, in order for results from different tests to be comparable, they must be expressed on the same scale. The comparison between the individual's scores on Tests I and II in the example given became more meaningful after we had *transformed* the raw scores to scores on a standard-score scale. Later we shall see how comparisons between scores on different distributions can be made even more meaningful if we also *normalize* them.

232

A transformation of raw scores to scores on another distribution can be made so that every individual retains exactly his relative position on the distribution. This is a *linear transformation*. The transformation can also change the form of the distribution by changing the size of the scale units at different levels of difficulty, so that a normal distribution of scores is obtained after the transformation. This is called *normalization*. We can perform normalization without performing linear transformation at the same time.

16–2 LINEAR TRANSFORMATION

A linear transformation involves changing the scale so that the mean and/or the standard deviation are changed, while exactly retaining the distribution's form and hence the individuals' relative positions on the distribution. We change the mean of the distribution by adding a constant to every score on the distribution. This merely means that the whole distribution is moved along the scale by the amount of the constant. If we wish to change the mean of a distribution of scores on a school readiness test from 30 to 100, we add the constant 70 to every raw score. The only effect of this is that the whole distribution, with the same form and standard deviation, has been moved 70 points upwards along the scale. We can also change the standard deviation of the distribution without changing the distribution's form or affecting the individuals' relative positions. Every deviation from the mean of the original distribution is thus multiplied by a constant, which gives the relation between the original and the desired standard deviation. In the example with the school-readiness test, we can increase the standard deviations from 10 to 20 by multiplying every deviation from the mean by 2. The distribution we finally obtain will have mean 100 and standard deviation 20. The distribution still has exactly the same form; it is merely 70 units higher on the scale and has been increased in width.

In Eq. (3–13) we have an expression for the prediction of a y-score (Y') from a x-score when the correlation between x- and y-scores (r_{xy}) is known:

$$Y' = r_{xy}(s_y/s_x)(X - M_x) + M_y.$$

Since, when we make a linear transformation, every individual is to retain his relative position on the distribution, the correlation between scores on the original distribution and scores on the transformed distribution will always be 1.0. Thus we obtain the following equation for determining every score on the transformed distribution from the score on the original distribution:

$$Y_j = (s_y/s_x)(X_j - M_x) + M_y, \qquad (16\text{–}1)$$

where Y_j is individual j's score on the transformed distribution, s_y is the standard deviation of the transformed distribution, s_x is the standard deviation of the original distribution, and X_j is individual j's score on the original distribution.

What score will a child obtain on the distribution with mean 100 and standard deviation 20, if he had a score of 45 on the distribution of school-readiness test results with mean 30 and standard deviation 10? Inserting the given values in Eq. (16–1), we obtain the transformed score $(20/10)(45 - 30) + 100 = 130$.

When we wish to make as accurate intra- or interindividual comparisons as possible, we often express values as z-scores, i.e., scores on a scale with the origin as the mean of the distribution and with the standard deviation as unit. However, z-scores have certain disadvantages which sometimes make them rather unsuitable. First, half of the scores on the distribution are negative, and second, we must work with decimal scores in order to obtain a sufficiently fine differentiation among individuals.

Both these difficulties can easily be avoided by a further linear transformation on the distribution. We can, of course, give the distribution any mean and standard deviation whatsoever. However, it should be observed that by doing so we have in no way affected the distribution's form or the individuals' relative positions on the distribution. If we carry out a linear transformation on a positively skewed distribution, the result will be a distribution with exactly the same positive skewness. If we have no reason to expect equal intervals in the distribution being transformed, we have as little reason to do so for the distribution of transformed scores.

In no way do we change the individuals' relative positions, so long as we make linear transformations of the raw-score distribution. The transformed scale has exactly the same qualities as the raw-score scale. Since it is very infrequently that we obtain distributions of raw scores which are exactly normal, a transformation of raw scores to standard scores without at the same time normalizing, and thus changing the form of the distribution, leads to certain consequences for the interpretation of the data. If the distribution

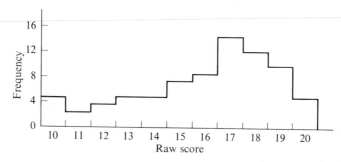

Fig. 16–1 A negatively skewed distribution of scores.

of raw scores is skewed, the mean (e.g., the zero point on a distribution of z-scores) will not lie exactly between the highest and the lowest 50% of the scores of the distribution, i.e., exactly on the median. Nor will the percentage of scores between -1.0 and 0 equal that between 1.0 and 0. The situation can be illustrated by Fig. 16–1, where data are shown for a *negatively* skewed distribution.

If the raw scores had been symmetrically distributed along the whole range, the mean of the distribution would have been 15.0. It is in fact 16.0. In the skewed distribution a considerably greater number of scores will lie in the area between the mean and 18.76 ($M + 1s$) than in the area between the mean and 13.24 ($M - 1s$). In non-normalized distributions a standard score has not, therefore, the same unequivocal statistical meaning as in a normalized distribution.

What we have said about standard-score distributions obtained by means of linear transformation of raw-score distributions also holds for all other distributions obtained in the same way.

16–3 NORMALIZATION

We showed previously that a score on a raw-score distribution or a distribution obtained from one by linear transformation seldom has an exact statistical meaning. This is such a serious disadvantage that such scores cannot be used in many practical situations. The relative position of some standard score on a non-normalized distribution of scores depends entirely on the form of the distribution. The more this approaches a normal distribution, the more concisely a standard score on the distribution can be interpreted. The disadvantages of raw scores or their linear transformations can be avoided by changing the form of the distribution so as to obtain a normal distribution of scores, i.e., by performing a normalization. This is almost always done in conjunction with a linear transformation.

On a normalized distribution every score has a concise statistical meaning. The percentage of individuals above and below each score is known exactly on a scale with known mean and unit of measurement. This is important when, for instance, test results are presented for use in selection and counseling situations. Here, importance is attached not to comparison between differences at different score levels, but to the relative position an individual has on a distribution whose properties are known.

Normalization can be required for other purposes as well. When we wish to use differences, interindividual or intraindividual, we need the individuals' values for the variables in question as scores on an interval scale. For the construction of instruments for measuring on an interval scale, we now return to the assumption discussed in the introductory chapter about normal distributions of scores for psychological variables.

There are as a rule no insurmountable difficulties in constructing measuring instruments which will give normal distributions for performance variables. It is more difficult, however, for other variables—for instance, those measured by questionnaires. As a rule we obtain distributions which are heavily positively skewed, even when we have good reason to assume that a normal distribution of scores exists on a hypothetical continuum. Figure 16–2 shows the distribution of a number of responses on a questionnaire intended to measure psychosomatic disturbances. In this case the skewness is considerable; in other cases it can be less striking, but nevertheless of such magnitude that we cannot assume that the raw scores give the individuals' positions on an interval scale. If the assumption of a normal distribution is reasonable, and we nevertheless obtain a skewed distribution of raw scores, this means that the instrument does not give a true record of the individuals' positions with respect to each other. However, in such cases we can normalize the skewed distribution of obtained scores, i.e., modify the distribution form so that we obtain a normal distribution of scores.

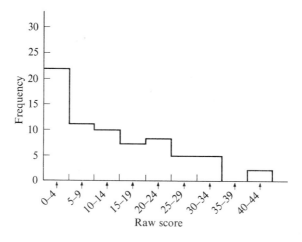

Fig. 16–2 A positively skewed distribution of scores on a psychosomatic inventory.

Column 2 in Table 16–1 shows frequencies for each raw score in a distribution of obtained scores. In the third column (cf_1) cumulative frequencies have been computed. The cumulative-frequency score 28 in this column for raw score 5 thus means that there are 28 scores of 5 or less in the distribution of obtained scores. In the fourth column (cf_2) the frequencies have been transformed to cumulative frequencies for the class means in each class interval. The cumulative frequency for a raw score in the fourth column thus gives the number of scores in the distribution which fall below the class mean in the interval represented by the raw score. Ten scores lie in the class

Table 16–1 Normalization of a distribution of raw scores

Raw score, X	f	cf_1	cf_2	p	Normalized standard score, z
1	2	2	1	0.013	−2.24
2	4	6	4	0.050	−1.64
3	4	10	8	0.100	−1.28
4	8	18	14	0.175	−0.93
5	10	28	23	0.288	−0.56
6	10	38	33	0.413	−0.21
7	12	50	44	0.550	0.13
8	8	58	54	0.675	0.45
9	8	66	62	0.775	0.75
10	6	72	69	0.863	1.09
11	6	78	75	0.938	1.54
12	2	80	79	0.988	2.26

interval for raw score 5. If we assume that the individuals are rectangularly distributed within the class, we see that half (i.e., 5 scores) lie below the class mean and 5 scores lie above. Since we have 18 scores below the class interval 5, and 5 below the class mean within the interval, the cumulative frequency for the class mean will be $18 + 5 = 23$. In the fourth column in Table 16–3 the cumulative frequencies for class means in different intervals have been transformed to proportions. The interpolation made within class interval 5 is based on the assumption of a rectangular distribution of scores in the class interval. We can see immediately that this is not entirely correct in a normal distribution, but so long as we have sufficiently small intervals the approximation we make will produce errors so small that they lack practical significance.

The cumulative-frequency score 23 for the class mean in interval 5 corresponds to the proportion 0.288. Hence, 0.288 of the total distribution of obtained scores lies below the class mean in interval 5. Now that we know the proportion of the total distribution which lies below the class mean in interval 5, we can obtain, from a table of cumulative proportions for a normal distribution, the position on a normal distribution which corresponds to this proportion. We find that the standard score corresponding to the score 0.288 is −0.56. The class mean in interval 5 on the raw-score scale thus divides the obtained distribution of raw scores in the same proportions as the standard score −0.56 divides a normal distribution. The raw score 5 will therefore correspond to the standard score −0.56 in the distribution of normalized scores. Similarly, we compute the positions on a normal distribution corresponding to the class means of the other intervals.

If we now mark the scale values we have computed on a scale of standard scores and draw a frequency polygon of obtained frequencies, we shall obtain a distribution which, as far as is possible with the rough measurements made, corresponds to a normal distribution.

It was pointed out in the previous section on linear transformation that this procedure does not involve any change in the individuals' positions with respect to each other. The correlation between scores on the original and the transformed distribution is 1.0. This is *not* the case for normalization. The purpose of the process is to change the form of the distribution, a change which must, of course, alter the relative distances between the individuals' positions on the distribution. The regression line for prediction of normalized scores from scores on the original distribution will not be linear.

In many practical situations, data are most easily obtained in the form of ranking data. This is true, for example, when we collect criterion data in the form of ratings. When individuals who are unused to psychological rating techniques have to rate their observations, it is often easiest to break down the raters' spontaneous resistance to making such judgments by letting them make them in the form of rankings. However, we can easily normalize these ranking data if we feel justified in assuming that the individuals' true scores follow a normal distribution. In principle we obtain the standard scores which correspond to the respective ranking scores in the manner demonstrated in Table 16–1. Column f will then contain only ones (if we assume that no two individuals are given the same rank). Thereafter the normalization is carried out in the same way as in Table 16–1.

In practical situations where we wish to transform obtained ranking scores to z-scores in a normal distribution, we can easily do this by using special tables which are available (cf. Fisher and Yates, 1953).

Normalization is merely a special case of *nonlinear transformation*. Any transformation which changes the form of the distribution is nonlinear, and any form of distribution may be chosen. However, in practice, the normal distribution is nearly always chosen. The only significant exception to this rule is the nonlinear transformation into a scale, for instance, a percentile scale (see below), which yields a rectangular distribution. Incidentally, the reader will notice that rank numbers (when considered as scale values on an interval scale) are rectangularly distributed (each with the frequency 1).

16–4 PERCENTILE SCALE

The simplest way of making comparisons possible between scores from different distributions is to give an individual's result as a *percentile*. A given percentile can be defined as the point on the scale below which a fixed percentage of the distribution falls. The use of percentile scores often involves interpolation within a class interval in which we assume that the individuals are rectangularly distributed.

Table 16–2 Transformation of a distribution of raw scores to a percentile scale

X	f	%	cf	%	Percentile score, P
1	1	2.5	1	2.5	1.25
2	2	5.0	3	7.5	5.00
3	2	5.0	5	12.5	10.00
4	4	10.0	9	22.5	17.50
5	5	12.5	14	35.0	28.75
6	5	12.5	19	47.5	41.25
7	6	15.0	25	62.5	55.00
8	4	10.0	29	72.5	67.50
9	4	10.0	33	82.5	77.50
10	3	7.5	36	90.0	86.25
11	3	7.5	39	97.5	93.75
12	1	2.5	40	100.0	98.75

Table 16–2 shows a frequency distribution. The frequency (f) and the cumulative frequency (cf), both also transformed to a percentage of the total number of scores, are given for each raw score (X).

If we wish to obtain a percentile score for an individual whose raw score is 5, we must thus, by definition, find the point on the percentile scale which corresponds to score 5. We must remember, however, that score 5 is the class mean of an interval which stretches from 4.5 to 5.5. From the table we can see that 22.5% of the distribution clearly falls below the class limit 4.5; 12.5% (we assume a rectangular distribution of scores) lies between 4.5 and 5. Thus 22.5 + 6.25% falls below the class mean 5. The percentile score for raw score 5 is then 28.75. The percentile score (P) corresponding to each raw score in Table 16–2 has been computed in this way and is given in the final column of the table.

If we wish instead to compute the raw score which corresponds to a certain percentile score, we merely interpolate in the opposite direction. In Table 16–2 we can compute the raw score corresponding to the percentile score 40. We then see that 35% falls below the class limit 5.5, and 12.5% of the distribution lies within the class interval 5.5–6.5. In order to find the point on the raw-score scale corresponding to 40 on the percentile scale, we need 5/12.5 of the class interval 1.0. The raw score corresponding to the percentile score 40 will then be 5.5 + [5/12.5] × 1.0 = 5.9.

The percentile scale makes it possible to estimate the value of individual scores in relation to other scores in the same population. Percentile scores are readily comprehensible and they give a clear and lucid presentation of results. The most important weakness of the percentile scale is that it does not take into account the form of the score distribution. The distribution we obtain when we transform raw scores to percentile scores will be rectangular,

Table 16–3 Standard scores corresponding to different percentile scores

Percentile scores	1	5	10	20	30	40
z	-2.33	-1.64	-1.28	-0.84	-0.52	-0.25

Percentile scores	50	60	70	80	90	95	99
z	0.00	0.25	0.52	0.84	1.28	1.64	2.33

irrespective of the form of the distribution of raw scores. When we estimate differences on a percentile scale, we exaggerate the differences in the middle of the distribution compared to those at the extremes, if the assumption of a normal distribution of true scores is correct. However, percentile scores can easily be transformed to standard scores for corresponding positions on a normal distribution. Table 16–3 gives the z-scores which correspond to given percentile scores.

Table 16–3 can confirm what was said previously about the relation between differences on the percentile scale and on a standard-score scale. While the difference between percentile scores 40 and 50 is only $0.25z$, the difference between percentile scores 70 and 80 is $0.32z$ and the difference between percentile scores 80 and 90 is $0.44z$.

16–5   NORMALIZED SCALES

When a distribution of raw scores has been normalized, we can place the distribution wherever we want on the scale by means of linear transformation, and give the distribution any standard deviation desired. Some of the reasons for normalization are (a) certain expectations derived from differential psychology, (b) the mathematical properties of the normal-distribution function, the convenience of available statistical tables, etc., and (c) probably to some extent the satisfaction derived from conforming to a long tradition. The procedure is also simplified if the transformation of the normalized scale takes place to some known scale for normalized data. Since even normalized standard scores have certain disadvantages mentioned earlier, they are seldom used. Instead, other scales have become more common. Scores on normalized scales are often expressed as *T-scores, stanine scores,* or *I.Q.-equivalents.*

When an obtained score is expressed as a *T*-score, stanine, or I.Q.-equivalent, it refers to a score on a normalized distribution. These terms should thus *not* be used for other data. We do not obtain *T*-scores merely by linearly transforming a raw-score distribution to a distribution with mean 50 and standard deviation 10.

Table 16–4 Stanine distribution

Stanine score	1	2	3	4	5	6	7	8	9
Percentage for each score	4.0	6.6	12.1	17.5	19.7	17.5	12.1	6.6	4.0

When we normalize a raw-score distribution into T-scores, we give the distribution of normalized scores mean 50 and standard deviation 10. The unit is thus $0.1s$ on the T-scale.

The stanine scale takes nine values from 1 to 9 with mean 5 and standard deviation 2.* When we normalize a distribution to a stanine scale, the frequencies are distributed in the following way. The lowest 4% are given the score 1, the next 7% score 2, the next 12% score 3, the next 17% score 4, the next 20% score 5, the next 17% score 6, the next 12% score 7, the next 7% score 8, and the next 4% score 9. The exact percentages of frequencies for different scores are given in Table 16–4.

The percentage for each score corresponds to the part of the distribution which lies on a $\frac{1}{2}s$. The percentage 20 for score 5 is thus the proportion of the distribution which has as its limits the standard scores -0.25 and $+0.25$, that is, $\frac{1}{4}s$ on each side of the mean. Since approximately 27% of a normal distribution falls between the mean and $\frac{3}{4}s$, and 10% falls between the mean and $\frac{1}{4}s$, 17% will lie in the part of the distribution which has as its limits $0.25s$ and $0.75s$ and the percentage of frequencies in the distribution with score 6 will be 17%.

The T-scale allows finer differentiation among individuals than the stanine scale. So long as a sufficiently high reliability justifies a stricter differentiation, we will lose a certain amount of information about the individuals by giving their results as stanine scores. For a reliability of 0.91 the standard error will be $0.3s$, and for a reliability of 0.96 the standard error will be $0.2s$. For a T-scale where $s = 10$, these figures indicate standard errors of 3 and 2 units respectively. The standard error is so small that the scale can be said to differentiate so accurately that one would lose valuable information if the results were to be given on a stanine scale instead of a T-scale.

One of the most misused and misinterpreted concepts in the field of differential psychology is that of the intelligence quotient. Alfred Binet introduced the concept mental age, by which he wished to express a child's level

---

* This is not exactly correct, since the two extreme categories at each end of the distribution have been grouped together to make one category, thus making 9 instead of 11 categories.

of intellectual development based on the result of his individual intelligence test. He determined what was an average performance on the test, measured by the number of correctly solved items, for a sample of children of a given age, e.g., ten-year-olds. Any other child who was then able to solve an equal number, but not necessarily the same items, was judged to have the same level of intellectual development as an average ten-year-old and was assigned the mental age ten, no matter what his chronological age was. Clearly a mental age of ten could be obtained by children of any age. Children whose chronological age was lower than their mental age had attained a level of intellectual development higher than that attained by the majority of the same age group; the opposite was true of children whose chronological age was higher than their mental age.

Mental age did not express an individual child's relative level of development. In order to express this, one needed also to know the child's chronological age. Wilhelm Stern placed the two values in relation to each other in the equation for computing the intelligence quotient (I.Q. = $100MA/CA$). A number of important facts concerning the interpretation of the intelligence quotient can be derived from this equation. The intelligence quotient will be 100 for all children who have the same level of development as the average child of the same age, i.e., who have the same mental and chronological age. This is true for children of all ages. For those who have a lower level of intellectual development than the average for their group, i.e., a lower mental than chronological age, the intelligence quotient will be lower than 100. It will be greater than 100 for children who have developed more quickly than their peers, i.e., have a higher mental than chronological age. In order to interpret an individual intelligence quotient, it is also necessary that the standard deviation of the distribution of the intelligence quotients be approximately the same for all age groups. In other words, the same intelligence quotient must give approximately the same relative position on the distribution from year to year. The standard deviation of the distribution of intelligence quotients on the Stanford-Binet test was approximately 16 in the sample used for standardization.

We have just described the intelligence quotient in its classical form. However, it has so many weaknesses that it is scarcely used to express performance on more recently constructed intelligence tests. One weakness is that the individual scores included in the same distribution have not been compared with the same norm. Children of the same chronological age, say ten-year-olds, are compared with mental-age norms which vary considerably with respect both to level and to what is measured. A further weakness is that the standard deviation is not exactly the same for different ages. This means that the same intelligence quotient does not give the same relative position on distributions for different ages. Even more important, perhaps, is the fact that the standard deviation of the distribution of intelligence quotients varies from test to test. One effect of this variation is that intelligence quotients obtained from these tests vary for the same child, even if they give exactly the same relative positions.

In new tests in which the result is expressed as an intelligence quotient, e.g., the Wechsler Intelligence Scale for Children (WISC), the scores are obtained differently, so as to avoid the shortcomings of the classical intelligence quotient based upon mental age. The test is standardized and normalized into a distribution of I.Q.-equivalents for each individual age group, with mean 100 and standard deviation 15. The performance of every child of a certain age is then compared with the same norm. Furthermore, a given intelligence quotient always has the same relative position on the distribution of intelligence quotients. Thus, the procedure does not differ from that applied to the standardizing of a test for a given age group in order to give the results on, for instance, a T-scale. Apart from practical considerations, it is immaterial whether we express our test results on a T-scale or on an I.Q.-equivalent scale. Since the concept of the intelligence quotient has been

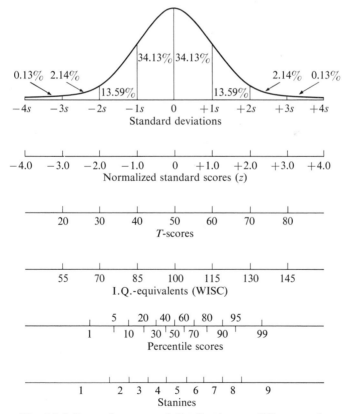

Fig. 16–3 Scores in a normal distribution on different scales.

misused and misinterpreted so often, we have good reason for using some other normalized scale more frequently. Incidentally, it may be observed that the latest version of the Binet test (1960), for which the classical I.Q. was invented, has been standardized for each age group without the use of the concept of mental age.

The scales discussed in this chapter are shown in Fig. 16–3.

16–6 NORMS AND REFERENCE GROUPS

By means of linear transformation and normalization we can satisfy the need for precise statistical significance in the data with which we make intra- and interindividual comparisons. If, say, A has obtained a stanine score of 6 on test X, we know that he has performed better on the test than approximately 60% of the group and worse than approximately 23%. However, in many practical situations where test scores are used as a basis for decision-making, counseling, or diagnosis, it is insufficient to know that A has obtained the stanine score 6 on the test. We must also know with which group of individuals A has been compared. For whom has the distribution been normalized and transformed into a stanine distribution? How old were the members of the group, what education did they have, what occupation? How homogeneous was the group with respect to other relevant variables? Suppose that A is a college student and the stanine distribution with which he has been compared has been obtained for a randomly drawn sample of fourteen-year-olds. His score cannot then be considered particularly outstanding, if the test measures some form of intellectual performance. If, on the other hand, the stanine distribution has been obtained for a representative sample of college students at the same level as A, the result can be considered rather good.

In the introductory chapter we stated that it is impossible to make absolute measurements of psychological variables. We can only make comparisons between individuals, using the variation of the individuals as units of measurement. But when we judge a certain performance we must know what to compare it with, i.e., which *norm* we want to use. We must know the mean and variation in performance on the test for the group with which we compare an individual score. A result can appear good when compared with one norm and poor when compared with some other norm.

When using a single test score for counseling, decision-making, or diagnosis, we must obviously base the assessment of the test scores on a comparison with the performance of a relevant, comparable group. If we wish to employ an individual as an office worker, we should base the assessment of his capabilities on a comparison with what good office workers achieve on the test battery, not on a comparison with what good factory workers achieve. In this case the group of office workers makes up a relevant *norm group* or *reference group*.

Most tests are used for several purposes and for several groups of individuals. If results from one test are used for comparison with various groups, we need norms for each of these groups, unless it has been empirically shown that the several groups have the same mean and deviation on the test results. In order for the test administrator to be able to decide whether a certain group of individuals is a relevant reference group, he should have access to information about factors (age, sex, education, etc.) which can affect the results for the norm group.

If an individual is to be compared with the correct reference group, the sample of individuals for which the norm has been computed should be a fair representation of the relevant population. The norm should be based on a representative sample of the population and not, as sometimes happens, on data obtained from individuals whom one just happened to test for one reason or another. When we present norm data, we should make their representativeness clear by giving the procedure used to select the sample.

The representativeness of the sample depends not only on the care taken in its selection, but also on the number of individuals included. This figure should also be given in the presentation of norm data, in order to help the test administrator to estimate the reliability of the comparisons he can make between individual test scores and norm data.

When norm data are used for comparisons in decision-making situations, great caution must be shown if the sample's representativeness is questionable or the number of individuals in the sample is small.

Norm data are not always necessary when one has to assess test scores in practical situations and use them as a basis for making decisions. If we are to make a simple selection and accept a certain number of individuals from a given number of applicants, we accept those who best meet the requirements, to the extent that these can be measured, for instance, by tests of relevant traits. We then accept those with the highest scores and reject the others.

PROBLEMS

1. Assume a normal distribution with $M = 5$, $s = 2$. Only whole numbers are used, 1–9 (the stanine scale).

   Determine the corresponding scores on the T-scale, i.e., a normally distributed scale with $M = 50$, $s = 10$.

2. The following values were obtained in a study with 625 subjects: $M = 15$, $s = 7$. The range was 1–30. Perform linear transformations and determine new scores which correspond to the original 1, 6, 11, 15, 20, 25, 29.

   (a) $M = 0$, $s = 7$ (b) $M = 0$, $s = 1$ (c) $M = 50$, $s = 7$

   (d) $M = 50$, $s = 10$ (e) $M = 100$, $s = 15$

3. Draw the frequency distribution of the scores below.

   (a) Characterize the skewness of the distribution.

   (b) Were the items too easy or too difficult to give a normal distribution?

Score	1	2	3	4	5	6	7	8	9	10	11
Frequency	3	4	8	15	19	21	17	6	4	2	1

4. (a) Determine the percentile score which corresponds to scores 4, 7, and 9 in Problem 3.

   (b) Which scores correspond to the percentile scores 25, 42, and 80?

5. Perform a linear transformation of the frequency distribution given in Problem 3 to a distribution with $M = 120$ and $s = 15$.

6. The following results, summarized in a frequency table, were obtained from a study.

X	1	2	3	4	5	6	7	8	9
f	2	6	10	18	24	44	46	32	18

   (a) Draw the frequency polygon.

   (b) Characterize the form of the distribution.

   (c) Determine the percentile score corresponding to each X-score.

   (d) Normalize the distribution and transform to z-scores. Draw the frequency polygon and compare with (a).

   (e) Transform to T-scores.

   (f) Transform to I.Q. equivalents.

   (g) Transform linearly to standard scores from raw scores and compare with the result of (d).

7. Construct a frequency distribution of the following raw scores obtained from testing with Raven's matrices. Normalize to a stanine distribution.

24	33	23	16	32	11	14	30
35	25	25	13	37	34	36	11
35	15	32	20	22	27	30	31
27	26	22	20	6	25	20	27
18	9	24	31	23	19	23	24
19	32	16	16	25	31	26	19
21	28	34	22	30	29	24	17
							18

8. Transform the distribution in Problem 7 to a T-distribution.

REFERENCE

FISHER, R. A., and F. YATES (1953). *Statistical tables for biological, agricultural and medical research* (4th ed.). London: Oliver & Boyd.

Suggested reading

CRONBACH, L. J. (1960). *Essentials of psychological testing.* New York: Harper & Bros.

FLANAGAN, J. C. (1951). Units, scores, and norms. In E. F. LINDQUIST (Ed.) *Educational Measurement.* Washington, D.C.: Am. Council on Educ.

LORD, F. M. (1962). Estimating norms by item-sampling. *Educ. Psychol. Measmt.*, **22,** 259–267.

THORNDIKE, R. L., and E. HAGEN (1961). *Measurement and evaluation in psychology and education.* New York: Wiley.

Answers

Chapters 1 and 2

1. The distribution is rectangular.

0.10	0.10	0.10	0.10	0.10	0.10	0.10	0.10	0.10	0.10
3	2	4	5	1	9	8	7	6	

2. The distribution is approximately normal.

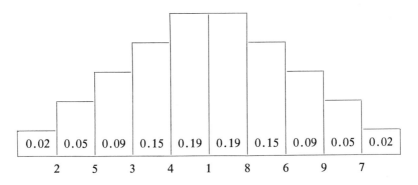

0.02	0.05	0.09	0.15	0.19	0.19	0.15	0.09	0.05	0.02
2	5	3	4	1	8	6	9	7	

3.

Item	1	2	3	4	5
p	0.034	0.127	0.159	0.258	0.500
%	3.4	12.7	15.9	25.8	50.0

Item	6	7	8	9	10
p	0.684	0.709	0.773	0.936	0.962
%	68.4	70.9	77.3	93.6	96.2

4. (a)

z	-2.25	-1.75	-1.25	-0.75	-0.25
Area to the left	0.012	0.040	0.106	0.227	0.401

z	0.25	0.75	1.25	1.75	2.25
Area to the left	0.599	0.773	0.894	0.960	0.988

(b)

Area	0.012	0.028	0.66	0.121	0.174	0.198

Area	0.174	0.121	0.66	0.028	0.012

5. (a)

	1	2	3	4	5
p	0.50	0.80	0.90	0.70	0.60
z	0.00	-0.842	-1.282	-0.524	-0.253

	6	7	8	9
p	0.10	0.20	0.30	0.40
z	1.282	0.842	0.524	0.253

(b)

	1	2	3	4	5
p	0.50	0.98	0.84	0.69	0.93
z	0.00	-2.054	-0.995	-0.496	-1.476

	6	7	8	9
p	0.16	0.02	0.31	0.07
z	0.995	2.054	0.496	1.476

6. (c) E.g., items 1, 2, 3, 6, 8, 11, 13, 16, 18, 19, and 20

(d) The distribution is approximately normal.

7. (a) 1,   (b) 1,   (c) 0,   (d) 0,   (e) 1,   (f) 1

8.

Item	1	2	3	4	5, 6
Variance	0.0475	0.0900	0.1275	0.1600	0.1875

Item	7	8	9, 10	11	12
Variance	0.2100	0.2275	0.2400	0.2500	0.2400

Item	13, 14	15	16	17	18
Variance	0.2275	0.2100	0.1875	0.1600	0.1275

Item	19	20
Variance	0.0900	0.0475

9. $s = 6.06$

10. (a) $\dfrac{\Sigma X}{N} = 10.20$,   (b) $\Sigma p = 10.20$

Chapter 3

1. (b) $a = -1.85$, $b = 0.22$
2. (b) $s_{\text{test}} = 5.97$, $s_{\text{final ex.}} = 1.43$,
   (c) $b = 0.918$
3. $r_{xy} = 0.918$
5. $r_{xy} = 0.918$
6. All the regression lines go through M_x and M_y, that is, 15/50.
   (a) $b_{yx} = 1.5$, $b_{xy} = 0.06$,
   (b) $b_{yx} = 3$, $b_{xy} = 0.12$,
   (c) $b_{yx} = 4.5$, $b_{xy} = 0.18$

7. (b)

X	10	11	12	13	14	15	16
M_y	101.45	101.94	102.62	103.57	104.16	105.06	105.60

   (c) The best prediction for each column is the mean given in (b).
   (d) $b_{yx} = 0.723$

9. Since linearity is not present, r_{xy} should not be computed; $b_{yx} = 0.66$; $b_{xy} = 0.80$.

10. (a)   Item

Item	1	2	3	4	5
1		−0.135	0.522	0.522	0.356
2			−0.258	0.258	0.076
3				0.556	0.293
4					−0.098

(b) Items 5, 3, 4, 2, and 1

11. (a) 0.19,   (b) 0.23,   (c) 0.023.
The large group differences are located below 11.5 (which does not thus reveal these differences). They are apparent in (a) and (b) when one dichotomizes at the top point in each group.

12. Two-tailed test: $z = 2.39$. Deviates significantly at the 5% level.

13. $\pm 1.96 \times 0.116 = \pm 0.228$

14. $1.65 \times 0.116 = 0.192$

Chapter 4

2.

Item	1	2	3	4	5
p	0.9167	0.8333	0.7500	0.7500	0.5833
q	0.0833	0.1667	0.2500	0.2500	0.4167
s^2	0.0764	0.1389	0.1875	0.1875	0.2431
s	0.276	0.373	0.433	0.433	0.493

Item

Item	1	2	3	4	5
1	0.0764	−0.0139	0.0625	0.0625	0.0486
2		0.1389	−0.0417	0.0417	0.0139
3			0.1875	0.1042	0.0625
4				0.1875	−0.0208
5					0.2431

3. (a) $\sum s_i^2 + \sum C_{ik} = 1.472$,   (b) $s_t^2 = 1.472$

4. (a) 9.25,   (b) 25.0,   (c) 2.5

Chapter 5

1. (a) 0.45,   (b) 0.71,   (c) 0.66
2. (a) 0.58,   (b) 0.78,   (c) 0.44
3. $r_{tt} = 0.50$
4. (a) $s_{3T}^2 = 27$,   (b) $s_{3e}^2 = 9$,   (c) $r_{tt_3} = \frac{27}{36} = 0.75$
6. (a) 0.887,   (b) 46 items
7. 50
8. (a) 0.824,   (b) 0.875,   (c) 0.903,   (d) 0.921
9. (a) 2.25 times,   (b) 4.75 times
10. 210 raters (impractical)
11. 0.775
12. $r_{uu} = 0.84$
13. $s_u = 6.24$

Chapter 6

1. (a) 3.162,   (b) 3.354,   (c) 0.775
2. (a) $55 \pm 1.96 \cdot 3.162 = 55 \pm 6.20$,
   (b) $60 \pm 1.96 \cdot 3.354 = 60 \pm 6.57$,
   (c) $6 \pm 1.96 \cdot 0.775 = 6 \pm 1.52$
3. $p \leq 0.001$
4. (a) $p = 0.16$,   (b) $p = 0.04$,   (c) $p = 0.003$
5. $p_{46} = 0.16$, $p_{42} = 0.02$, $p_{38} = 0.003$
6. $p_A = 0.03$, $p_B = 0.03$
7. 90 ± 10.4
8.

Group	I	II	III	IV
Reliability	0.75	0.89	0.75	0.89

9. (a) $s_e = 2.86$,   (b) $s_e = 3.57$,   (c) $s_e = 2.14$
10. 23.13–36.14
11. 46—72%

12.

Score	8	29	42
Upper	3.23	3.49	1.97
Lower	1.97	3.79	3.23

13. (a) 0, 2.165, 2.932, 3.423

Chapter 7

1. $a - b = 1.96 \times 3.742 = 7.33$, $a - c = 1.96 \times 4.583 = 8.98$,
   $b - c = 1.96 \times 5.00 = 9.80$
2. $p_{A-B} = 0.24$, $p_{A-C} = 0.11$, $p_{B-C} = 0.30$
3. $p = 0.046$ (4.6%)
4. $p = 0.143$ (14.3%)
5. (a) The score on the I.Q. scale is better ($z_1 = 1.0$, $z_2 = 1.5$)
   (b) $p = 0.84$
6. 95%: $a - b = 1.645 \times 4.123 = 6.78$, $a - c = 1.645 \times 3.742 = 6.16$,
   $b - c = 1.645 \times 3.873 = 6.37$
   99%: $a - b = 2.326 \times 4.123 = 9.58$, $a - c = 2.326 \times 3.873 = 9.01$,
   $b - c = 2.326 \times 3.742 = 8.70$
7. $r_{dd} = 0.55$
8.

		r_{gh}						
	$\bar{r}_{gg}$	0.10	0.20	0.30	0.40	0.50	0.60	0.70
s_d	0.70	13.4	12.6	11.8	11.0	10.0	8.9	7.7
r_{dd}	0.70	0.67	0.63	0.57	0.50	0.40	0.25	0.0
s_{e_d}	0.70	7.7	7.7	7.7	7.7	7.7	7.7	7.7
5%	0.70	34	32	28	25	20	15	10
10%	0.70	46	43	40	37	32	27	20

Chapter 9

1. (a) $r_{tt_8} = 0.859$, (b) $r_{tt_8} = 0.863$, (c) $r_{tt} = 0.441$
2. $r_{tt} = 0.755$ (The magnitude depends on the order in which items with the same frequency of correct solution are placed in the test halves.)
3.

	1	2
(a)	$r_{tt} = 0.83$	$r_{tt} = 0.750$
(b)	$r_{tt} = 0.83$	$r_{tt} = 0.750$

4. KR_{20}: $r_{tt} = 0.71$ ($s_t^2 = 3.34$, $\sum pq = 1.28$)
   KR_{21}: $r_{tt} = 0.46$ ($n\overline{pq} = 1.99$)
5. $$r_{tt} = \frac{n^2\overline{C}_{ik}}{s_t^2} = 0.543 \qquad (\sum C_{ik} = 0.639,\ s_t^2 = 1.472)$$
   $$r_{tt} = \frac{n}{n-1}\,\frac{s_t^2 - \sum pq}{s_t^2} = 0.543 \qquad (\sum pq = 0.8334)$$
6. $r_{tt} = 0.84$

Chapters 11 and 12

1. (a) -0.70,   (b) 0.00,   (c) 0.525,   (d) 0.980
2. The best possible estimate is the score 9. ($Y' = 9.475$, $s_{yx} = 2.810$)
      (a) 9.475 ± 2.810,   (b) 9.475 ± 5.51
3. (a) $Y' = 4.36$,   (b) approx. 8%,
4. 7.19 ($Y' = 4.24$, $s_{yx} = 1.503$)
5. (a) approx. 28%,   (b) approx. 4%
6. (a) approx. 5%,   (b) approx. 20%,
      (c) approx. 56%,   (d) approx. 69%
9. (a) $r_{TG} = 0.74$,   (b) $r_{tG} = 0.68$
10. $r_{tG} = 0.69$
11. $r_{tt_4} = 0.97$, $r_{t_4 g} = 0.68$
12. 61.9
13. $Y' = 15.89$, 10% risk of failure
14. (a) $z_x = 2.71$,   (b) $z_x = 0.20$

Chapter 13

1. (a) $h^2 = 0.53$,   (b) $r_{tt} = 0.53 + 0.25 = 0.78$,   (c) $u^2 = 0.47$

2.

Test	1	2	3	4
1	—	0.20	0.27	0.17
2		—	0.00	0.42
3			—	0.39
4				—

3.

Test	1	2	3	4	5
1	—	0.605	0.525	0.480	0.698
2		—	0.559	0.224	0.505
3			—	0.606	0.549
4				—	0.541
5					—

4.

Test	1	2	3	4	5
Validity	0.675	0.390	0.398	0.480	0.717

5. (a) $r_{tt} = 0.865$, $r_{gg} = 0.930$,   (b) $r_{tg} = 0.465$,

    (c) $r_{tG} = 0.482$,   (d) $r_{tg} = 0.482$,

    (e) $r_{tg} = 0.723$,   (f) $r_{tg} = 0.526$,

    (g) $r_{tg} = 0.805$,   (h) $r_{tg} = 0.832$,

    (i) $r_{tg} = 0.759$,   (j) $r_{tt(\text{max})} = 0.882$

Chapter 14

1.

Item	p	r_{pbis}	y	r_{bis}
1	0.95	0.063	0.1031	0.133
2	0.80	0.416	0.2800	0.594
3	0.75	0.480	0.3178	0.655
4	0.65	0.611	0.3704	0.786
5	0.55	0.641	0.3958	0.806
6	0.40	0.679	0.3863	0.862
7	0.25	0.608	0.3178	0.829
8	0.15	0.582	0.2332	0.892

2.

Item	r_{phi}
1	0.229
2	0.250
3	0.346
4	0.524
5	0.503
6	0.612
7	0.577
8	0.420

3. (a) $r_{\text{pbis}} = 0.3386$. There is a weak positive correlation between being a boy and having good test results.

(b) No. The sex categories are not distributed on an interval scale.

4. (a) $r_{\text{pbis}} = 0.535$,   (b) $r_{\text{bis}} = 0.670$

5. $\dfrac{r_{\text{bis}}}{r_{\text{pbis}}} = 1.253$

6. We cannot obtain r_{bis} when p_u or $p_l = 0$ or 1. For item 4, $r_{\text{bis}} = 0.62$.

7.

Item	Reliability index
1	0.0137
2	0.1664
3	0.2080
4	0.2913
5	0.3188
6	0.3328
7	0.2635
8	0.2080

8. $s_t = 1.803$, $\sum r_{ti}s_i = 1.803$

9. (a)

Item	Reliability index
1	0.0000
2	0.1917
3	0.3244
4	0.3244
5	0.3391
6	0.1769
	1.3565

10. (a)

Item	Validity index
1	0.0000
2	0.0063
3	0.1521
4	0.2788
5	0.1014
6	0.0570
	0.5956

(b) $s_t = 1.3565$

(b) $\dfrac{\sum r_{gi}s_i}{\sum r_{ti}s_i} = 0.439, \quad r_{xy} = 0.439$

12. $r_{KR} = 0.896$

13. 3, 1, 4, 2

14. $r_{KR} = 0.52$, $r_{tg} = 0.56$. Item 7 should be removed in case (a), item 3 or 8 in case (b). In case (a), $r_{KR} = 0.543$. In case (b), $r_{tg} = 0.598$.

Chapter 15

1. 34

2. 109

3. 85

4. (a) 33,   (b) 108

Chapter 16

1.

Stanine	1	2	3	4	5	6	7	8	9
z	-2	-1.5	-1	-0.5	0	$+0.5$	$+1$	$+1.5$	$+2$
T-scale	30	35	40	45	50	55	60	65	70

2.

	(a)	(b)	(c)	(d)	(e)
	$M = 15$ $s = 7$	$M = 0$ $s = 7$	$M = 0$ $s = 1$	$M = 50$ $s = 7$	$M = 50$ $s = 10$	$M = 100$ $s = 15$
1	-14	-2.0	36	30.0	70.0
6	-9	-1.3	41	37.1	80.7
11	-4	-0.6	46	44.3	91.4
15	0	0.0	50	50.0	100.0
20	5	0.7	55	57.1	110.7
25	10	1.4	60	64.3	121.4
29	14	2.0	64	70.0	130.0

3. (a) The distribution is positively skewed.

(b) The items are too easy.

4. (a) 22.5, 78.5, 95.0

(b) 4.2, 5.1, 7.1

5.

Raw score	1	2	3	4	5	6
Transformed score	86.25	93.75	101.25	108.75	116.25	123.75

Raw score	7	8	9	10	11
Transformed score	131.25	138.75	146.25	153.75	161.25

$$M = 5.5, \quad s = 2$$

6. (b) negatively skewed

	(c)	(d)	(e)	(f)	(g)
X	P	z (normalized)	T	I.Q.	z (linear)
1	0.5	−2.58	24.2	61.3	−2.86
2	2.5	−1.96	30.4	70.6	−2.31
3	6.5	−1.51	34.9	77.3	−1.76
4	13.5	−1.10	39.0	83.5	−1.21
5	24.0	−0.71	42.9	89.4	−0.66
6	41.0	−0.23	47.7	96.6	−0.11
7	63.5	0.35	53.5	105.2	0.44
8	83.0	0.95	59.5	114.3	0.99
9	95.5	1.70	67.0	125.4	1.54

7.

Stanine	Raw score	Percentage distribution
1	6–9	3.5
2	10–14	7.0
3	15–18	12.3
4	19–22	17.5
5	23–25	19.3
6	26–30	17.5
7	31–33	12.3
8	34–35	7.0
9	36–37	3.5

8.

Raw score	T-score	Raw score	T-score
6	26	24	50
9	31	25	52
11	34	26	53
13	36	27	54
14	37	28	55
15	38	29	56
16	40	30	57
17	41	31	58
18	42	32	60
19	43	33	62
20	45	34	63
21	46	35	66
22	47	36	69
23	48	37	73

Appendix

TABLE A The Normal Distribution

Standard scores (z) corresponding to different magnitudes of p and q respectively, together with the ordinate (y) for these standard scores

Area from $z = 0$	z	Ordinate (y) at z	Area from $z = 0$	z	Ordinate (y) at z	Area from $z = 0$	z	Ordinate (y) at z
0.000	0.000	0.3989	0.165	0.426	0.3643	0.330	0.954	0.2531
0.005	0.013	0.3989	0.170	0.440	0.3621	0.335	0.974	0.2482
0.010	0.025	0.3988	0.175	0.454	0.3599	0.340	0.995	0.2433
0.015	0.038	0.3987	0.180	0.468	0.3576	0.345	1.015	0.2383
0.020	0.050	0.3984	0.185	0.482	0.3552	0.350	1.036	0.2332
0.025	0.063	0.3982	0.190	0.496	0.3528	0.355	1.058	0.2279
0.030	0.075	0.3978	0.195	0.510	0.3503	0.360	1.080	0.2226
0.035	0.088	0.3974	0.200	0.524	0.3477	0.365	1.103	0.2171
0.040	0.100	0.3969	0.205	0.539	0.3450	0.370	1.126	0.2115
0.045	0.113	0.3964	0.210	0.553	0.3423	0.375	1.150	0.2059
0.050	0.126	0.3958	0.215	0.568	0.3395	0.380	1.175	0.2000
0.055	0.138	0.3951	0.220	0.583	0.3366	0.385	1.200	0.1941
0.060	0.151	0.3944	0.225	0.598	0.3337	0.390	1.227	0.1880
0.065	0.164	0.3936	0.230	0.613	0:3306	0.395	1.254	0.1818
0.070	0.176	0.3928	0.235	0.628	0.3275	0.400	1.282	0.1755
0.075	0.189	0.3919	0.240	0.643	0.3244	0.405	1.311	0.1690
0.080	0.202	0.3909	0.245	0.659	0.3211	0.410	1.341	0.1624
0.085	0.215	0.3899	0.250	0.675	0.3178	0.415	1.372	0.1556
0.090	0.228	0.3887	0.255	0.690	0.3144	0.420	1.405	0.1487
0.095	0.240	0.3876	0.260	0.706	0.3109	0.425	1.440	0.1416
0.100	0.253	0.3863	0.265	0.723	0.3073	0.430	1.476	0.1343
0.105	0.266	0.3850	0.270	0.739	0.3036	0.435	1.514	0.1268
0.110	0.279	0.3837	0.275	0.755	0.2999	0.440	1.555	0.1191
0.115	0.292	0.3823	0.280	0.772	0.2961	0.445	1.598	0.1112
0.120	0.306	0.3808	0.285	0.789	0.2922	0.450	1.645	0.1031
0.125	0.319	0.3792	0.290	0.806	0.2882	0.455	1.695	0.0948
0.130	0.332	0.3776	0.295	0.824	0.2841	0.460	1.751	0.0862
0.135	0.345	0.3759	0.300	0.842	0.2800	0.465	1.812	0.0773
0.140	0.359	0.3741	0.305	0.860	0.2757	0.470	1.881	0.0680
0.145	0.372	0.3723	0.310	0.878	0.2714	0.475	1.960	0.0585
0.150	0.385	0.3704	0.315	0.897	0.2669	0.480	2.054	0.0484
0.155	0.399	0.3684	0.320	0.915	0.2624	0.485	2.170	0.0379
0.160	0.413	0.3664	0.325	0.935	0.2578	0.490	2.326	0.0267
						0.495	2.576	0.0145
						0.499	3.090	0.0018

TABLE B The Normal Distribution

Proportions of the total area corresponding to different standard scores

z	Area	z	Area
0.00	0.000	1.65	0.451
0.05	0.020	1.70	0.455
0.10	0.040	1.75	0.460
0.15	0.060	1.80	0.464
0.20	0.079	1.85	0.468
0.25	0.099	1.90	0.471
0.30	0.118	1.95	0.474
0.35	0.137	2.00	0.477
0.40	0.156	2.05	0.480
0.45	0.174	2.10	0.482
0.50	0.191	2.15	0.484
0.55	0.209	2.20	0.486
0.60	0.226	2.25	0.488
0.65	0.242	2.30	0.489
0.70	0.258	2.35	0.491
0.75	0.273	2.40	0.492
0.80	0.288	2.45	0.493
0.85	0.302	2.50	0.494
0.90	0.316	2.55	0.495
0.95	0.329	2.60	0.495
1.00	0.341	2.65	0.496
1.05	0.353	2.70	0.497
1.10	0.364	2.75	0.497
1.15	0.375	2.80	0.497
1.20	0.385	2.85	0.498
1.25	0.394	2.90	0.498
1.30	0.403	2.95	0.498
1.35	0.411	3.00	0.499
1.40	0.419	3.05	0.499
1.45	0.426	3.10	0.499
1.50	0.433	3.15	0.499
1.55	0.439	3.20	0.499
1.60	0.445	3.25	0.499

Indexes

Index of Notation

The following notation is used throughout, unless information to the contrary is contained in the text.

b	regression coefficient
C	covariance
e	error component
f	frequency of correct solution
g, h	any test or variable
h^2	communality
i, k	any item
j, l	any individual
m	number of factors
M_x, M_y	means of the distributions of x- and y-scores respectively
n	number of items in a test
N	number of individuals
p	proportion
P	percentile score
q	the proportion $(1-p)$
r	correlation coefficient
r_{bis}	biserial correlation coefficient
r_{pbis}	point-biserial correlation coefficient
r_{phi}	ϕ-coefficient
r_{tt}	reliability coefficient
s	standard deviation
s^2	variance
t	obtained score
T	true component
u^2	unique variance
v^2	specific variance
x, y	the difference between raw scores (X, Y) and means (M_x, M_y) of respective distributions $x = X - M_x$ and $y = Y - M_y$
X, Y	raw scores for the variables x and y
y', Y'	predicted scores for the y-variable
y	the ordinate for a normal distribution with standard deviation 1.0 and area 1.0
z	standard score

Author Index

Subject Index

ABCDE6987